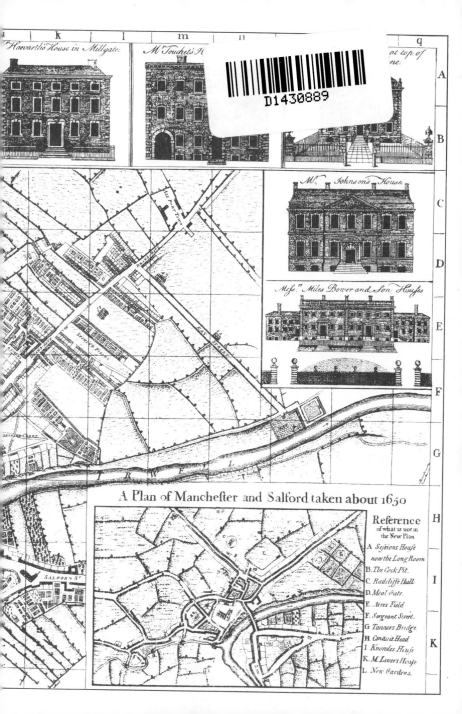

A Plan of Manchester and Salford taken about 1650

i k l m n q

Havarth's House in Millgate.   M.r Touchet's H...   ...at top of ...ne.

M.r Johnson's House.

Mess.rs Miles Bower and Son. Houses

SALFORD S.t

Reference
of what is not in
the New Plan

A Sessions House
  now the Long Room
B. The Cock Pit.
C. Radcliffe Hall.
D. Meal Gate.
E. Acres Field
F. Sergeant Street.
G Tanners Bridge.
H. Conduit Head
I Knowles House.
K. M.r Levers House.
L. New Gardens.

A B C D E F G H I K

ANN THE WORD

ANN THE WORD

The Story of Ann Lee, Female Messiah,
Mother of the Shakers,
the Woman Clothed with the Sun

RICHARD FRANCIS

FOURTH ESTATE • *London*

First published in Great Britain in 2000 by
Fourth Estate Limited
6 Salem Road
London W2 4BU
www.4thestate.co.uk

10 9 8 7 6 5 4 3 2 1

A catalogue record for this book is available from the
British Library.

ISBN 1-85702-969-0

Typeset in Caslon 540 by
Rowland Phototypesetting Limited,
Bury St Edmunds, Suffolk.
Printed in Great Britain by
T J International Ltd, Padstow, Cornwall

For Jo, William and Helen

'To such as addressed her with the customary titles of the world, she would reply, "*I am* ANN, *the* WORD;" signifying that in her dwelt the Word.'

Contents

Author's Note

I've been interested in Shakerism for some time, ever since working on nineteenth-century utopian experiments in New England. A couple of years ago I realised that no satisfactory free-standing biography of Ann Lee herself had ever been written, despite her astonishing and adventurous life and the scale of her achievement. Though she could write nothing down herself, her salty, humorous, impassioned voice comes to us across the centuries from the records of her followers. These testimonies were made after her death, by American believers who only knew about Ann's early days in Manchester second-hand, through anecdotes by herself and the small group of expatriates who came over the Atlantic with her. For this reason there is, perhaps appropriately, a kind of old and new testament to Ann Lee's life, with her early experiences taking on a rather stylised, almost allegorical form, while the later, American episodes have a richness of detail and an immediacy that come from eye-witness accounts. Because of this imbalance, and because her final decade in America is by far the most fascinating and significant period of her life, I have devoted two-thirds of this biography to her experience in New York State and New England.

The most important source of material is a book compiled by two Shakers, Rufus Bishop and Seth Youngs Wells, in 1816, and called *Testimonies of the Life, Character, Revelations and Doctrines of Mother Ann Lee, and the Elders with Her*, or, more romantically, the 'Secret Book of the Elders'. For more information on this and other sources please turn to the Bibliographical Note at the end of the book. I have not attributed any facts or utterances to Ann Lee or her contemporaries that have not been recorded in accounts and reminiscences by those who knew her.

I would like to express my gratitude to the staff of the following institutions for their assistance in my research: the Albany Institute of History and Art, the American Museum, Bath, Bath Spa University College, the British Library, Chetham's Library, the Fruitlands Museums, the Lancashire Archive Office, the Library of Congress, the Archive of Manchester Cathedral, the John Rylands University Library of Manchester, the Manchester Public Library, the New York Public Library, the Sabbathday Lake Shaker Library and the Western Reserve Historical Association.

The following people have helped me with advice, hospitality and encouragement: Ann Armitage, Otto Bergman, Roberta Bienvenu, Vera Brice, Roben Chapman, Pat Cummings, Gareth Davies, Jean and Barry Day, Rose Gore, Clio and Anthea Harrison, Helen Johnson, Peter Marshall, Sue Phillpott, Michael Schmidt, Alex Sherwood, Michael Volmar, Ian Walker, John Walker, Dick Yerkes, and special thanks to Christopher Potter and Sarah White at Fourth Estate, to my agent Caroline Dawnay, and to my wife Jo Francis.

PART ONE
ENGLAND

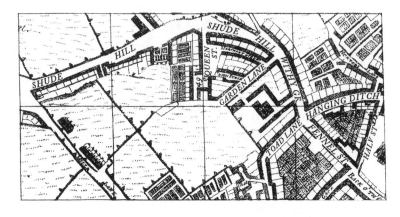

Toad Lane, where Ann was born.
(endpaper map ref. He)

I

Toad Lane

Ann Lee was born on 29 February (as one might expect of a miraculous person) in 1736, second oldest of the eight children of a blacksmith and his wife living in Toad Lane, Manchester, a fairy-tale address if not a fairy-tale place. Toad Lane is still there – it's the approach road to Victoria Station, slightly separated from what is now the heart of the city, but linked to it by the new developments that have followed the enormous damage caused by an IRA bomb in 1996. Now, mundanely, it's called Todd Street. Back in 1552 it had been Towd Lane; in 1609 it was described as 'Crooked Lane alias Tode Lane'. By 1618 it had become New Street alias Toade Lane. Names seem to slide and mutate in Ann Lee's vicinity. Spelling was only just becoming standardised, and in any case Ann herself was illiterate. Her family was actually called Lees, but the s somehow got lost during her travels. She married a man called Abraham Standerin, whose surname is also recorded as Stanley or Standley, but reverted to her maiden name when she rejected earthly marriage.

Manchester in the mid-eighteenth century is not likely to be equated with the city as it is now; but equally it shouldn't be confused with the Manchester of the period

South-west prospect of Manchester from
Casson and Berry's map of 1746.

of Dickens's *Hard Times*, with its thundering machinery
and factory chimneys belching out smoke. That mid-
nineteenth-century industrial city is almost as far away
from Ann's childhood as we, on the other side, are from
it. When Ann was about ten years old two Manchester
engravers and booksellers called Casson and Berry published a new edition of their *Plan of the Towns of Manchester
and Salford*. Their map is illustrated by a view of the town
from the north-east. In the foreground we see huntsmen,
fields, the River Irwell with its boats and fishermen;
beyond, buildings rise picturesquely from the rural scene.
The two mapmakers had their business in Manchester
and it was in their interest to give their locality a good
gloss, but the map itself meticulously depicts the little

4

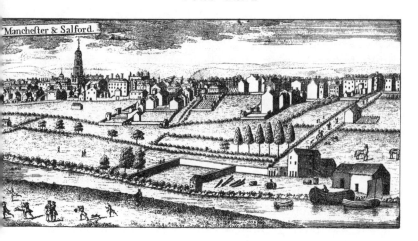

Manchester & Salford.

fields and allotments peppered among the Manchester streets. Toad Lane, like most of the other thoroughfares, has courtyards behind the houses and then a patchwork of strips of land behind the courtyards. There were fields to the south of it (the *Plan* shows south at the top), with Shude Hill circling them beyond, and then the country-side. St Ann's Square was the most elegant part of the town; its paved surface, its charming church and its neatly spaced trees are all shown to advantage in an engraving inset on the border of the *Plan*. Thirteen years previously, however, St Ann's Square was known as Acres Field, and as late as the 1780s aged locals could remember how in bad seasons the corn had to be harvested before it was ready because the lord of the manor insisted on his right to set up the annual Acres Fair promptly on 19 September each year.

Of course, at the time of Ann's birth and during her life

there, Manchester was growing and developing. Daniel Defoe, visiting it during the 1720s on his tour of England and Wales (at the time when locals were still growing their corn and potatoes in Acres Field), described it as 'the greatest meer village in England', and in the subsequent decades it became greater, while retaining, to modern eyes at least, some of the qualities of an overgrown village. An issue of the *Gentleman's Magazine* of 1739 claimed that there had been substantial development in the town over the previous twenty years, and proportionately that was true, but one must bear in mind the proportions: what it was talking about was two thousand houses. In 1717 Manchester had had a population of around eight thousand. By 1757, the total for Manchester and Salford combined was 19,839. The first proper census, which was taken in 1773 – the year in which the thirty-seven-year-old Ann, having disrupted a church service, found herself in the local House of Correction cheek by jowl with a highwayman called Long Ned – gave the joint Manchester and Salford population as 27,246.

Ann was born into an environment where you could still see fields and trees. Her father, John Lees, practised one of the most evocative of all trades, though epithets like 'village' or 'harmonious' hardly apply; he was the equivalent of the modern small-time mechanic, repairing people's horses when they broke down. He almost certainly ran his own business, and in a town with a growing population and economy it is likely that his services were in demand. Ann's beloved brother William took up the same trade, and her husband Abraham was a blacksmith too, living at their house, so almost certainly these two at least were employed in her father's business. Nevertheless, she claimed to have been poor and by modern standards she certainly would have been.

It was undoubtedly a crowded household, with up to ten people crammed into a few rooms, no money to spare for luxuries and, even more significantly in view of Ann's later development, no privacy. In common with members of artisan families from medieval times to the late nineteenth century, she would have been able to hear her parents, and perhaps in later years married siblings, having sex through partition walls or even in the same room. Her followers recorded that Ann's hatred of 'fleshly cohabitation' dated from early youth, and that she often warned her mother, who was a pious woman also called Ann, about its snares. The story goes that on one occasion her father got wind of this threat to his sex life and tried to whip the child, 'upon which she threw herself into her mother's arms, and clung around her to escape his strokes'. She seems to have been a preoccupied, introverted girl in any case, with a neurotic or at least a melancholy edge to her nature. 'When I was a child,' she later told her followers, 'my mind was taken up with the things of God, so that I saw heavenly visions, instead of trifling toys.' On another occasion she said that in her childhood she would lie in bed at night seeing beautiful colours and heavenly scenes, but even in the midst of these visions she felt distraught at the prospect of them coming to an end, and dreaded the sound of her mother getting up in the morning, because she would open the windows and let them escape.

Toad Lane was in the large shadow of Christ Church, Manchester's most important place of worship, which dates from the late medieval period, though it has been so modified and worked upon over the centuries that not much survives to give a sense of its age. Under the choir stalls, however, there are some carvings, misericords, dating from the late fifteenth century, including a charming one which shows a family of piglets dancing to a tune played by their mother pig. It had been founded as a collegiate church, that is, one with an extra retinue of clergy, but it did not become a cathedral until a century after Ann's birth, when Manchester itself had grown to a scale commensurate with its bulky parish church (the reason for its original collegiate status was simply that its parish responsibilities stretched over large tracts of south Lancashire). St Ann's Church had been erected in 1708, twenty years before the square that took its name, to provide a slightly lower form of worship, halfway, it was said, (both geographically and ritually) to the Cross Street Chapel where the nonconformists worshipped. Ann's fate, however, was tangled up with the church nearest her home, and in 1742 when she was six years old she was christened there.

The baptism is recorded in the Christ Church register as a private one. In the mid-eighteenth century the poorer classes often went through two of the three most important sacramental occasions of their lives, baptisms and weddings, *en masse*, like Moonies do nowadays, with anything up to a whole churchful being processed at once, and expenses consequently being shared around. Ann's older sister Nancy had been baptised in 1734, one of a party of six, and her brother Joseph was one of a similar group in 1741. William, the brother whose life was to be intertwined with her own, preceded Ann by two months though he was four years her junior, being baptised in April 1742, one of twelve on that day. Given that she was the second oldest child, it's odd that Ann was number four to receive the sacrament, though illness might explain both the delay and the privacy of the service when it eventually came. In any case her brothers James and Daniel and her sister Mary have no baptismal entries; the last sibling, George, was entered in 1749.

Like other English artisan children of her time Ann had to go to work instead of to school, and as a result did not learn to read and write. Once again we should avoid judgement from a modern or even Victorian perspective. Dickens and the other great nineteenth-century agitators have made us aware of underfed pasty-faced children being turned into units of mechanical production by the factory system. There were no large-scale factories in the mid-eighteenth century, and people then did not see the issue in those terms. Work, even for very small children, was regarded by social commentators as an opportunity, not a curse. Daniel Defoe noted that one of the great benefits of the clothing trade was that 'the very children after four or five years of age, could every one earn their own bread'. Casson and Berry, in the notes to their *Plan*, give their customary optimistic spin to the fact that women, and children as young as five or six years old, could earn more in Manchester than anywhere else in the country at the trades of spinning, winding or weaving. In the early 1770s, when Ann was just beginning to cross swords with the authorities, the agricultural reformer Arthur Young arrived in Manchester and noted approvingly that 'large families in this place are no incumbrance; all are set to work'. The clothing industry had been important in Manchester since Elizabethan times, and Ann was employed preparing cotton for the looms. This work would have been undertaken in a house or a small workshop. It was a harsh way of life but it operated on a human scale. At some point she moved on to being a cutter of velvet.

The fact that Ann's experience in this respect was normal for her time and class doesn't mean that she herself enjoyed it or approved of it. When she was in her forties, and far away in America, she had occasion to give advice to a poor woman called Beulah Rude, who had five children, hardly an unusual number at the time. 'Five! Five!' Ann exclaimed. 'When you had one, why did you not wait and see if you were able to bring up that as you ought before you had another? And when you had two, why did you not stop then? But now you have five! Are you not ashamed to live in the filthy works of the flesh? You must go and take up your cross, and put your hands to work, and be faithful in your business; clothe your children, and keep them clean and decent; and clean up your house and keep that in order.' One can picture the poor woman's dismay or even rage at being on the receiving end of such a tirade, particularly since the advice was coming a bit late in the day.

Ann's fury may have been triggered in part by a kind of jealousy at seeing a woman with five children when she had lost four of her own. But some of the vitriol is no doubt traceable further back, to childhood experience. In fact she goes against the wisdom of her own time, contradicting Defoe, Casson and Berry, and Arthur Young, with her insistence on seeing children as an economic responsibility rather than as an economic resource. Perhaps in this respect, as in others, she is playing her own small part in forming modern attitudes, despite her uncompromising and unsympathetic tone. One can also wonder, given the stress she always gave to the need for cleanliness, decency and good order, just how clean and decent and orderly the house in Toad Lane had actually been when she was growing up in it.

Ann's childhood is lost to us, just as, in various respects, it seems to have been lost to her. There is a suggestion that her mother died during this period, but she was alive in 1749, when Ann was thirteen, because her name appears on her son George's baptismal record, and there is no record of her death in the following decade. The only glimpse we get of her comes in a testimony from the last years of Ann Lee's own life. In 1780, when Ann was at Harvard town in central Massachusetts (not to be confused with the distinguished university in Cambridge, Massachusetts, some forty miles away), she described a vision she'd had of multitudes of the present and past generation: 'I saw them clothed with blackness and darkness, many of whom I knew.' These were lost souls, who had not the path to salvation. 'I saw my own natural mother in the same condition, and when I saw her, I cried to God; for I had thought that my mother was a good woman, if there were any good upon earth.'

It is appropriate that all we see of Ann's mother is this poignant vision, because the people who surrounded her in her early days all have a spectral quality, and Ann herself is only marginally less transparent. This is hardly surprising given that what remains to us of the inhabitants of the past is largely what they have written down or what has been written down about them. These were ordinary people who would normally make little impact on politics or culture or society, and like most of their generation, and every generation, they mostly vanished without leaving much of a trace behind. When, later, Ann began to make her mark, even though she herself was illiterate others began to make their own marks on her behalf: the recorders of the Quarter Sessions, the Manchester constabulary, the local newspapers and, after she began her ministry in America, her followers. But the only event of note we know that occurred during her childhood was a public one: the Jacobite rebellion of 1745.

The Glorious Revolution had taken place more than half a century earlier, in 1688, when William of Orange had deposed the Catholic James II and restored Protestant rule in the combined kingdoms of England and Scotland. Twenty-seven years later, James Edward Stuart, the Old Pretender, had attempted to seize back the throne his father had lost and restore the Stuart dynasty in the doomed rebellion of 1715. Thirty more years passed, and his son Charles Edward, the Young Pretender, tried the same again with the sponsorship of the French government. He landed in Scotland, began to assemble an army, and in the autumn of 1745 marched south into England.

There were many gentlemen with Catholic sympathies in Lancashire, and Manchester had provided important support for the Stuart (or Jacobite) cause during the Fifteen, so the Young Pretender probably expected some solid recruitment in the region. The lesson had been learned, however, and while the local Jacobites were happy to toast the 'king over the water' they were a little wary as the amateurish Scottish army of just about four thousand men drew nearer. An attempt was made to collect together a Manchester regiment, but only around a hundred volunteers had enlisted when a quixotic character called Sergeant Dickson appeared on the scene with a blunderbuss, and swelled the force by a further one hundred and eighty.

The Young Pretender brought his men into town on 28 November 1745, met with sympathisers, recruited some more supporters and marched south towards Derby on 1 December. He had nowhere near enough troops, however, and just over a week later he returned to Manchester in retreat. One of the local loyalists, Peter Mainwaring, a physician and Justice of the Peace who was to cross paths with Ann Lee in both capacities in later life, ordered the town bellman to go the rounds calling on the people to arm themselves with guns, swords or, more realistically, shovels, and prepare to beat off the Jacobites for a few hours until the Duke of Cumberland could bring his troops to their aid. As a result crowds of people pelted the vanguard of the Young Pretender's army as it passed by Hanging Ditch. Nonetheless the rebels got into the town and some of them went to Mainwaring's house at 12 King Street where, according to Beppy Byrom, daughter of the Manchester poet Dr John Byrom, they were 'a little rough' with him. The army headed north the following day, towards disaster at Carlisle followed by utter catastrophe at the battle of Culloden.

The Manchester Regiment was picked out for particularly harsh treatment and many of its members paid with their lives during the bloody reprisals that followed. The heads of two of them, Captain Thomas Deacon and Ensign Syddall, were pickled in spirits and sent back from their place of execution in London for public exhibition outside the Manchester Exchange. Syddall's own father's head had been similarly displayed after the rebellion of 1715; Deacon's father, meanwhile, took off his hat and bowed deeply in respect for his son's head, or at least for his manner of losing it. This gruesome spectacle was in place for three years (while Ann Lee, living a couple of hundred yards from it, went from ten to thirteen), until one night in 1749 both heads disappeared. An eighteen-year-old medical student called Edward Hall had run out a plank from Mrs Raffald's coffee house next to the Exchange and crawled along it to free them from their spikes, later burying them in his own garden.

At some point Ann moved on from cutting velvet to cutting fur for hats. The hatting trade in Manchester had really taken off at about the time she was born, and a national reputation for high-quality products was being established, as the use of fur suggests. But in 1752 a further career opportunity began to arise, with the establishment of the Manchester Infirmary in a small house in Garden Street, off Shude Hill, just yards away from Toad Lane. For the first year only twelve beds were available, but this doubled when the hospital was extended into the house next door, and by 1755 the infirmary was so successful – or, to be more accurate, the population's need had proved so great – that it moved into premises built for the purpose on land which had been granted on generous terms by the lord of the manor, Sir Oswald Mosley, in what is now Piccadilly. The plot was known as 'daub-hole field' because it contained a six-hundred-foot pond created by the practice of digging out daub or clay for house-building in earlier times. The infirmary was built facing the pond (complete with ducking stool), and remained there till early last century when it was demolished and replaced by public gardens which, despite the civic importance of the site, seem nowadays to be given over to a tatty funfair for the greater part of the time, a suitable complement perhaps to the brutalist concrete architecture of the 1960s development on the western edge of the square. At some time near the opening of the infirmary on its new site, Ann got a job there as a hospital cook.

The enlargement of the infirmary was an important event in Manchester history, and the bells of Christ Church rang out on the day it opened. It was run by a matron and had three visiting surgeons, one of whom was the young Jacobite, Edward Hall, who had retrieved the rebel heads a few years earlier. There were also three physicians, including loyalist and pillar of the community ('rather dull', according to Beppy Byrom), Peter Mainwaring.

Of course, Ann was at the bottom of the working hierarchy – in fact her name isn't even recorded in the infirmary records. She was now around twenty years old. We can get little more physical impression of her at this (or any other) period of her life than we could of her mother. The only descriptions we have of her appearance come from devoted followers in America many years later, and they are more a testament to the importance she assumed in their lives than a reliable account of how she looked. She is inevitably beautiful to them. What we can glean from their reports is that she had light chestnut hair, a fair complexion and blue eyes. She was a little below average height, with a stocky, 'rather thick', build.

We can get some inkling of the kind of cooking Ann had to provide by looking at a diet sheet used by the hospital a few years later, in 1769. Patients on a 'low diet' were given water gruel or pottage for breakfast, and broth or two ounces of veal or four ounces of root vegetables, or a pint of rice milk, or eight ounces of bread pudding, for their dinner. Supper was a repeat of breakfast or a small portion of bread and butter or cheese. Patients were given a pint of beer a day. The more substantial 'common diet' provided a pint of panada or milk pottage for breakfast, eight ounces of meat or vegetables for dinner, and a bigger helping of cheese or a pint of milk pottage for supper. This meagre, simply cooked food was the staple of ordinary people like Ann herself, and the catering arrangements at the infirmary anticipate some of the Shaker meals Ann would share in America. Three pounds of mutton or veal, or two pounds of beef, went into the making of every gallon of broth.

In 1757, two events occurred which must have affected Ann Lee in a number of ways: as a resident of Toad Lane, as an artisan woman in Manchester, and (at least as far as the second event was concerned) as an employee of the infirmary. On 7 June of that year two women were 'cheapening some Potatoes in the Market', as the *Manchester Mercury* put it in its issue of the following week – in other words, haggling about prices. Riots in the mid-eighteenth century tended to be about the price of food, and were often started by women. In the Manchester case the women tipped the potatoes out of the sacks and sent them bouncing along the ground, where they were grabbed by boys and women in the crowd (five years later, in the 'Great Cheese Riot' at Nottingham's Goose Fair, a similar thing happened with whole cheeses being rolled down the streets). A mob then formed and decided to turn its attention to the meal-house, where the market's grain was stored. During the ruckus the authorities got the upper hand and locked some of the looters inside the building, where they were left for a few hours to cool off before being released. Instead of going home as ordered by the magistrates, they regrouped and broke the windows of a shop belonging to a deeply unpopular corn-dealer called George Bramhall. They stormed in, insulted and terrorised his wife, and stole his supplies of bread.

The town constables managed to seize two of the

women in the crowd, and imprisoned them in the old dungeon on Salford Bridge. The rioters promptly stole some large forging hammers from a nearby smithy (whether it was John Lees's or not we cannot know), marched up to the dungeon and knocked the door from its hinges. They threw it in the River Irwell, released the two women and carried them off in triumph. They then made their way to Toad Lane, where Bramhall had his warehouse, broke in, and helped themselves to the grain, flour, meal and cheeses that were being kept there.

The situation was obviously getting out of hand, and the magistrates and leading citizens met together to decide what to do. They concluded the only thing for it was to meet force with force, armed themselves with heavy sticks, and called on their servants to assist them. As darkness came on they proceeded down Toad Lane and dispersed the mob, securing the peace of the town for that night.

Next day the whole thing started again. The mob was beefed up by the presence of some colliers from Clifton, a town on the way to Bolton, who marched across the bridge into Manchester, past the dungeon with its gaping doorway, and into Hanging Ditch. At this point, though, they were confronted by a group of gentry and tradesmen on horseback, and were unable to get any further. At mid-afternoon, the High Sheriff of Lancashire, James Bayley, rode into town with a retinue of fifty of his tenants, neighbours and friends. Within an hour he had assembled a substantial force, a vanguard of three or four hundred tradesmen and servants brandishing sticks, followed by sixty of the gentry armed with muskets and swords, and backed up by a further eleven or twelve hundred men, armed 'promiscuously' (as the excitable *Mercury* had it) with guns, swords and clubs. The numbers were no doubt exaggerated somewhat, but clearly the force was formidable enough to enable Bayley to stop at each of the town's flash-points, and, 'in a very concise and elegant Manner', point out the dangers arising to the poor from tumults.

This event, on her own doorstep, triggered by the price of bread and potatoes (the food of the poor), and initially led by women, must have had an impact on Ann Lee. One assumes that her allegiance was with the rioters, but ironically what would have been significant in the long run was the insight it must have given her into the volatility and violence of mob behaviour, of which she was herself to be the victim over and over again in later life.

The tensions that had led to the riot of June 1757 had been calmed by the High Sheriff, but not dissipated. Riots at this period tended to be caused not by hunger as such but by a sense of injustice in the operation of the retail trade. That motive is particularly evident in the next Manchester eruption, the most famous (or notorious) event of its kind until the Peterloo Riot of the early nineteenth century: the Shude Hill Fight of 15 November 1757.

This time the problem began with a march on the town by some rioters from Ashton-under-Lyne, on Saturday 12 November. Once again the meal-house in Market Street was the target. Perhaps as a result of the disturbances earlier in the year, a military force from Liverpool called the 'Invalids' was quartered in the town, and after some scuffles and arrests the rioters were dispersed. Back in Ashton on the following Monday they gathered together again, and raided some huxters' stalls. The following day they made for Clayton where they did considerable damage to the mills there. Then they marched towards Manchester in a very large body – nine hundred, according to one source. The High Sheriff got wind of what was happening and with a party of gentlemen and militia intercepted them just outside the town. He met with the leaders and asked to know their demands. These were that for the next twelve months oatmeal should be sold at twenty shillings, and potatoes at four shillings, per load, and flour at five farthings a pound. This attempt at price control anticipated similar endeavours in various parts of the country in the ensuing years. In the Thames Valley in 1766, for example, gangs of men working on the turnpike road cried out 'with one Voice, Come one & all to Newbury in a Body to make the Bread cheaper', and styling themselves the 'Regulators' enforced a popular price on foodstuffs in various towns and villages of the region.

The Ashton rioters, making their pitch on the outskirts of Manchester, were not so successful. Sheriff Bayley told them he had no power to make the sort of guarantees they wanted. As in June, however, he did his best to strike a conciliatory note, saying that he would serve the poor as far as he legally could. This time his attempt at reasonableness didn't work: one of the rioters struck at him with a scythe fastened to a pole, crying out, 'God damn you, you shall be the first to suffer', and another one tried to unhorse him. He was unhurt, but, along with his party of gentlemen and militia, decided it was time to retire back into the town. This proved to be a strategic error.

Crowds of locals, out on the streets in sympathy with the marchers from Ashton, interpreted the tactical withdrawal on the part of the forces of law and order as an admission of weakness, and abused them as they went past. The Sheriff and his men positioned themselves in Shude Hill (a hundred yards or so from the top of Toad Lane). The rioters, buoyed up by the mood of the locals, moved in to the attack, pelting the militia with stones and brickbats. They killed one of the soldiers, a corporal in the Invalids – whose brains, according to a letter to the *Mercury* written after the event, were clearly visible upon the stone that killed him – and injured nine others. In return the soldiers fired off a volley, killing two rioters outright and wounding fifteen, one fatally. There was a large clump of willows to the north of Shude Hill, remembered today in the name of Withy Grove (withy meaning 'willow'), which connected Shude Hill itself with Toad Lane. A young man called John Newton, the son of a substantial farmer and therefore more likely to be siding with the militia than with the rioters, climbed one of the willow trees to watch the spectacle and was picked off by a musket bullet for his pains.

If Ann Lee wasn't working she would probably have been one of the crowd that day, or at the very least have heard the uproar from her home in Toad Lane. More likely, though, she was at her station in the infirmary kitchen when the injured were carried in. According to *Whitworth's Manchester Advertiser and Weekly Magazine* for 22 November 1757, the task of caring for the victims was both a challenge to, and a vindication of, the new hospital. 'Thro' the great Care and Skill that has attended this Charity, since its Institution, the rest [of the injured], its hop'd will recover,' it claims, adding darkly, 'tho' the Loss of Limbs of two of them will mark 'em as the unfortunate Examples of this seditious and lawless Attempt.'

The firepower of the militia dispersed the rioters for the moment, but two hours later they regrouped and were joined by numbers of local people. They made their way to a mill belonging jointly to the inevitable George Bramhall and a merchant called Hatfield, and virtually destroyed it, along with Hatfield's house that stood nearby. The mob then marched to the dungeon, which had been repaired since the June disturbances and now housed one of their number who had been captured during the Shude Hill Fight. They demanded his release and the authorities, remembering what had happened last time, obliged. After this the whole affair more or less fizzled out, though the tensions it left behind were great enough for the Secretary at War to order Sir Robert Rich's Dragoons into the town on 23 November. In a conciliatory gesture the Manchester authorities advertised for any information that could lead to charges of hoarding and price-tampering of corn, meal and other provisions. When another, smaller, disturbance broke out in 1762 the ever unpopular Bramhall was led to put a price on his own head, by offering a reward of £5 to anyone who could find evidence that he personally had manipulated the price of corn.

Food riots during the second half of the eighteenth century were part of a process whereby unenfranchised people were beginning to find a political voice, and ultimately to establish themselves as the 'working class', with its own social identity and its own agenda. Of course this process took place in other areas of life apart from the purely economic one, vital though that was as far as the well-being of the poor was concerned. Equally important for many was the spiritual arena, and the whole history of Protestantism since the Reformation can be seen as an attempt by ordinary people to make themselves responsible for their own inner lives, or at least to establish that only God was their master there.

It was in this particular struggle that Ann Lee was to make her extraordinary contribution. In her own way she was to tap into, and represent, the combination of resentment and self-assertion that led to the riots of 1757, though ironically her stance was to make her as much a victim of mob violence as George Bramhall ever was.

In 1758, the year following the market-place disturbance and the Shude Hill Fight, Ann Lee became a Shaker.

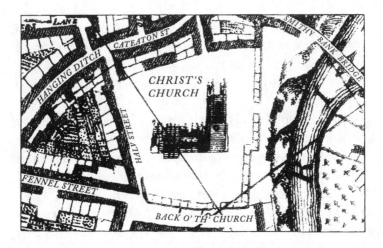

Christ Church, Manchester.
(endpaper map ref. Hg)

2

Clothed with the Sun

Shakerism had been going for just eleven years when Ann Lee joined the sect in 1758. It was started by a married couple called John and Jane Wardley, tailors from Bolton, a small town a dozen miles north of Manchester, who had broken away from their Quaker faith in 1747. The clue to the Wardleys' motives comes with the very word 'Shaker'.

An account of the origin of this name is given in an early-nineteenth-century Shaker textbook which offers an evocative and poetic description of those early meetings in Bolton under the Wardleys' ministry:

Sometimes, after assembling together, and sitting a while in silent meditation, they were taken with a mighty trembling, under which they would express the indignation of God against all sin. At other times they were affected, under the power of God, with a mighty shaking; and were occasionally exercised in singing, shouting, or walking the floor, under the influence of spiritual signs, shoving each other about, – or swiftly passing and repassing each other, like clouds agitated by a mighty wind. From these strange exercises, the people received the name of *Shakers*, and by some, were called *Shaking Quakers*.

The last phrase is obviously tautological, since shaking and quaking amount to the same thing. Moreover, this account of Shaker behaviour could easily be describing meetings of the Quakers, properly known as the Society of Friends, nearly a century earlier.

The first important proselytising mission of the Society of Friends had happened in north-west England, where Shakerism too was to begin, and those meetings held in the 1650s were characterised by trembling and shaking just as the Wardleys' services were to be in the 1740s. George Fox, the original leader of the Society, described speaking to a great meeting of priests in the church at Ulverstone in 1652 to such effect that one of them claimed 'ye steeplehouse shooke & hee was afraide & trembled & thought that the steeplehouse woulde fall on his head'. Margaret Fell, who was to marry Fox and become one of the leaders of the Society in her own right, herself shook when she first had experience of inner light the same year. One convert, John Gilpin of Kendal, had an extraordinarily strenuous experience that eerily repeated itself, like a transcendental version of the film *Groundhog Day*. He first quaked when in bed after a Quaker meeting in 1653; then was thrown off a chair while attending another meeting, twisting about involuntarily upon the floor all night; next, having had to resist a terrible compulsion to cut a hole in his own throat in order to give outlet to the language of the spirit, he had a third quaking episode which convinced him that the Lord had finally entered his soul. After a while, though, he began to doubt the validity of all these violent experiences, became disillusioned with the whole business, and wrote an anti-Quaker tract that accidentally predicts the name applied to the Wardleys' group a century later, *The Quakers Shaken* (London, 1653).

The origin of the common name, or rather nickname, for the Society of Friends is given by George Fox in his journal. In 1650 Fox appeared before Justice Gervase Bennett in Derby and told his Lordship that he ought to tremble at the name of the Lord (in her day, Ann Lee would be equally uncompromising in her dealings with judges). Justice Bennett replied that it was Fox and his followers who were quakers, not him. As with homophobia and racism, so with religious abuse: terms intended to express contempt can be appropriated by the victims and used with pride. As the Shakers said of their own label, 'the name (though by the world intended for derision) was very properly applied to the people'.

The strenuousness of the early Quaker conversion experiences, plus a sense of something paradoxical in the combination of enthusiasm and passivity that characterises them, can be seen in the phrase 'Lamb's War' which the Quakers gave to this phase of their evolution. But by the eighteenth century, Lamb's War was long over; the lamb had, in effect, been victorious. Quaker meetings were known for their peace and calm, for the silent meditation and self-questioning that took place in them. The term 'Quaker' was still in use, as it is to this day, but it no longer described, either literally or ironically, the normal behaviour of the Friends at their meetings; quaking had given way to Quietism, the term used by the Friends to describe this inward exploration. Whether a more enthusiastic tradition survived in outposts of the north-west, or whether the Wardley group had spontaneously rediscovered the raw emotionalism of the first generation of believers, hardly matters. What is clear is that in the very act of repudiating their affiliation with the Society they can be seen to be tapping into its original energies.

Shaker historians support this interpretation, praising the early Quakers for enduring persecution 'unto death', and claiming that as soon as they achieved public accept-ance they lost their spiritual purity; but their explanation goes one step further, suggesting that the Wardleys left the Society of Friends on 'receiving the spirit of the French prophets'.

The French Prophets, or Camisards as they were known in their home country, were a sect that arose in the late seventeenth century, in those dangerous years after the revocation of the Edict of Nantes in 1685 outlawed Protestantism in France. Worship involved paroxysms, writhing, fainting, trembling and twitching, a process that would culminate in prophecies, with particular emphasis on the imminence of the millennium when the heavens would open, anti-Christ be defeated, and humankind receive deliverance. Many of those inspired were women or young girls; in fact the first of the Prophets was a fifteen-year-old called Isabeau Vincent, who in 1688 led services while apparently asleep, a handy circumstance that established both integrity of inspiration and her lack of personal res-ponsibility, and one which was to characterise the prophecies of various of her successors: 'It is not I that speak, but the spirit that is within me.'

Persecution inevitably began, with villages being razed to the ground, Prophets being shot, some believers getting burned at the stake and broken on the wheel. In 1706 three of the French Prophets escaped to England, and for a few years made a stir there, especially in the London area, attracting up to four hundred believers in all. By 1712 they had made sufficient impact to warrant exposure in a book by a certain Charles Owen entitled, crushingly, *The Scene of Delusions Open'd in an Historical account of Prophetick Impostures, ... wherein the Pretensions of the New Prophets, are Considered and Confuted*. Owen surveys the predecessors of the French Prophets, amongst whom he numbers several female mystics, including the 'Holy Maid of Kent', Elizabeth Burton, 'who was subject to *Fits*, and often fell into *Trances*, which were accompanied with Convulsions and strange Motions of Body; in which she pretended to Inspirations and Revelations'. Despite this odd behaviour, in other respects, Owen tells us, 'she liv'd a regular, and a very austere Life'. Sadly, however, one of her prophecies suggested Henry VIII's downfall, and she was executed for the prediction in 1534.

Owen's point, of course, is that this prophetical tradition is at best absurd, and at worst threatening. His attack was hardly necessary, as it happened, because the French Prophets were beginning to pass into near-oblivion at about the time his book was published. This has cast doubt on the Shakers' claim that, more than thirty years later, the Prophets were to provide the impetus for their own faith. On the other hand, if one is aware of an influence it must, on some level or other, be real. There is no reason for the

Shakers to have known of the French Prophets if the sect had been completely defunct. Moreover, in his book Owen tantalisingly mentions certain prophetic meetings at Great Budworth in Cheshire, presided over by Thomas Dutton during the course of April 1711, and there is evidence of adherents in Manchester in 1712. One can surmise that these marked the beginning of some sort of tradition in the north-west of England which, however sketchy and attenuated it might have been, was still available as an influence when the Wardleys experienced their spiritual crisis more than thirty years later. Certainly the occasional French Prophet had popped up during the intervening period. A Welsh evangelical preacher called Howell Harris wrote in his diary for 1744 that he'd been given 'an account of the French prophets and of the devils acting in them, and how they design on Mr. Wesley'. The mention of the Methodist leader is a reminder that there was a strand in that movement too that encouraged ecstatic and millennialist worship, associated not with Wesley himself, who remained cautious about it (thus triggering the scheming by stray French Prophets), but with George Whitefield, one of the founders of Methodism, whom Ann heard preach in Manchester in the early 1750s.

Both the Quakers and the Camisards were notable for accepting female ministry. Women like Margaret Fell and Elizabeth Hooten achieved positions of leadership in the seventeenth-century Quaker movement, and George Fox himself wrote a tract entitled (in part) *The Mysterie of the womans Subjection to her Husband*, in which he argued that men and women were equal before the Fall; that men were then dominant; but women were made equal once more through the ministry of Christ. Quaker women preached and had their own meetings in parallel with those of men, and one of the seventeenth-century Quaker martyrs admired by the Shakers was a woman, Mary Dyer. When the Massachusetts General Court published a law outlawing Quakerism on pain of death in 1659, Mary Dyer deliberately went to Boston to challenge it. She was duly sentenced to death and underwent a mock execution, being paraded through the streets to the gallows, then bound and the noose put round her neck. She was then released and deported. Not content with that close escape, she returned the following year and was hanged for real (it has been estimated that of the first eighty-seven Quaker ministers to visit New England between 1656 and 1700, twenty-nine, exactly a third, were women). But comedy was possible as well as tragedy: in the early period, the Quaker Elizabeth Adams stood outside Parliament for two days with a great earthenware pot upside down on her head, explaining simply that 'Many things are turned and turning.'

Similarly, many female French Prophets followed the example of Isabeau Vincent in prophesying and ministering to their followers. One of the London converts, Mary Keimer, would on occasion speak with God's voice, once telling a religious rival, in language that must have had a very challenging edge to it coming from a woman's mouth, 'Who art thou O man that Exaltest thyself? . . . How durst thou presume to speak unto me? I can this moment strike thee dead.' Another, an elderly woman called Dorothy Harling, identified herself as the 'Permanent Spring'. She would whip her disciples, and even – living up to her self-awarded title – urinate on the sinful parts of their bodies.

Being able to identify the background and traditions that produced Shakerism does little, of course, to explain the religious experience of the followers of this strange sect. The only contemporary account of Shaker worship before the emigration to America was published in an American periodical (oddly enough), the *Virginia Gazette*, in 1769, more than twenty years after the Wardleys had founded the sect and at a time when Ann herself was rising to ascendancy within it. The participants would sit and quietly converse at first, and then begin to scratch themselves. After this they would move their heads from side to side, at the same time '*trembling, shaking, and screeching* in the most dreadful manner'. Eventually they would begin to sing and dance 'to the pious tunes' (some heavy sarcasm here) 'of Nancy Dawson, Bobbin Joan, Hie thee Jemmy home again, &c'. As would happen later in America, the Shakers would disturb neighbours far and wide in meetings that often lasted through the night.

The Bible, the Old Testament in particular, can be resonant on the subject of shaking:

And they shall go into the holes of the rocks, and into the caves of the earth, for fear of the Lord, and for the glory of his majesty, when he ariseth to shake terribly the earth. (Isaiah ii, 19)

*   *   *

So that the fishes of the sea, and the fowls of the heaven, and the beasts of the field, and all creeping things that creep upon the earth, and all men that are upon the face of the earth, shall shake at my presence, and the mountains shall be thrown down, and the steep places fall, and every wall shall fall to the ground. (Ezekiel xxxviii, 20)

There are plenty more references to shaking in the Bible, and the early-nineteenth-century Shakers, when they established a theology for their creed, were ready and willing to cite them. Nevertheless, the central mystery of their faith defies solution. One can find justifications and point to precedents, but that is not the same thing as providing answers, and ultimately there is no point in trying to explain away the bizarre antics of the Wardleys and their little group of followers. Our distance in time and behaviour is too great; in any case Shaker worship is intrinsically inexplicable, something that happened outside the scope of ordinary life and beyond the realm of rationality. The most one can do, perhaps, is to point to a teasing ambivalence at the heart of their doctrine. God shakes terribly the earth, while all living things shake at the presence of God. Shaking is an individual's reaction in the face of God, and at the same time the sign of God making His presence felt in the spirit. It is human; it is divine. It is a characteristic of the temporal and a symptom of the eternal: 'Yet once more I shake not the earth only, but also heaven' (Hebrews xii, 26).

The whole point of Shakerism is that these oppositions are not resolvable. Shaking takes place at the very moment when the human and divine encounter each other. In common with other radical Protestant sects, we find at the heart of Shakerism (at least as the Wardleys and, later, Ann Lee herself promulgated the faith) a direct and unmediated encounter with God. This access cuts through social class and religious hierarchy; it ignores family ties and national loyalties, cares nothing for conventions and codes of conduct, and gives the participants an absolute authority to follow their impulses, no matter how irrational, disruptive and ridiculous their consequent behaviour might seem to an outsider. In terms of the growing self-confidence of common people, Shakerism can be related to secular forms of self-assertion like the 'cheapening' of potatoes by the women at Manchester market, or the stoning of the militia by the mob at Shude Hill, though its Quaker affinities encouraged a passive and indeed pacifist stance in dealings with the civic authorities, and in due course made its followers victims of mobs rather than members of them.

The Wardley Society, as the first group of Shakers was originally known, began meeting in private houses in Bolton. While it had a distinctive mode of worship it didn't possess a clear body of doctrine in any other way: except that its reliance on the inspiration of the Holy Spirit was in itself a creed, not to mention an agenda, one that perhaps made all other theological complexities irrelevant. Nevertheless certain beliefs became established, and anticipated Shakerism's later development under the leadership of Ann Lee. Mrs Wardley gained dominance over her husband, and in due course became known as Mother Jane. She also began to lay emphasis on the importance of confession which, by the time of the movement's major American expansion, was to become the cornerstone of the whole conversion process. Equally significant was her insistence on the desirability of sexual abstention, telling Ann that she and her husband did not touch each other any more than if they were 'two babes'.

In the sympathetic climate of north-west England, this austere and eccentric religion began to make converts. The most important, in terms of the first phase of its development, was a man called John Townley, a wealthy builder who lived in Canon Street in Manchester. In due course his house became the centre of Shaker activity, and he brought the Wardleys (who, like most of the believers, were in 'low temporal circumstances') down to Manchester and supported them there. It would probably have been difficult or even impossible for a working woman like Ann to make the long journey to Bolton regularly; and the communication barrier makes it unlikely that she would have been able to find out much about the sect until they became established in her neighbourhood, so it's a fair guess that this happened earlier than Ann's conversion in 1758.

We cannot reconstruct the nature of Shakerism, or Ann Lee's role within it, during her early years of membership of the Wardley Society. The fact that she got married in Christ Church, where she had been christened, early in 1762, is of little significance as far as her current religious allegiances were concerned. While some Shakers did get their marriages solemnised in-house, so to speak, for a wedding to be legally binding a minister of religion from a recognised church would have had to officiate. What is probably more relevant is her age at the time of the service: just coming up to twenty-six, quite advanced for a woman of her class and period. It suggests the possibility of reluctance or at least of a lack of enthusiasm, and lends support to Ann's later claim that she felt revolted by sex from the time of her early childhood. Her husband was a blacksmith like her father, and the married couple lived in the Lees family house; while not conclusive in itself, this probably means that Abraham Standerin worked in Ann's father's business, a normal enough set-up, but it could suggest that from Ann's point of view this was a marriage of convenience, undertaken under family pressure. Later she claimed to have gone through nine years of spiritual travail before achieving the revelation that she was Ann the Word. But since this moment seems to have taken place sometime in the year 1770, the long struggle must have begun at about the date of her wedding.

The wedding certificate is still preserved in the archives of what is now Manchester Cathedral. Both husband and wife made a cross in lieu of their signature, as did many other uneducated couples at that time. That wavering mark is the nearest we can now get to Ann Lee physically, a strange irony for a woman who was going to dedicate herself with such intensity to the destruction of marriage as an institution; it's even more ironic to reflect that the woman who was to turn herself into the Word couldn't form the two words that belonged to her.

Four children were born to Ann and Abraham Standerin, though only one appears in the Christ Church records, their daughter Elizabeth who was baptised on 15 July 1764. Unlike her mother's ceremony this was a mass baptism, a group of twenty-eight infants in all, one of whom may have been her cousin: Thomas, son of a William and Elizabeth Lee. The parallelism of female names, coupled with the fact that William was the name of the devoted brother who accompanied Ann through her spiritual and indeed her geographical odyssey (along with the fact that he is known to have had a child), suggests this may have been a family occasion. Any rejoicing, however, was to be short-lived. Elizabeth, daughter of Abraham Standley, that is, Standerin, appears in the church's burial record for 7 October 1766.

Of the three other babies born, the last delivery was a difficult one, requiring forceps. Like their sister all of these children died in infancy, and there may not have been the opportunity to baptise them beforehand. On the other hand the omission may have been caused by Ann's increasingly extreme divergence from orthodox religious belief. During the 1760s the Shakers consolidated their position in Manchester, rising to a membership of around thirty, and also began to establish a base in north Cheshire. John Townley's wife had a brother called John Hocknell who lived in Cheshire, twenty-four miles from Manchester, probably in the town of Kermincham. Hocknell had left the Church of England to become a Methodist and held meetings at his house. In due course he visited the Shakers in Manchester, fell under the influence of

John Wardley, and became a member of the sect in about 1766. His spiritual trials were by no means over, however. His wife, Hannah, came from a family of 'wealthy and high-spirited people', and three of her brothers demonstrated their high spirits, or at any rate their wealth, by conniving with a magistrate to have John Hocknell put in prison at Middlewich, four miles from his home. Eventually, however, he was released and after a time succeeded in converting Hannah and their daughter, Mary. On their way to the Hocknell house, the Manchester Shakers had to pass by the house of another believer, John Partington, who lived in Marton, about three miles from Congleton, and often stopped over for one of their services.

This journeying over the countryside led to a number of adventures which Ann Lee and John Hocknell recounted to their American followers in later years. On one occasion, Ann claimed, she found herself being pursued by a mob, and had to run to the far side of a small hill where she came to a frozen pond. 'I laid myself down upon the ice,' she told a Shaker called Abigail Babbit, 'and remained there all night, in great peace and consolation, and did not take cold.'

Another more elaborate and detailed tale has echoes of the story of the Good Samaritan. Again, Ann was attacked by a mob, and driven along a road, being kicked every few steps over a distance of several miles. A certain nobleman (there's something rather abstract and stylised about the phrasing of this story) living some distance away began to develop a sensation of unaccountable anxiety and a desire to go somewhere, though he didn't know where.

Meanwhile John Hocknell was following Ann as best he could. Unfortunately, however, he was spotted by the attackers, and thrown into a bulge-place (a cesspit, as we would call it now). 'With much difficulty,' he later explained to a Shaker called Mehitabel Farrington, 'I got out, and went to a fountain of water, and washed myself; then went and changed my garments, and pursued after Mother [Ann].' Sadly his troubles didn't end there. When he caught up with the mob, they took hold of him again, knocked him about, and rolled him in a mud-slough. Despite being considerably the worse for wear, he 'did not suffer anger to arise in the least degree', as he proudly informed Mehitabel, testifying to Shakerism's affinity with Quaker pacifism. A poor widow came out of her house and bandaged up his head, and he took the opportunity of going inside and having another wash.

Meanwhile, the fidgety nobleman asked for his horse to be saddled and set out to find what was worrying him. He was drawn to the fracas and ordered the mob to disperse. He then asked Ann if she had any friends nearby. At that moment along came the newly clean John Hocknell, and took care of her.

Many of the anecdotes from this phase of Ann's life have an almost allegorical quality. There's enough corroboration and incidental detail to suggest a basis of truth – would Hocknell have invented the need for two washes in quick succession on his way to a rescue? – but the desire for a religious lesson, and indeed the process of memory, or of forgetting, seem to have given the narrative

an unnaturally sharp and simple focus. The nobleman may
not have been as noble as all that; his arrival might be
down to happy chance rather than divine intuition. Possibly Ann Lee lay on the icy pond for some minutes rather
than a whole night. The later, American anecdotes have
their own religious agenda, a miraculous content which
is often quite simply detachable, but they also have a
supporting tissue of observation, along with names and
dates and places, that gives their reality a richer texture
than this earlier, English material.

But while our knowledge of the external events of Ann
Lee's life at this stage is unreliable and sketchy, we get
a vivid picture of the spiritual journey she was under-
taking, and of the pain it cost her. Indeed in the Shakers'
parlance the process was indistinguishable from the suffering that accompanied it, since they punned on, or perhaps
simply failed to distinguish between, travel and travail,
using both words indiscriminately to describe the quest
for salvation. What made the spiritual journey so arduous
was its loneliness, and the austere divinity who awaited
the pilgrim. 'Many times, when I was about my work,'
Ann said later, 'I felt great gifts of sorrow; and I used to
work as long as I could to keep it concealed, and then
run to get out of sight, lest some one should pity me with
that pity which God did not.' By 'gift' Shakers referred
to any impulse or mood which might sweep over them,
and which they attributed to the Almighty. The descriptions Ann later gave to her American converts of her
developing religious experience paint a poignant picture
of a lonely woman in a crowded house, trying desperately

to cope with repeated tragic pregnancies, and to find herself in finding her God: 'I often rose from my bed at night, and walked the floor in my stocking feet, for fear of waking up the people. I did not let my husband know my troubles, lest I should stir up his affections; and I was careful not to lay any temptation before him. I also prayed to God that no man might suffer in hell on my account. Thus I labored, in strong cries and groans to God, day and night, till my flesh wasted away, and I became like a skeleton; and a kind of down came upon my skin.'

What is particularly striking about this account of spiritual crisis is its physicality. It is as though, to borrow imagery from a mid-nineteenth-century Shaker, we are watching the metamorphosis of an insect mutating from larva to pupa to imago. There is nothing abstract about this process, and nothing metaphorical about Ann's account of it. We will find similar examples over and over again when the American converts to Shakerism describe their experiences. A kind of down came upon Ann Lee's skin. To her this was obviously the mark of a struggling soul; to us it looks more like a symptom of anorexia nervosa.

When Ann described her nine years of suffering to another American Shaker convert, Mary Tiffany, she used similarly physical language: 'In my travail and tribulation, my sufferings were so great, that my flesh consumed upon my bones, and bloody sweat poured through the pores of my skin, and I became as helpless as an infant.' Perhaps her suffering is most vividly conveyed in yet another account she gave, where she describes her efforts to avoid sleeping during times of religious crisis. For a woman who constantly experienced visions of the spiritual world, sleep was a challenging state that could indicate the real whereabouts of the soul. A nightmare for Ann Lee did not take place in the subconscious, a concept that would not be available for more than a century; instead it was located in the geography of the spirit. 'When I felt my eyes closing with sleep, I used to pull them open with my fingers, and say within myself, I had better open my eyes here, than open them in hell.'

The sequence of events which led to Ann's full conversion and its consequence has to be somewhat conjectural. Shaker sources claim the conversion took place in 1770, and relate it to Ann's experience in prison. The record makes it quite clear, however, that she first got into trouble with the law in 1772, and it seems logical that her increased aggression was a product of conversion rather than a prelude to it. Since we also know that she was confined for a period in an asylum it seems likely that this was the location for the final stage of her spiritual drama. Half a century later, in 1822, the elderly Mary Hocknell remembered the confinement in a bedlam as being Ann's 'first imprisonment'.

In 1766 the Manchester Infirmary where Ann Lee had been a cook opened a Lunatick Ward for the mentally ill, and if this reconstruction is correct, four years later Ann herself became one of the patients. Her fourth child was still alive at the time she was admitted, because her sister Nancy carried her to the hospital windows and held her up so that Ann could see her. It is not hard to understand how this woman, who had lost three children and who may

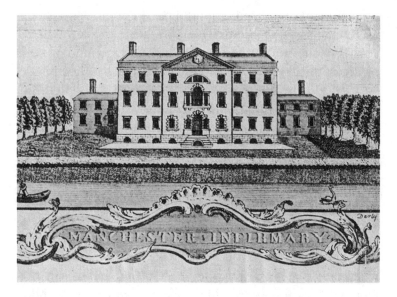

Manchester Infirmary, 1756.

have been suffering from what we would term postnatal
depression after the birth of a fourth, and who had every
reason to experience the most agonising postnatal anxiety
– this woman who walked the floor in stockinged feet at
night, or who lay in bed with her fingers holding her
eyes open, who was wasting away because she wouldn't
eat and whose body had become covered in a fine down
– could seem to be a prime candidate for the lunatic
ward of the local hospital. It's important, however,
particularly given the brushes with the law that were
shortly to commence, not to jump to conclusions about
Ann's confinement in the asylum. The records, which

43

unfortunately are missing for the period when Ann herself was an inmate, show that patients were regularly cured and discharged. In other words, as its association with the infirmary itself suggests, the institution was a therapeutic one, not a cage for lost causes, some savage eighteenth-century bedlam filled with the gibbering of the insane. Certainly Ann was released into the community after a short period of confinement. Moreover, in her own terms, and those of her followers, the most beneficent possible transformation had taken place. She had been born again.

It is a familiar phrase, part of the armoury of funda-mentalist Christianity, but for Ann it was not ultimately metaphorical. When you live in more than one dimension metaphors lose their vitality: they move inexorably towards the state of the literal. 'My soul broke forth to God; which I felt as sensibly as ever a woman did a child, when she was delivered of it. Then I felt unspeakable joy in God, and my flesh came upon me, like the flesh of an infant.' She uses similar language in other accounts of this moment of revelation. We have seen how she told Mary Tiffany that in her distress she became as helpless as a baby; it turns out there is a bonus to be collected from this vulnerable state: 'And when I was brought through, and born into the spiritual Kingdom, I was like an infant just born into the world. They see colours and objects, but they know not what they see; and so it was with me, when I was born into the spiritual world. But before I was twenty-four hours old, I saw, and knew what I saw.' It is tempting to make an equation between the woman who has lost her infants in childbirth or soon after, and the visionary who sees herself as a baby being born. What is clear is that the experience of rebirth for her was a real event, something that affected her physically, and that made her not just see the world in a new light but actually put on weight and have a new sense of her own body and personality.

This process was best described by one of the most philosophically acute minds Shakerism threw up, Elder Frederick Evans, when in the middle of the nineteenth century he wrote his *Compendium of the . . . Doctrines of the United Society of Believers in Christ's Second Appearing*. He says that the procreative principle that kept humankind on the animal plane was merely a stepping-stone to a superior order. He then switches to the example of the metamorphosis of insects: 'as the worm state to that of the butterfly', and points out that after the task of producing and continuing the human race has been completed, this developmental phase can be discarded and then be 'supplanted by the opening of the next discrete degree – the Divine-spiritual – in the soul, which is the ultimate and final resurrection'. As we move to the next evolutionary stage (Evans was writing at the time Darwin was completing his *Origin of Species*) we cast off not our bodies, exactly, but our body-reproducing capacity, and progress thereby from a temporal to an eternal state. We have moved on to a new 'discrete degree': we have begun again.

But it's Ann's own account that conveys the grandeur and excitement involved in beginning again. And her very phrasing gives a sense of what she has become. The declarative force of her last sentence – 'I saw, and knew what I saw' – suggests a new assertiveness and authority that would bring her to leadership of the Shakers, not merely in organisational terms but in an absolute spiritual sense. She was in a position to reveal to the Shakers whom she now gathered round her at John Townley's house that she was the woman clothed with the sun, as described in the Book of Revelation, the witness to whom the light and power of God were revealed: Ann the Word.

In terms of Shaker theology she now assumed the status of the counter-Eve and counterpart of Jesus: for many people, though this was not a claim she specifically made herself, this new Ann was the female messiah. There is of course an element of hindsight, of retrospective logic, in this claim, as there is in the case of Jesus himself, the male messiah. One of the key texts of Shakerism, a book published by Calvin Green and Seth Youngs Wells in 1823 and entitled (in part) *A Summary View of the Millennial Church*, gives a detailed account of the calculations involved in establishing the date of the millennium when humankind would find salvation on earth. The book quotes Revelation xi, 3, 'And I will give power unto my two witnesses, and they shall prophesy a thousand two hundred and threescore days, clothed in sackcloth.' According to the Shaker commentators, days in prophetic language equal years. They claim that the two witnesses prophesied in sackcloth while anti-Christ was triumphant. This dark period began with the accession of Pope Leo I, who established the supremacy of the papacy in AD 457. If 1,260 is added to 457, we get 1,717, and 1717 happens to be the year when Peter the Great permitted liberty of conscience in Russia and inaugurated an era of tolerance that slowly spread through Europe.

We are also told, in the same chapter of Revelation, that for a period of forty-two months the Holy City was being trodden down by the gentiles. Forty-two months equals 1,278 days, that is to say, in prophetic language, years. If 1,278 is added to 457 we get 1,735. This year marks the beginning of the reinstatement of the Holy City. 'It may be noted,' the commentators point out, 'as a remarkable circumstance, that Ann Lee was born the very next year, viz. 1736.'

It is necessary to understand both the importance and the limitation of these two central figures, Jesus and Ann, the two 'witnesses' in the history of Christianity, according at least to Shaker doctrine. They are, each in his or her own generation, unique, but only in the sense that they provide a lead which others can follow. They are the two people who, at historically significant moments, were spiritually pure enough to be aware of the coming of the spirit of God to redeem humankind. The name of that spirit is Christ. In witnessing the arrival of the spirit, Jesus and Ann participated in it; they therefore became embodiments of Christ, as can we all. This is an important feature of Shaker theology, one which clarifies the status awarded to Mother Ann. She was the facilitator, so to speak, of the Christ-spirit, the vanguard of a new phase in the spiritual evolution of the human race. In this respect she is performing the exact function of her male predecessor. And it is possible for any of us, through a rigorous process of purification, to open our hearts to God sufficiently to take our place alongside, or at least only just behind, these great spiritual leaders. An early-twentieth-century Shaker sister, Catherine Allen, probably described Ann's status best: 'We recognise the Christ Spirit, the expression of Deity, first manifested in its fullness in Jesus of Nazareth. We also regard Ann Lee as the first to receive in this latter day the interior realisation that the same Divine Spirit which was in Jesus might dwell within the consciousness of any man, woman or child.' As Thankful Barce, one of Ann's American converts, was to put it: 'If I ever saw the image of Christ displayed in human clay, I saw it in Mother Ann.' This is a doctrine that acknowledges spiritual hierarchy, or at least precedence, but at the same time offers egalitarian possibilities. It is therefore a reflection of the aspiration of the Manchester people who brought it into being and profoundly compatible with the developing democratic spirit of America, where it would take root.

Despite the qualifications and codicils, the Shakers were making a breath-taking claim, that 'Christ did verily make his second appearance in *Ann Lee*'. In addition to the account of the witnesses in the eleventh chapter of Revelation there were a number of other texts that could be interpreted as prophesying the female messiah, including a reference to an 'Elect Lady' in the second epistle of John, and, most importantly of all, the extraordinary vision described in chapter 12 of Revelation: 'And there appeared a great wonder in heaven; a woman clothed with the sun, and the moon under her feet, and upon her head a crown of twelve stars.'

It is a strange and haunting image, and one that

resonated with Ann herself. The woman clothed with the sun was suffering the pangs of childbirth: 'and she being with child cried, travailling in birth, and pained to be delivered'. She was locked in battle with a great red dragon that was waiting for her child to be born, in order to devour it. Quite clearly this imagery spoke to the experience Ann had already gone through, but miraculously it transmuted her bereavement into a spiritual drama, and thereby made it meaningful. The child was the new spiritual dispensation, the return of the Christ-spirit to the world, and would provide the means for the human race to become united with the divine. In due course, Revelation tells us, the man-child of the woman would be 'caught up unto God, and to his throne'.

This powerful vision, traditionally taken to refer to the Virgin Mary, had inspired other women before Ann Lee – indeed, sixty years earlier, five of the French Prophets (somewhat incompatibly) had each staked a claim to be 'the woman clothed with the sun'. But Ann was to give the twelfth chapter of Revelation a force and impact no other female religious leader could lay claim to. A few years later an American convert to Shakerism named Cornelius Thayer was to confess his sins to her. In return she made him a promise of eternal life, and told him to 'read a chapter in the Revelations, concerning the woman clothed with the sun'.

Ann, as the second witness to the Christ-spirit, was born only a year after the date calculated on the basis of chapter 11 of Revelation. In another sense she was born thirty-four years later, in the year 1770, when she was released from

49

the Lunatick Ward and took over the leadership of the Shakers. 'I love the day when I first received the gospel,' she said later, 'I call it my birthday.' Her words had 'the most astonishing power of God' and the Wardleys immediately relinquished the leadership of the sect to her.

At this moment Ann Lee, the obscure artisan woman, steps into history, and demonstrates it by getting herself into trouble with the authorities.

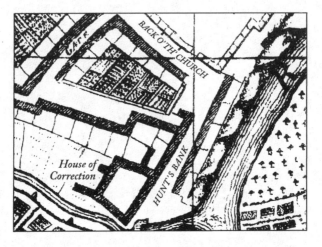

The Manchester House of Correction.
(endpaper map ref. If)

3

The House of Correction

Shaker worship was loud and unruly. It involved singing of an impassioned kind, very out of kilter with the great British tradition of mouthing hymns in a combination of boredom and respect. What the Shakers would have lacked altogether, from an orthodox point of view, is any sense of spiritual etiquette. Indeed, as the writer in the *Virginia Gazette* had pointed out, they didn't scruple at using folk tunes, some of which had distinctly racy connotations. This was home-made religion, which would have offended the decorum of the established churches and, perhaps more importantly, challenged the class structure and social regulation that were implicit in it. It is hardly surprising that the Manchester constables put spies and vigilantes in position to keep an eye on Shaker behaviour on the Sabbath.

On Sunday 11 July 1772, the Manchester Shakers assembled at John Lees's house in Toad Lane for worship. In the streets round about, twenty-four 'assistants', employed by the constables at sixpence apiece, were lying in wait.

We know nothing about John Lees's conversion, beyond the fact that it had happened. Of course, a lot of water had flowed under the bridge since Ann as a child had aroused his fury by trying to persuade her mother not to have sex with him – at least twenty years' worth, in fact, since Ann was now a woman of thirty-six. There's no mention of her mother, so it's reasonable to infer that the good woman had long ago joined other lost souls in that blackness and darkness where, years later, Ann was to find her again in a vision. Other members of the family had been won over by Ann the Word as well: Nancy Lees (not her sister but a niece), Betty, who was probably a second cousin, her brother James, and above all her brother William. Her piety didn't strike a chord with everyone, though. Another of her brothers became so enraged at seeing her writhing and singing that he threatened her with a staff the size of a broom handle. When she refused to answer him he began beating her with it, until he had to stop for a drink. Ann describes sitting there unharmed while he became 'out of breath, like one who had been running a race'.

William, four years younger than Ann, possessed some of the charisma and drive of his beloved sister. At the beginning of his adult life he had put these assets at the service of a secular career, and had become a sergeant of horse in the Oxford Blues, one of the regiments entrusted with royal guard duties, a position he no doubt achieved because of an expertise in handling the animals that had been shoed in his father's shop all his life. He was married and had one son, perhaps that Thomas who had been christened with Ann's daughter Elizabeth in 1764. William was a commanding figure, above middle height, thick-set and strongly built, with an open countenance; a bit of a gay dog, with a love of his uniform and other fine clothes. But he was also Ann Lee's brother, and at some point in his young adulthood he became abruptly overwhelmed by a conviction of sin.

This crisis must have taken place just before Ann took over leadership of the Shakers – in the late 1760s, in other words. He went to see his sister, who briskly took him in hand, telling him to throw off his ruffles and silks and 'put his hands to work and his heart to God'. He duly did so, and left the army, returning to the trade of blacksmith and working in his father's shop. His experience at this point gives us an interesting little glimpse of the rift that was taking place between Ann and the Wardleys. William frequented the society of John and Jane Wardley and when in spiritual distress confided his 'trials and feelings' to them. Their policy was to encourage and build him up, so that he gained peace of mind. As soon as he went back to his sister, however, she would 'spoil his comfort, overthrow his false hopes, and again plunge him into deeper tribulation than before'. By a process of osmosis his distress developed the intensity, and the symptoms, of hers. There is something eerie about the closeness and complexity of the relationship he had with Ann. 'I love my Mother,' he once said, 'although she is my sister; yet she has become my Mother, and the Lord God made me to love her.' Just as Ann would lie in bed at night not daring to fall asleep in case she should wake up in hell, so he describes working so hard that 'I would have given anything if I could have set down and rested myself upon my anvil one minute; but I durst not; for I felt my soul, as it were, upon a needle's point.' Like Ann, he developed an aversion to food, feeling that he was unworthy to put 'any of the creation of God' into his mouth, but wept instead, and went back to his interminable work. He was, as we shall see, to become well known as a weeper. Finally he was able to make a full confession of his sins. He then cried to God, day and night, till eventually he heard 'an audible voice from Heaven, saying, *William thy sins are forgiven*'.

First thing on that Sunday morning in July 1772, Ann Lee had an inkling that something was amiss, and it illuminates both her relationship with her brother and the importance he had already achieved in the Shaker fellowship that her reaction was to tell William to leave the house and get out of Manchester straight away. Some time later, while the Shakers were at worship, the constables' assistants broke in, rushed up to the 'garret, or third loft of the house', and seized everyone there. They were disappointed not to find William, and interrogated Mary Hocknell, the twelve-year-old daughter of John and Hannah Hocknell, the wealthy couple from Kermincham in Cheshire who had converted to Shakerism some years before, 'to make her tell where *Bill Lee* was, as they called him; but she refused to answer or even speak'. The Shakers were then taken down the stairs. Ann herself was dragged down by her ankles, a fate that was to befall her on a number of occasions, one which cunningly combined sexual humiliation (by sending her skirts skidding up to the top of her legs) with physical abuse. This violence may have been spurred on by drink. The constables' accounts covering this episode include five shillings and sixpence 'To Ale for 24 Persons about apprehending the Shakers'.

Five of the Shakers were imprisoned in the local lock-up, that same dungeon on Salford Bridge that had been used to accommodate rioters in the two disturbances of 1757. At this point we move out of the sphere of facts and into that of legend, as we do on a number of occasions in this early phase of Ann's career. When talking about this period to her American converts, she was to remember being left in a cell that was too small for her to 'straighten' herself, for two weeks without food. According to the constables' accounts, however, the Shakers were brought out the following day to face a remand hearing. This seems to have taken place in a tavern, because there is an item of 1s 2d paid to a Mrs Hulme for drink when the 'Shakers was brought before the Justice'. Three were then released while Ann and her father were remanded to the House of Correction pending the assizes, which were to take place in Manchester on 23 July.

Not that the House of Correction represented an easy option. The Houses had been set up by Elizabeth I 'for the suppressing and punishing of rogues, vagabonds and other idle and disorderly persons'. By the mid-eighteenth century they tended to be 'evil, disease-ridden places, managed by corrupt officers', whose conditions shocked the reformer John Howard more than those of prisons. The cells of the building as it was in Ann's time there, were on the first floor and looked out over the street below by means of grated windows. It was the custom of the

The House of Correction at Hunt's Bank as it was when
Ann was an inmate. Notice the prisoners 'fishing' for
alms from their cell windows.

inmates to solicit money and food by lowering bags to
passers-by (prisoners received no allowance except 2d per
day when sick). When the House was modernised, a year
or two later, this begging by bags was no longer possible
because none of the new cells directly overlooked the
street. But even that didn't reflect an architectural repudiation of the principle involved, because a sign was erected
on the outer wall quoting Matthew xxv, 43: 'Sick and
In Prison and Ye Visited Me Not', with a drop aperture
underneath it so that friends and relatives of the prisoners
would have their consciences pricked and insert
donations.

The fact that prisoners in effect had to beg for food

gives some credence to Ann's claim that she wasn't fed during her imprisonment, and that she would have perished had it not been for the ingenuity of one of her most devoted followers, a weaver by the name of James Whittaker, and his stratagem of the pipe.

James Whittaker, like Ann, was born on the last day of February, though in his case that was the 28th, in 1751, the son of an Oldham couple, Jonathan Whittaker and his wife Ann, whose maiden name had been Lee and who was, apparently, a distant relative of her namesake. Ann Whittaker had become a Shaker, and was followed into the faith by her husband, though this commitment did not save them, as we shall see, from eventually being on the receiving end of a spectacular onslaught from their devout son. The young James went with his mother to the Wardleys for worship, and in due course came under Ann's influence. His own conversion experience took classic Shaker form, though he seems to have begun with an unusually clean slate. 'I was brought up in the way of God by my Mother, and knew no unclean thing,' he claimed, the mother concerned at this point presumably being his biological one, but the second phase of his spiritual development has all the hallmarks of the agency of the other Ann Lee, his mother in God, and takes the shattering and traumatic form which characterised her own experience, and that of her brother William. Interestingly, James's account highlights the ambiguity about where shaking actually comes from, discussed in Chapter 2: 'I ... cried mightily to God: I do not think I spoke more than five words in a day; and I verily thought that the earth trembled under me, for the space of a whole year; but I suppose it was my body that trembled, which caused this feeling.' James Whittaker was to rank with William Lee as Ann's most trusted elder, and indeed took over leadership of the sect when she died.

James was just twenty-one when Ann Lee was put into prison, and was much exercised about how he could help her. Eventually he went out and bought a pint flask which he could conceal in his pocket, and some wine. He continues, in a way which reminds us how bucolic Manchester still was: 'About milking time, I went and bought a half pint of milk, and put it into my bottle. I then considered how I should convey the wine and milk to Mother. At length I thought of a pipe, so I bought one and put it into my hat.' After dark, he mixed the milk and the wine, went to the prison, put his mouth to the keyhole, and whispered to Mother Ann to put *her* mouth to the other side of the keyhole and he would give her something to drink (presumably her cell didn't overlook the street, or a lowered bag would have been a simpler solution). Unfortunately, ingenious as this plan was, it foundered at this point, because the clay pipe's stem proved too wide to go through the aperture. James thought of whittling it away with a penknife, but decided that would be too risky, so returned home feeling 'very heavy'.

The next day he went to the store and bought another pipe, a yard long but presumably with a narrower bore, the sort you see being held at arm's length by men in frock coats in eighteenth-century engravings. A detail that suddenly brings a past moment to life: this time, it being a longer pipe, James carried it home in the buttonholes of his coat. Again he went off to Ann's cell in the dead of night, and on this occasion he was successful in nourishing her.

This is a great anecdote if one wants to create a religious mythology. There's the parallel with Jesus being given a sponge of vinegar to drink on the cross, along with the potent symbolism of milk and wine, the nourishment associated with the female redeemer, the sacramental blood with the male one. The picture of Ann receiving this brew through the stem of a pipe conjures up a heady combination of suckling and sexual images. But the fact that the symbolism is powerful does not mean the story is untrue. Just as the tale of the benevolent nobleman is grounded by John Hocknell's account of the two washings he needed en route to Ann, so this anecdote too has its share of convincing detail: the pipe in the hat, the wait for milking time, the question of paring the stem, the second pipe carried in the buttonhole.

The main sticking point in the story, as told years later by Ann herself and by James, is that since the cells were on the first floor they would have to be reached from *inside* the prison. But the set-up in the House of Correction at this time seems to have encouraged interaction between inmates and those outside. A historian writing just thirty years after Ann's imprisonment says that the profits of the bags which the prisoners lowered from their cell windows 'were but too often exchanged for spiritous liquors, which were very improperly, permitted to be sold in the house'. The governor in the early 1770s was Thomas Whitlow who, according to the Quarter Sessions records for October 1772, received £12 10s per half-year for his services. Whether he made any more out of providing alcohol for sale to the prisoners or through other forms of venality is not clear, but it would have been consonant with the mood of the times if he had, and with or without his connivance trading went on inside the House of Correction. We know that when Ann was jailed in Albany in America she in effect held court to her followers in her cell. It seems perfectly possible therefore that James Whittaker might have gained access to the corridor where the cell doors were set. The quote from Matthew's gospel that was later put on the outside wall of the prison also suggests that at that time too the public were allowed in. These arrangements seem, by modern standards at least, a trifle informal, and indeed many inmates at this period managed to escape from the House of Correction. At the same time, however, Ann herself might have been subject to an unusual degree of constraint because of her unruly and unpredictable behaviour. When she was being held in Albany, years later, she had to be moved out of prison into a fort because she and her followers made such an intolerable amount of noise. So it is perfectly possible that members of the public were free to walk the corridors of the House of Correction and hobnob with the prisoners; equally, Ann could have remained locked in her own cell while this was going on, giving scope to Whittaker's ingenuity.

On 23 July 1772 Thomas Whitlow escorted Ann and her father, along with other prisoners, to court to appear before her old employer Peter Mainwaring, Doctor of

Physic and Justice of the Peace, assiduous attender at board meetings of the Manchester Infirmary and general pillar of the establishment – the same man who twenty-seven years before had tried to organise the citizenry to resist the entrance of the retreating Pretender into the town, and had been roughed up by the Jacobites for his pains. Once again a tavern was taken over for the hearing, this time the Mule, where the expenses came out at the sum of 2s 7d. The charge was an assault on a person called Mary Ashley. The background to this charge can never be known now. The incident could have taken place prior to the Sunday morning raid and indeed have provided the legal justification for it. Alternatively, Mary Ashley could have been involved in what we would nowadays term the 'stake-out' of the Lees household on Toad Lane, assuming the constables had considered it wise to have 'assistants' of both sexes. Certainly, half of the eight witnesses called for the case were women. They were all paid a generous fee for attending court (three shillings each for the women, four and six for the men), as well as being provided with meat and drink.

Ann and her father were found guilty but the court does not appear to have been minded to take a harsh view of the case. There is no reason to doubt later Shaker claims that Ann Lee had been a model employee of the infirmary, and Peter Mainwaring would probably also have remembered that only two years before she had been treated there for mental disturbance. He simply asked for them to provide sureties for their good behaviour until the next Quarter Sessions. This, however, they were not willing to do.

Their intransigence in this respect would be repeated by Ann and other Shakers at similar hearings in America. They followed the dictates of their own consciences, or rather, as they saw it, the direct instructions of God, and were therefore not in a position to offer any guarantee that their behaviour would satisfy legal or social norms. On the day when Ann had been born again, she had prayed to God that he would give her *'true desires'* and it was these that determined all her subsequent behaviour. Mainwaring therefore must have felt he had no choice but to fine Ann and her father sixpence apiece and sentence them to one month's detention in the House of Correction, still a mild enough punishment compared with those received at the same court by other defendants. William Eastwood, for example, was convicted of felony and like Ann and her father was ordered to be sent back to the House of Correction for a month; after that, however, he was to be transported to the American colonies for seven years. Two other fellow-prisoners, Alexander Bell and Thomas Clough, who were also found guilty of felonies, were ordered to be taken to the public Rogues' Post in Manchester, and 'being Stripped from the Middle Upwards shall be tied thereto and severally severely whipped 'till Blood comes'.

After her release in late July it did not take Ann long to find herself in the thick of trouble once more. By now she and the other Shakers were obviously the focus of public suspicion and resentment. One of the items of expense claimed in relation to the July court case was 2s 6d for 'Cryers Fees', so information about the affair must have been broadcast at full volume over the streets of Manchester. In October of 1772 there is evidence of a couple of disturbing episodes. On the 3rd, the constables claimed the sum of 5s 6d 'To sundry persons and expences Quelling a Mob who were beginning to pull down the House of John Townley a Skaker', and an additional 2s 6d on behalf of the Widow Shepley 'for Ironwork when the Shakers were apprehended'. A couple of weeks later, on 19 October, there's an entry for another 5s 6d 'To repairs making good the breaches at Lees's in Toadlane in order to apprehend a gang of Shakers lock't up there'. It may have been on this occasion that a gang broke into the Leeses' smithy and struck William over the head with a firehook, fracturing his skull. It sounds as if some small-scale sieges had been taking place, though it's interesting to note that the legal authorities felt obliged to make good the damage caused in mounting their assault on the Leeses' home just as they did at Widow Shepley's.

It was perhaps on 19 October, when the Leeses' house with its complement of Shakers was under assault, that an incident occurred which Ann later recounted to followers in America. She got out of her house with a mob at her heels, hoisted her apron over her head so she couldn't be readily identified, and ran to the home of a sympathetic neighbour who lived only a few doors away. He took her to the upper loft of his house where there was a large quantity of wool lying under the roof, pulled out several fleeces, told her to get down and covered her with them so that she lay 'safe and comfortable'. The mob arrived, called for a key, and began to search the house.

But when they got to the loft she heard them say: 'She is not here; there is nothing here but wool.' And so this time she escaped.

Her brother James was not quite so lucky – or perhaps not so fleet of foot – because on 20 October the constables claimed two shillings 'To the like apprehending and detaining James Lees while he could find Sureties'. James seems not to have shared his sister's disapproval of giving guarantees of good behaviour and perhaps as a consequence there is no record of his case, or any other arising from these October incidents, actually coming to court. There were, of course, other problems for the authorities to concern themselves with. Immediately after the entry dealing with James there is one claiming expenses for the arrest of eight persons for 'destraining a Cow under false pretences' all day and all night, followed by another for apprehending a 'Gang of Imposters one of whom was a woman pretending to be of super natural Strenght having with them a set of dancing Dogs with several Assistants'.

On other occasions Ann, too, failed to outwit her antagonists. She relates an episode where a mass of people came to her house by night, and dragged her out by her feet – face downwards this time because they tore the skin off it. There was also an occasion when a mob drove her through the streets in a cart, while people threw mud, horse dung 'and all manner of filthy stuff' at her. Ann didn't again bring herself to the official notice of the authorities until the following year, however: Sunday 23 May 1773, in fact, when John Townley, John Lees, Betty Lees

and Ann Lees were arrested for wilfully and contemptu-
ously disturbing divine service at Christ Church.

It is perhaps significant that this time, unlike the case
the previous summer, Ann was indicted in her maiden
name. This could have been a signal that she'd now fully
evolved her radical stance; after all, it was no longer a
matter of the authorities interrupting Shaker worship, but
Shakers interrupting a service of the Church of England.
There were precedents in the history of the French
Prophets and the early Quakers for such attacks: George
Fox once found himself so enraged at the sight of three
church spires as he was walking near Lichfield – 'they
strucke at my life' – that he entered the town and walked
the streets for several hours, crying out, 'Woe unto ye
bloddy citty of Lichfeilde.' Such aggression would never
again be associated with the Shakers, but perhaps for Ann
it marked a necessary repudiation of the community into
which she had been born, and the beginning of a search
for a new world in which to operate.

The disruption of a service at the Old Church, as it was
familiarly known, was almost certainly the cause of Ann
Lee's interrogation by ministers of the cloth, an event
which she recounted on a number of occasions after her
migration to America, making it sound like some sort of
formal tribunal, even an appearance before the Inqui-
sition. The way she saw it was that her enemies had falsely
accused her of blasphemy, and she was taken before four
church officials to have the judgement confirmed against
her. But she presented her case movingly, and also spoke
in tongues, with the result that the judges, impressed,

ruled in her favour. The mob, however, demanded blood, and she, along with other leading Shakers, was taken to a hillside where there was an attempt to stone them all to death. Luckily the mob proved to be poor shots, and only caused a slight wound to one of the Shakers.

What probably happened was that the church dignitaries asked her some questions, pending the arrival of the constable, to find out what all the fuss was about, and then while the Shakers were being taken off to prison some angry bystanders threw missiles at them, a nasty enough experience but not quite the same thing as a formal stoning. As far as the speaking in tongues was concerned, we can only conjecture what the church officials made of it. This was a regular occurrence for Ann and probably helped to trigger the charges of drunkenness that were sometimes levelled at her. Once when recounting the tale of this religious interrogation, Ann said she spoke for four hours and the ministers – the 'greatest in those parts' (suddenly we hear the illiterate daughter of a blacksmith talking) – 'said that I spoke in seventy two different tongues, and that I spoke them more perfect than any in their knowledge were able to do. After this they tried to persuade me to teach the languages; but I did not regard their flatteries.'

These priests, 'great' or not, seem to have been rather more naïve than was Timothy Dwight, President of Yale, when he went to visit the Shaker community in New Lebanon in upstate New York more than a quarter of a century later, in 1799. He heard a woman speaking in tongues and pointed out to her that she was making sounds that were not articulated, and which therefore could not be called words. She replied, 'How dost thee know but that we speak the Hotmatot language? The language of the Hotmatots is said to be made up of such words.' Dwight suggested that it would be simple enough to do a test if instead of speaking Hottentot they essayed a more familiar language, like Greek, Latin or French, but the woman wisely declined. An eccentric commentator called Thomas Brown, who was fascinated by Shakerism and who joined the sect for a while, described, indeed transcribed, his own experience of speaking in tongues at about the same time as the woman who spoke to Dwight: '*Hiero devo jirankemango, ad gileabono, durem subramo, deviranto diacerimango, jaffa vah pe cu evangalio; de vom grom seb crinom, as vare cremo domo*', the commas adding a nicely fussy touch. Brown makes a shrewd point about the serendipity involved: 'When a person runs on in this manner of speaking for any length of time, I . . . thought it probable that he would strike into different languages, and give some words in each their right pronunciation.' In other words, this apparent gibberish is an oral equivalent of the eternal monkey at the typewriter.

This time Ann spent two days in some sort of holding cell, possibly the lock-up on Salford Bridge once more, but more likely a room in a tavern requisitioned for the purpose, as often happened at that period, since a kind of rent seems to have been payable: 'To Ann Lees a shaker appre[he]nded for disturbing the Congregation in the old Church detaining her in the Prison room two days 2s'. Certainly at this stage there was no attempt to starve her, because the constables' accounts continue: 'maintaining her with meat & drink and her attendant 2s 3d wages 2s . . . 6s 3d'. This sizeable investment does not seem to have been thought necessary for her fellow-accused, which probably means they had been allowed, or had allowed themselves, to give sureties for their later appearance in court. This took place on 24 July 1773, one day after the anniversary of Ann's previous appearance. Whether she had been incarcerated in the House of Correction from 30 May or whether she had been allowed to go free in the meantime is not clear. It is possible that the authorities felt they had bigger fish to fry – they had just arrested a highwayman called Long Ned, for example (actually one Edward Edwards, though pleasingly the constables use his professional name in their accounts). The court records do not indicate whether, on this occasion, Ann and the others made their appearance before Peter Mainwaring in the custody of Thomas Whitlow. This time the fine was considerably more swingeing, however: £20 apiece. Perhaps Doctor Mainwaring was becoming impatient with his ex-employee and her followers. There is no record of the Shakers serving time in lieu of payment, so it may be that the wealthy members – John Townley, himself one of those convicted, and John Hocknell – coughed up the required sums. All we have is a note in the accounts for 28 July, when the amount of three shillings is claimed 'To attending Ann Lees two whole nights'. This may have been while the fine money was being found, but the other three Shakers are not mentioned and the word 'whole' suggests that Ann might have needed especially attentive supervision, possibly because of a perceived tendency to violence or instability.

There is no record of payment to the town criers on this occasion, but the case received publicity all the same, in the *Manchester Mercury* of 27 July 1773. This weekly paper was mainly devoted to news reports from London and abroad (except at times of local crisis, like the Shude Hill Fight of 1757), allowing just a half-column for Manchester news; but it did cover this court appearance and detailed the fines of the four Shakers cheek by jowl with news of other, severer sentences, like the seven years' transportation passed on John Crowder for obtaining under false pretences enough cloth to make himself a coat and waistcoat, along with another unpleasant titbit: the death by cancer of the throat of Sarah Sharrock, a woman over fifty years of age, whose tongue fell out of her mouth into her hand twelve days before she expired.

We have now reached a turning point in the history of Manchester Shakerism. Ann Lee would not be keeping her annual date before Peter Mainwaring at the July Sessions in 1774 because by then she and a small number of her followers would be on the high seas, aboard the *Mariah*, en route to the New World.

PART TWO
AMERICA

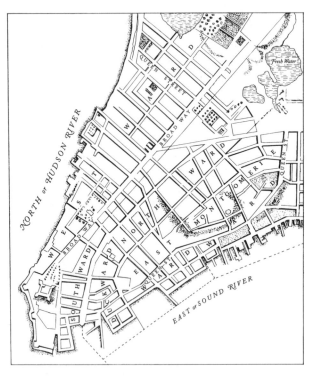

New York City, showing Broad Way and
Queen Street.

4

The Mariah

B ecause persecution had become routine, the Shakers used to make the twenty-mile journey for worship at the Townley and Partington residences in Cheshire by night. One Saturday, as they sat down by the roadside in the darkness to eat their victuals, young James Whittaker – the one who had thought up the pipe ruse for feeding Ann while in prison – had a vision of America.

Countless people have had a parallel experience in the five centuries since Columbus made landfall. John Winthrop, one of the original pilgrim fathers, foresaw a 'city on a hill' as his ship the *Arbella* approached the wild New England shoreline in 1630; in 1924, Scott Fitzgerald, writing the conclusion of *The Great Gatsby*, imagined the early Dutch explorers seeing with wonder a 'fresh, green breast of the new world'. This latter would have been an inappropriately sensual image for a Shaker seer; what Whittaker himself perceived was 'a large tree, and every leaf thereof shone with such brightness as made it appear like a burning torch, representing the church of Christ, which will yet be established in this land [of America]'. The vision was so powerful that it lingered on after the meal was over, and Whittaker had to be led by his fellow-believers for some distance before he came into focus on his surroundings again.

The tree was an important icon for the Shakers. Once, as she neared the end of her life, Ann pointed to an apple tree in full bloom and talked in parable style about some apples falling before becoming ripe, and others that would stay in place until they were ready. In a footnote to this anecdote, a Shaker commentator pointed out that Ann's tree comparison does not signify what 'must take place' but what 'actually does take place'; in other words, we are not dealing with a forced simile but a parallelism in the very nature of things. The same is true of a vision like Whittaker's. It was an experience that had the force of an imperative behind it, and would ensure that instead of being simply a cranky religious sect in northern England, Shakerism would become entwined with the developing culture of America.

This does not, of course, mean that there were no rational motives for emigration, though our reconstruction of them must be rather speculative. George Whitefield's American missions undoubtedly had their influence. Whitefield, like his colleagues the Wesleys, was a great evangelical preacher. He made six trips to America during the course of his career, starting in the late 1730s. On his second mission, between 1739 and 1741, he was an enormous popular success, preaching to gatherings in their thousands. He also addressed enormous crowds in Manchester on a number of occasions (in 1750, 1753 and 1767), and Ann attended one or more of these meetings, where she may well have been given some idea of the scope for proselytising on the other side of the Atlantic. Whitefield would have been an inspiration, but Ann nevertheless had her reservations about him. Some years later, in the early 1780s, she was at the house of a believer in New Lebanon when she was visited by three leaders of the local community – Eleazer Grant, shortly to prove her bitter enemy, a Dr Averill, and Elisha Gilbert – all curious to find out about the persecution she had suffered in England (perhaps Grant wanted some tips on how to mete out the same treatment to her in America). In the course of the conversation she told them that Whitefield had made the great mistake, when on the receiving end of adversity similar to that which she had experienced, of asking for the king's protection. The result of this appeal to – and therefore recognition of – secular authority had been the loss of the power of God; Whitefield had 'become formal', she went on, 'like other professors'. In other words, by sacrificing his independence he had lost his authentic spiritual voice, and had to make do with a religion of external observances no different in essence from those of the established creeds. The fact that White-field had had to compromise himself in this way (in Ann's view, at least), coupled with the extraordinary impact of his American missions, must have acted as both stick and carrot for the Shakers, giving them a reason for leaving England and an incentive for heading across the Atlantic.

Ann needless to say had her own vision, though it was a considerably less radiant one than James Whittaker's. America, it must be remembered, was not just a land of opportunity but also a dumping ground for social misfits, some of whom Ann herself had met in the House of Correction. In Harvard town, Massachusetts, in 1781, a woman called Phoebe Spencer was converted to Shakerism and was then taken by one of the elders to meet Mother Ann, who said, 'I have seen you before; and I knew that you and your family would come and embrace the gospel with us. Poor woman! you little know what you have lived amongst. I saw the lost situation of the people in America, before I came from England, how deeply they were all sunk in their pollutions; and so did brother William.' A messiah does not have the same motive for emigration as an ordinary person. Just as the Christ-spirit came into the world precisely because it required redemption, so Ann could be drawn to America precisely because it was sunk in its pollutions.

There was one huge drawback to American emigration at this time, but it is impossible to tell from this distance whether Ann and her followers even knew of it, though it would certainly cast a shadow over them in the years to come. In December 1773 three ships containing tea arrived in Boston harbour. A short time previously, Lord North's government had given the East India Company the right to export tea directly to the American colonies, but had at the same time passed a law levying a tax on it, and some disaffected colonists, resentful of being governed at a distance, had seen in this legislation an issue of principle, their opposition being pithily summed up in the slogan 'No taxation without representation'. On the night of 16 December fifty Bostonians covered themselves with war paint and dressed up as Indians. They then rushed down to the harbour, boarded the ships and threw the tea overboard, a symbolic act that opened the way to the War of Independence which was to begin in earnest eighteen months later, when the tea party would be transformed into a battlefield.

The Shakers were provincial, mainly poor, English people who could be expected to have limited horizons, though the very fact that they had embraced Shakerism shows independence of spirit. Nevertheless, the attraction to America felt by three of the sect's leading members (if we include William, on Ann's say-so) was not shared by most of the others, and we can only guess at the agonised soul-searching and the heated discussions that must have taken place. Though they may have had little or no knowledge of the colonial ferment that was beginning, they would be fearful of the dangers of travel and the uncertainty of the future, and aware that they faced the loss of their community, of the whole world they had known. It was one thing to believe, and to behave, in defiance of men such as Mainwaring and the ministers of the Old Church, but quite another to leave one's friends and family behind for ever.

John Townley, who had stood in the dock with Ann and her father at the July Quarter Sessions in Manchester, and whose house on Canon Street had provided living quarters and meeting rooms for some of the believers, was one of those who decided not to go. Others may already have been repelled or disillusioned as the result of the increasing stridency and radicalism of the sect under Ann's leadership – it had never earned an entry in the constables' records or the local newspapers before Ann took over. John and Jane Wardley, now getting along in years, overtaken, superseded and contradicted by their forceful protégée, never settling down to their odd double-billing as John the Baptists to her redeemer, also chose to remain in Manchester. It has been estimated that Shakerism in north-west England peaked at about sixty believers in the early 1770s; only nine went across to America in the *Mariah*, with a few more following a year later. Ann herself said goodbye for ever to her father and six of her brothers and sisters, including James who, eighteen months before, had been involved enough with the sect to have got himself on the wrong side of the law.

Schism, however, is not the word here, because the religion did not break into two parts: in the old country it ceased to exist altogether. Looking back at this period from their vantage point in 1808, some American Shakers briskly summed up what happened: 'those of the society who remained in *England*, being without lead or protection, lost their power, and fell into the common course and practice of the world'. Townley himself disappears completely from Shaker history; shortly after the *Mariah* set sail the Wardleys had to move out of his house into rented accommodation, and from there to the poorhouse, where they both died.

Luckily John Hocknell, fifty-one years old and a prosperous farmer in mid-Cheshire (courtesy of his wife Hannah), was willing and able to take Townley's place as the Shakers' chief patron, and he began by paying for passage on the ship for the handful of believers who

actually set sail: Ann, her husband Abraham, her brother
William, her niece Nancy, James Shepherd (an old friend
who had been one of the witnesses at Ann's and Abraham's
wedding), James Whittaker, Mary Partington (her husband
John stayed behind to clear his affairs) and John Hocknell
himself, along with his son Richard. It was Ann's own circle,
a group composed of close relatives and friends. Not that
this guaranteed fervour or even commitment – Abraham
never seems to have been anything more than a puzzled
bystander of his wife's religion, and would shortly go his
own way, while in due course Nancy and Richard would
fall in love, breaking one of the Shakers' cardinal rules and
therefore having to leave the sect in their turn. It seems a
very small foundation to build a major religious and commu-
nitarian enterprise on; yet it proved enough.

There were limits to John Hocknell's generosity, or at
least to his supply of ready cash (his farm wasn't sold until
the following year), and the berths on the *Mariah* were
cut-price because the ship had apparently been condemned. Nevertheless it set sail from Liverpool on 19
May 1774, under the command of Captain Smith of New
York, with its consignment of pilgrim fathers, and, more
significantly, mothers. As a clincher, the voyage had a
quality of *Pilgrim's Progress* about it as well, with its share
of real or imagined adversity and danger waiting to be
overcome.

This first generation of Shakers never made quiet citizens, neighbours or shipmates. As we shall be seeing, the
explosive sounds they were able to produce during their

meetings were considered phenomenal by those within earshot – and earshot was a considerable distance, one that could be measured in miles. In the close confines of the *Mariah* they were soon singing and dancing on deck, and it's not difficult to imagine how oppressive and claustrophobic the ship must have seemed to its other occupants. To make matters worse, Ann felt obliged to testify against the wickedness of the sailors. Predictably enough they responded by threatening to throw her overboard. There was probably an element of humorous exaggeration in this threat, but Shakers, like other fundamentalists, were not sensitive to irony, and in any case they had a tendency towards exaggeration themselves.

What dispelled this tension was a sudden crisis. The ship ran into heavy seas and a plank was loosened, a not wholly surprising occurrence if it is true that the *Mariah* wasn't fully sea-worthy to start with. At this dangerous turn of events Captain Smith, according to Ann, 'turned as pale as a corpse'. Fortunately she was able to reassure him: 'Captain, be of good cheer, there shall not a hair of our heads perish; we shall all arrive safe to America. I was just now sitting by the mast, and I saw a bright angel of God, through whom I received this promise.' Whether this information was enough in itself to cheer the captain up is not known, but the Shakers were prepared to supplement religious faith with practical effort, and zealously assisted the sailors at the pumps. According to one source this assistance in itself had a miraculous effect. The sailors had been able to do no more than keep the ship afloat, but once Ann and the other believers came to help, the situation was transformed. The *Mariah* began to make way again and eventually limped into New York harbour on 6 August 1774.

This account comes from a Shaker called Morrell Baker, who lived in the community at New Lebanon in the early years of the nineteenth century. He had a brother – that is, a 'natural' brother as opposed to his Shaker brethren – called Jedediah, who happened to be a sailor on the *Mariah* and who described these people with their 'strange religion' (his account obviously predated Morrell's conversion), the leak, and the danger they were in. He was forever grateful for the contribution of Ann and the other Shakers and 'believed the woman, and those who came with her, had a power above the natural power of man – and were the means of their ever arriving in America'.

Another source gives a more melodramatic version of events. A second large wave came along and struck the *Mariah* with such force and at such an angle that it reinstated the plank that its malign predecessor had dislodged, leaving the ship watertight once more.

There is ample biblical precedent for miraculous encounters with the liquid element, whether Jonah surviving in the belly of the whale or Jesus walking on the waters of the Lake of Galilee. The story of Ann's ship, broken and then conveniently repaired by the might of the Atlantic Ocean, belongs in this tradition, triggered as miracles so often are by the scepticism and hostility of non-believers.

Whether this event, so adventitious that it could count as truly magical, actually took place, or whether the

miracle was of a more routine sort, involving a certain
amount of good will and co-operation along with a fair
share of muscle power, some of it honed at an anvil, it
seems clear that solidarity and harmony between the
Shakers and the crew were achieved. Perhaps Ann's disciples simply became too busy (and tired) to perform their
more outlandish acts of worship. In any case no more
crises, natural or man-made, occurred before landfall, but
what happened immediately following the arrival of the
Shakers in New York seems, to modern eyes at least,
almost as magical as the tale of the plank.

The heat in New York must have struck Ann Lee and
her fellow-Mancunians with an alien intensity, but in other
respects the town would not necessarily have seemed
intimidating. It was smaller than Manchester, after all,
with a population of about twenty thousand. Back home,
James Whittaker had waited till milking time before
buying half a pint for his imprisoned leader, and that
acceptance of rural rhythms would have been possible in
New York too, with farms and streams on the northern
tip of Manhattan Island. On the hot August Sunday when
the Shakers disembarked from the *Mariah*, many of the
inhabitants of New York were sitting on chairs in the road
outside their houses.

The motley group of Shakers made their way up a wide
avenue called, appropriately enough, Broad Way (it's odd
to think of that name being a simple description rather
than a talisman for entertainment and night life), and
turned into Queen Street (which later on became Pearl

Street in order not to offend the sensibilities of the new republic). Ann Lee then went up to a woman who was sunning herself, and announced that an angel had told her to come to this very house, where she would be taken in. One can only speculate on what the consequences might be if a new immigrant tried this approach in the New York of today: what happened in 1774 was that the woman did indeed take Ann in, along with her husband Abraham.

As it happened, this family in Queen Street, who were called Smith, had a blacksmith's business, so they were in a position to make use of Abraham's skills. Quite probably it was this common ground, rather than the angel's announcement from on high, that had made Ann's direct appeal successful. She herself was given the job of washing and ironing for the family, and very soon 'gained the love and esteem of the woman of the house' by her 'meekness, humility, and amiable deportment'. It's not easy to see Ann in this relatively humble role, but one shouldn't assume that her tempestuous dealings with the authorities provide the only key to her character. She had knuckled down to work all her life and while she may not have struck those who encountered her as meek and humble, most of them found her amiable enough, albeit in a rather scary way. She had worked at menial occupations, had had children and subsequently lost them, knew what it was like to cope with adversity, physical violence, and jail. In short, though her experience had so far been confined to Manchester she was a woman of the world, and that was probably good enough for the inhabitants of small-town New York in the period immediately preceding the War of Independence.

The sharply increasing tension between the colonies and Britain would not yet have been a major problem. The conflict at this stage was, after all, between Briton and Briton, and there was no reason to see Ann as in any way a stooge of the authorities back at home – she had proved that point often enough. But the American Revolution is worthy of the name precisely because, as it took hold, it changed the nature of the very antagonism which had triggered it, so that one half of the adversaries began to define themselves in national and cultural terms over and against the other half. What began as a sort of civil war very soon became simply a war, and on a number of crucial occasions Ann Lee, through no fault of her own, was to find herself on the wrong side of it.

In the meantime, however, she and her husband had landed on their feet (there is no record of the digs found by the remainder of the small band of Shakers). Apparently she made such an impact that she was offered more remunerative work, but decided to remain loyal to the Smith family. This was, however, only a temporary arrangement. She had not come all this way to be a servant in a New York household. The Shakers needed a base to establish themselves in, and like so many other immigrants they were thinking in terms of a settlement in the wilderness. It was a romantic aspiration, to reject the burgeoning cities and the early industrial age in order to settle back into nature. It was a religious ideal as well, to search out a new Garden of Eden in the wilderness of

America, where a lost innocence could be rediscovered. These motives are the very fabric of American mythology, but for the Shakers they had an extra resonance and a sharper urgency, because they believed their leader to be the woman 'clothed with the sun' described in chapter 12 of the Book of Revelation.

After this woman had given birth she fled from the great red dragon 'into the wilderness, where she hath a place prepared of God, that they should feed her there a thousand two hundred and threescore days'. Just as in the case of the migration to America practical motives must ultimately have been secondary to a spiritual vision, so with the plan to leave the town of New York to seek out a new home in the unspoilt environment of upper New York State. A woman who had borne and lost children, who had, as she claimed, been herself new-born, and who faced the task of bringing into being the new final phase of human existence, needed to flee to the wilderness, in order to discover that place prepared of God.

In point of fact it was John Hocknell who found the spot. He, James Whittaker and William Lee went up the Hudson River to Albany to try to acquire land in that region, but found it too expensive. They then heard of cheaper land a little to the north-west and continued on their way another seven miles or so to find it. At this point Hocknell found his arm rising upward and going forward into a pointing position, a common if bizarre Shaker phenomenon that can perhaps be related to the old country tradition of water-divining. The best description we have of it is by one Valentine Rathbun, an American preacher who was converted to Shakerism six years later, left the sect almost immediately, and devoted much of his subsequent energy to attacking the faith: 'Sometimes their hand will stretch out, and after it they run, – through woods – cross lots – over fences, swamps, or whatever, till they come to a house; perhaps they will be stopt, several times, in their course, and head turn them round, as though they had lost their way; then take a new set off, and run again.' In its way, this behaviour reflects one of the two opposed beliefs that seem to underlie the nature of shaking itself, the notion that the divine spirit has actually invaded the body and taken over motor control (rather than the idea that shaking represents the body's *reaction* to an individual's encounter with the divine). What we are left with in the mind's eye is the middle-aged Hocknell, erstwhile respectable Cheshire farmer, scuttling over the vast brooding landscape of northern New York State in pursuit of his own quivering finger.

But it worked. In Shaker terms he found himself in Wisdom's Valley.

In fact it was an area of woods and swamp-land where the Iroquois still roamed, and with only a few scattered farms owned or tenanted by white settlers. It was known at this period by the Native American name of Nisqueunia or Niskeyuna, though later Dutch settlers would call it Watervliet and the Shakers would give it their own allegorical title in the 1840s, during a period known as Mother Ann's Work; nowadays it has been swallowed up by the township of Colonie, New York, and has become a nondescript tatty area, with the Shakers' original settlement hemmed in on three sides by a prison, Albany airport, and the Diamond Dogs' minor-league baseball stadium.

Here the Shakers were able to arrange the lease of two hundred acres of land at a very reasonable rate – eight bushels of corn annually for each hundred acres – from the greatest estate in the region, the Manor Rensselaerwyck. With this settlement in prospect, John Hocknell arranged to return to England to sell up his farm in Cheshire, and to bring back John Partington who had been winding up his affairs. The capital released by this would allow the Shakers to take over the property and develop it to the point where they could become self-sufficient. Indeed, on his own arrival in Niskeyuna, Partington would lease a further four hundred acres of land adjacent to that taken by Hocknell, and he and Hocknell would take over the leases of two farms that had already been set up there. John Hocknell later told a believer called Jonathan Wood that he had sold his farm in England for eight hundred guineas, an enormous sum at the time. In the meantime, James Shepherd joined William Lee and James Whittaker in Albany, where the three of them found temporary work pending the settlement at their trades of shoemaker, blacksmith and weaver respectively.

Meanwhile, back in New York, Ann Lee had run into a crisis.

Over time many couples would be converted to Shakerism, and the attitude of Ann and the other leaders towards their marriages was always quite clear. The experience of Hannah Goodrich and her husband Nathan a few years later provides an example. They came to what was by then the Shaker settlement at Niskeyuna in June 1780, just as a 'sharp testimony against sin' was being given, and Mary Partington was addressing a large company with the following words: 'Strip off your pride and abominations! – We know you; but you do not know us – We have men here that are not defiled with women, and women that are not defiled with men!' The next day Hannah went to see Ann, and asked about her husband, who had been separated from her in the community. Ann turned on her: 'Let your husband alone fastening your lust upon him!' There's something heartless in her reduction of a concerned enquiry to this sexual lowest common denominator. It's not surprising that during this period at Niskeyuna Ann had a vision of 'a large black cloud arising, as black as a thundercloud; and it is occasioned by men's sleeping with their wives'. The punishment, in the afterlife, would be grim indeed: 'their torment appears like melted lead, poured through them in the same parts where they have taken their carnal pleasure'.

On the other hand, the Shakers could be pragmatic, and knew that they couldn't always expect to split couples up immediately on conversion. A generation later a Shaker apologist, Benjamin Seth Youngs, claimed that husbands and wives should not be separated 'against their feelings' as long as they were willing 'to forsake all carnal desires'. Ann was even prepared to acknowledge on occasion that couples could give each other support as they embraced the severe tenets of her religion – but she also asserted that she had not received this sort of comradeship herself.

Some years after the conversion of the Goodriches, she spoke in the following terms to a number of Shaker sisters who had been converted along with their husbands: 'It is a great deal easier for you than it was for me. Your husbands will be a great help to you. I had no husband to help me, when I set out to obey the gospel; but I had to stand against my own carnal nature, and my wicked husband's too. I had, as it were, to tread the wine-press alone, and no man to help me.'

Ann called her husband 'wicked' because he was either an apostate or a non-believer, according to how his early commitment to Shakerism was regarded. A later verdict, by Shakers who couldn't have known him, is probably a judicious one: 'Tho he never had been considered as a faithful and substantial believer; yet he had hitherto supported his credit and reputation, and maintained an outward conformity to his faith.' He had gone through the motions, in other words, probably to keep his wife happy. In absolute terms, and these were the terms Ann was committed to in promulgating the Word, this made him wicked. On occasion, though, she was able to give a more tempered judgement: 'The man to whom I was married, was very kind, according to nature; he would have been willing to pass through a flaming fire for my sake if I would but live in the flesh with him, which I refused to do.' He hadn't passed through a flaming fire but he had endured an ordeal by water, crossing a vast ocean for his wife's sake, and the two of them were now living and working in New York. And at this point, sometime in the autumn of 1775, he became seriously ill.

Ann nursed him. It was her last act of secular responsibility. They had been married for fourteen years and gone through a lot together. He had been a kind husband, doing his best to cope with the strange metamorphosis that his wife had accomplished. In his illness the great bone of contention that lay between them, his desire to 'live in the flesh' with her, could be put to one side. Ann was stronger than he was, just as she was stronger than her father and her brother, all of them tough working men in an era when men were expected to dominate women; and now Abraham was completely dependent on her, helpless in her hands. She had worked in the Manchester Infirmary, admittedly as a cook, but was used to confronting sickness, and she had watched her own children die.

Abraham survived, but the crisis brought matters to a head. His illness seems to have soured the welcome given by the Smiths, and there was no work to return to. Instead he began to join with 'the wicked at public houses'. One can imagine how normal and human the 'wicked' must have seemed after years of the Shakers' frenetic spirituality. Shaker historians claimed, rather charmingly, that he 'loved his beef and his beer, his chimney corner and seat in village tavern'. The argument about sex resumed, and rapidly reached the point of no return. One day Abraham brought home a prostitute and gave his wife a choice: would she sleep with him, or would he have to resort to the whore?

The very question reveals his complete incomprehension of what had happened to Ann. We have seen that in the crisis of her conversion Ann Lee sublimated her terrible experience of motherhood into images of spiritual birth, and pictured herself, redeemed, as a new-born baby. By doing this she had transcended her trauma in two ways simultaneously: switching the terms of her experience from negative to positive by replacing tragic physical births with a glorious spiritual one; and consigning her previous miseries to a past that was as irrelevant as it was irretrievable. But much the same occurred with her sexual experience. She jettisoned physical love for the spiritual variety, but still saw herself in a male–female relationship. Indeed that was the whole point of her role within Shakerism. She was the new Eve, the female Christ. 'When I first gained victory over a carnal nature,' she said, 'I was brought into great clearness of sight. I saw the Lord Jesus Christ, and met with him, as a lover, and walked with him, side by side.' Abraham could not have been further out of his depth. Ann had taken as a lover his immeasurable superior, while he was hand in hand with her only-too-measurable inferior. His choice was body, not spirit. He stepped back into the streets of New York in company with the woman he had found there, and out of history for ever.

This was a bleak time for Ann. A year before she had had the support of home and family, and had been head of a sect that numbered its believers in dozens. Now she was in America with only a handful of supporters. Three of those were off in the north of the state, another had gone to England, her husband had left, and she had no proper home or job. A Shaker account in the early nine-teenth century gives her situation the full treatment, in a passage that has the same sort of grave melancholy about it as the story of Jesus in the Garden of Gethsemane. Ann was acquainted with a similar grief: 'her only shelter from the inclemency of the winter, was a small, uncomfortable room, without bed or bedding, or any other furniture than a cold stone for a seat, and her only morsel was a cruise of vinegar; and, as she afterwards testified, she sat down upon the stone, without any fire, sipped her vinegar, and wept'. She had every reason to be downcast, though as so often there's a stylised and exaggerated quality about this account: from a certain point of view it seems to be more closely related to Monty Python than to the Bible, the product of the sort of perverse zest for the dismal that leads people to claim they've been brought up in shoe-boxes. Even in a poor quarter of eighteenth-century New York it's hard to envisage a room furnished only with a stone, and a woman with nothing to drink but vinegar.

In any event Ann took several trips north up the Hudson River, to keep in touch with the pioneering Shakers who were preparing their base just above Albany. On the first of these she travelled with Mary Partington. The vessels that plied the river at that period were Dutch sloops, about seventy feet in length with a big, bellying mainsail. The packet sloops were roomy, with plenty of deck space where the passengers could socialise, and sleeping accommodation below. Their sloop moored in Albany itself and they lodged in it overnight. At some point, however, Ann woke up and felt the urge to leave the vessel. Prompted, as she saw it, by the power of God, she wandered the streets of the town until she came to a fortified building. As she stood outside its walls she had a premonition that one day she would be imprisoned within them. Five years later her vision came true.

Back in New York Ann had to cope with loneliness and poverty, as preparations for war became more and more evident all around. In the adjoining state of Massachusetts events moved swiftly towards confrontation. Coercive Acts had been passed in Parliament in order to restrain the turbulent New Englanders, and on 14 April General Gage, Governor of Massachusetts on behalf of the Crown, received a letter from Lord Dartmouth telling him to use force if necessary to uphold the Acts. He promptly moved troops out towards Concord, which was a major arsenal for the local militia (and only a few miles from the township of Harvard, the setting for so much Shaker drama in the years to come). Paul Revere set off on his famous ride to warn the Minute Men, and on 19 April 1775 the British and American forces faced each other at the village of Lexington. Someone then fired the shot that, as Emerson would later put it, was heard round the world.

A month later the man-of-war *Asia* appeared off the New York coast, which it patrolled for much of the summer, keeping a wary eye on developments there. In August some of the town-soldiers, that is to say the revolutionary militia, began to remove the cannon from the battery on the southern tip of Manhattan Island. The *Asia* fired on them; the militia fired back. One of the *Asia*'s crew was killed and several on both sides were wounded.

Drums were then beaten, and more militia assembled. The *Asia* fired a broadside that damaged several houses. The next day, 25 August, people began fleeing the city. Ewald Schaukirk, a Moravian minister, described New York on 28 August: 'Moving out of the city continues, and some of the Streets look plague-stricken, so many houses are closed. The dividing of all men between 16 and 50 years into Ward companies, increases the movement.' The following month the same witness gives an account of the Minute Men parading, marching, getting drunk and fighting each other. 'May the Lord have mercy on this poor City!' he exclaims devoutly. It may have been something of a phoney war in New York at this stage but it created a disturbed and uneasy atmosphere, and the increasing militarism in the air, coupled with the ambiguity of her own national status, must have been very oppressive for Ann, since the Shakers, like the orthodox Quakers, were committed pacifists, no matter how obstreperous they had occasionally been in their Manchester days on a one-to-one level. Disturbances continued in the city through the autumn.

On Christmas Day 1775, in the nick of time, John Hocknell arrived in America with his wife Hannah, his daughter Mary, and John Partington, and with sufficient cash to establish the Shakers at their base at Niskeyuna. The two men went up to Albany to complete the transactions on the land required for settlement. The war, meanwhile, was hotting up, and in the summer of 1776 the British occupied New York, where they were to remain for the duration of the hostilities. But by then Ann Lee was gone. Sometime in the spring the woman believed by her followers to be clothed with the sun had entered the wilderness that awaited her.

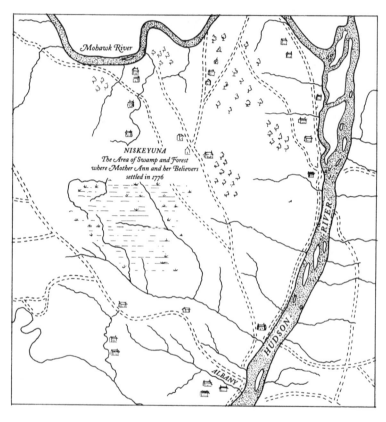

The wilderness of Niskeyuna.

5

Niskeyuna

The Shakers, like so many pioneers before and after them, lived in a log cabin (though John Hocknell and John Partington, the wealthy members of the group, had small farm-houses of their own), and spent their days cutting down trees, clearing stumps and draining swamp-land. There were wolves and bears in northern New York State; Indians, with whom the Shakers were to feel an affinity, roamed the forests. The north-east of America was peopled by a large complex of tribes known as the Iroquois Nation, with a subgroup of five tribes in the New York State region called the League of the Iroquois. In this culture the people lived in long-houses or lodges, but the League also thought of themselves as living in an extended 'lodge', the Ganonsyoni, that embraced their whole territory. The Mohawks, one of the five tribes, occupied the territory round Niskeyuna, and were known as the Keepers of the Eastern Door of the Lodge. They were accomplished farmers – Niskeyuna (more correctly *Nis-ka-yu-na*) meant 'extended corn flats'.

John Hocknell and John Partington were farmers too, though working on the tamed landscape of Cheshire could hardly have prepared them for a wilderness like this. Most of the other Shakers had learned and practised their trades in Manchester. They were practical people, however, and used to a tough life. Moreover, the years of struggle in England, the upheaval of emigration, the ordeal of finding somewhere to settle on the other side of the Atlantic, had filtered out the doubters and the faint-hearted, leaving this small residue of eleven hardy and focused people.

For three years nothing much happened except survival and consolidation. Initially they occupied a log cabin that had already been built on their land. They built a bigger dwelling-house but it burned to the ground shortly before completion; by 1778 they had erected another in its place. They kept themselves to themselves during this time, which was probably wise, given that the war was going on all round them. The Hudson River and its valley were strategically important because they could provide a British supply line from Canada right the way down to the city of New York. At the beginning of the conflict Fort Ticonderoga, which guarded the lake of the same name at the head of the Hudson, was taken in a surprise attack by the Rebels, but on 5 July 1777 it was recaptured by the British under General Burgoyne. Shortly afterwards, however, on 7 October, Burgoyne was defeated at the second battle of Freeman's Farm just south of Saratoga and only about thirty miles below the Shaker settlement. The British general Sir Henry Clinton – not to be confused with the Rebel officers George and James Clinton, whose paths Mother Ann and her followers would cross in due course – tried to make a diversion up the Hudson valley to cover Burgoyne's retreat. He took Forts Clinton and

Montgomery off his namesakes, but stopped short about forty-four miles from Albany. Nevertheless he sent off a marauding expedition which burned down Kingston, where the provisional state government was housed, causing antagonism and bitterness in the state.

During this politically sensitive time, faced with bruising work to do, the Shakers made only one convert, a woman from a neighbouring farm called Eleanor Vedder, and she remained an 'outside' Shaker, meaning that she did not actually join her fellow-believers bodily but instead stayed at home with her family. Her commitment and contribution were genuine enough, though: four of her five granddaughters, Eleanor, Catharine, Clarissa and Polly, were to become Shakers in their turn, and die in the faith.

It may be that during this period the Shakers formed a rapport with the Mohawks who lived around them. On at least one later occasion William is described as having the ability to speak to them in their own language, and they are observed showing reverence for Ann herself. This is not wholly surprising, since there were various points of similarity between Shaker doctrine and Iroquois culture. The Iroquois Nation gave women more status and power than did western society at that time. There was a system of matrilineal descent, with a son belonging to his mother's rather than his father's clan (all marriages were across clan boundaries), and matrons could appoint and depose clan chiefs. The Iroquois also had an equivalent of the Shakers' Manichean concept of the fundamental struggle of the world taking place between 'a woman clothed with the sun' and a great red dragon: in their case they perceived a conflict between the basic forces of the universe, the Twin Boys, one of whom was good and creative, the other evil and poisonous. On a more pragmatic level the Iroquois, like the Shakers, found themselves in a no-win situation as far as the Revolutionary War was concerned. Their fighting skills and knowledge of local terrain meant they were wooed by both sides in the conflict, and some tribes went one way, some the other. The Mohawks were broadly pro-British, mainly because the Indian agents of the king's government provided a degree of protection against the predations of white settlement. They wisely wished to remain neutral, but were eventually sucked into the conflict on the Loyalists' side.

Despite endeavouring to keep a low profile for similar reasons, the Shakers managed to attract a certain amount of hostile attention because of their weird behaviour at worship. One day in July 1778 some travellers buttonholed a military physician called James Thacher at West Point, on the lower reaches of the Hudson River, and described the way the sect spent whole nights in their revels, dancing extravagantly, so they claimed, with hardly any clothes on. These 'dancing Quakers' were led by a female called Ann Lee, who, Thacher speculated, must be the niece of Charles Lee, the British-born Rebel general. There was also some discussion about the Shakers in a newspaper. On 2 November 1778, a correspondent in the *Boston Gazette* attacked a suggestion by the Rev. Isaac Backus that government should refrain from interfering in matters of conscience, by making reference to the dangerous practices of a group of believers he doesn't name but who were obviously the Shakers: 'There is a sect whose conscience leads them into gross immoralities,' he claims sarcastically, 'and abominable prophane[ne]ss. Every Sabbath they have their meeting, when their mode of worship consists in dancing stark naked, one of them presiding whom they call their God. I would be glad to know of Mr Bachus, whether the plea of conscience is valid in such cases.'

The charge of dancing naked, which surfaced at this early phase of the Shakers' American experience, is one that was to be repeated on numerous occasions over the next few years by the sceptics and apostates who put pen to paper on the subject of the sect. Thomas Brown wrote an interesting book called *An Account of the People Called Shakers* in which he describes his own experiences during his brief membership of the cult, which he joined in 1800. He reveals himself to be obsessed with discovering whether his fellow-believers took their clothes off or not. He was fated to be disappointed, since nobody stripped while he was looking; he himself was not an adept dancer, joining in the 'stamping gift' with such vigour on one occasion that a baby had to be rescued from his approaching feet, and the other worshippers all fled the room. In February 1799 Brown had interviewed Mary Hocknell, who as a twelve-year-old had been in the Toad Lane house when the constable and his assistants raided it. She was by then a woman of forty, and, as we shall see, had been a close companion of Ann Lee and at the very heart of Shaker activities in America. She was adamant that no sort of hanky-panky took place: 'Because the brethren pulled of[f] their coats, or outside garments,' she told Brown, 'to labour, or as the world call it, dancing; and in warm weather the sisters being lightly clothed, they would report we danced naked.'

There was always an odd combination of extremeness and practicality about Shaker behaviour, and this may have been a case where the practical explanation is the most likely one. Certainly one can imagine how the wild and improvised nature of their worship could generate prurient speculation; and of course the accusation, which for us is likely to have a quaint hippyish resonance to it, was one that would have been taken seriously in the puritanical atmosphere of eighteenth-century America, so it was a handy way for the disillusioned or the disapproving to blacken their image – though interestingly one of the enemies of Shakerism, by the name of William Haskett, having made the usual charge against them went on to explain that nakedness was the Shakers' way of demonstrating that they had cast off sin and re-established the innocent state of the Garden of Eden.

Despite the occasional rumour or report, the Shakers were pretty much left in their isolation for three years, and eventually they began to feel it. They had never had an easy ride, but back in England they had at least had an opposition to define themselves against. Out here they must occasionally have felt their faith would drain away into the huge emptiness all round them. One can imagine them in the endless winters, with no work to do apart from their spiritual 'labours', as they called them, muffled in their log cabin by the deep snow outside. Their

determination to see their experience as spiritually meaningful is nicely illustrated by an event that took place in
their first winter. The Shakers did not celebrate Christmas
as a special day, but on the morning of 25 December 1776,
Hannah Hocknell found her hands were shaking so much
that she could not do up her shoes preparatory to starting
on the day's work. Ann appeared in the room and told
her to leave her shoes off, 'for the place whereon you
stand is holy ground'. The severe cold of New York State
in mid-winter would have provided a sufficient explanation of the problem, but as far as Ann was concerned
the shaking was a sign that no manual work should be
done and that Christmas from then on should be devoted
to cleaning the house of the spirit.

One day Ann led her little group into the woods, where
they praised God with songs and dances. Then, when
they were resting, there was a short, tense conversation.

'Do you believe the gospel will ever open to the world?'
her brother William asked.

Ann said the time was at hand when converts would
come like doves.

If repeated frequently enough, that sort of biblical lyri-
cism can wear a bit thin, and William replied, 'Mother,
you have often told us so, but it does not come yet.'

Ann told him to be patient, repeating her prophecy that
converts would come and in great numbers. William said
later that this moment of doubt gave him more anguish
than any sin he ever committed.

It is interesting that at this stage Ann took a passive
stance, waiting for things to happen. Because the early

part of her career is so sketchy, it's easy to gallop through it and lose one's sense of how much temporal investment there had already been. She had now been a Shaker for over twenty years; had experienced the revelation of her status and destiny nearly a decade before; had been in America for upwards of five years; and she was more than forty years old. Sometimes simple patience can develop a crushing weight and density. One day she stood on the bank of a small river near her house, and wept in despair, tears flowing down her cheeks.

This mood did not last for long. By 1779 the Shakers' farming was beginning to yield results in excess of the needs of the small community. In the spring of that year she insisted that the believers should grow a large quantity of crops, and when they were harvested she ordered the surplus to be stored rather than traded. Some of the community asked what was to be done with it, given that they lived in such isolation. Ann explained, 'We shall have company enough, before another year comes about, to consume it all.'

There are times when history seems a force separate from human cause and effect, making connections of its own accord, and triggering events. On the face of it there is no reason why the handful of Shakers should not have remained in obscurity in their clearing in the forests of northern New York State indefinitely, as William – and even Ann herself on one occasion – obviously feared. But in the summer of 1779 their American destiny began to catch up with them.

*   *   *

The eighteenth century, in the American colonies as in Europe, is seen as an epoch of increasing rationalism, scepticism and deism, with the American Revolution itself perhaps the most impressive single embodiment of those humanistic tendencies. But the strongest wave has an undertow in the opposite direction, and the spiritual forces which led to the seventeenth-century settlement of the north-eastern seaboard of America were still powerfully present, particularly in the smaller towns and villages of New England. A sense of human weakness, guilt and worthlessness, in the context of the absolute might and rightness of Almighty God, lay just below the surface of American energy and optimism, and on one occasion over thirty years previously (not a long interval in the life of the spirit) it had erupted and demonstrated its enormous power.

This was the religious revival known as the Great Awakening, which swept over large parts of New England in the 1740s. Its leader was not a messianic figure like Ann Lee, but a scholarly, reflective minister called Jonathan Edwards, a man who approached the spiritual heart of his belief with an unparalleled philosophical lucidity, and who was able to communicate his belief in the absolute nature of sin, and the ineffable possibility of grace, in a limpid prose that made the drama of the soul all the more urgent and immediate to his readers and hearers.

On 8 July 1741 Edwards gave a sermon in Enfield, Connecticut, entitled 'Sinners in the Hands of an Angry God', taking as its text a glum prophecy from Deuteronomy: 'Their foot shall slide in due time.' Time, in fact, was of the essence. Edwards believed it to be coming to an end, claiming that God seemed to be hastily gathering in the chosen, so that the process of salvation was reaching its conclusion. From an individual's point of view this process takes on an existential intensity. Edwards's wonderful and repellent rhetoric evokes exactly that terror of imminent spiritual disaster that made Ann Lee hold open her eyes when she was lying in bed, and forced William to work without respite on his anvil: 'It is nothing but His hand that holds you from falling into the fire every moment. It is to be ascribed to nothing else, that you did not go to hell the last night; that you was suffered to awake again in this world; after you closed your eyes to sleep. And there is no other reason to be given, why you have not dropped into hell since you arose in the morning, but that God's hand has held you up.'

It wasn't all bad news. Edwards concluded his sermon by announcing an 'extraordinary opportunity' (unwittingly anticipating the language of the secular hard sell in years to come): the process of conversion itself would be enough to allay the terror of this angry God, and guarantee salvation. But by this time it was too late in a quite different sense for many of the congregation, who were weeping in the aisles, even fainting dead away and being carried from the meeting-house by friends and family.

Nobody can live at crisis level indefinitely, and after a few years the Great Awakening faded away. Ministers and leaders cooled their message down, or stepped into the background. Eventually Edwards himself was dismissed by his own congregation in Northampton, Massachusetts, and went to the frontier outpost of Stockbridge where he acted as missionary to the Housatonnuck tribe and devoted himself to writing some of the most profound philosophical and theological works to be penned in pre-Revolutionary America. But New Lights ministers and lay-people – that is, those imbued with the evangelical spirit of the Awakening – continued to maintain the spirit of Protestant radicalism in New England with, every now and then, a new revival breaking out in some backwater or another.

There are two threads connecting Ann Lee with the Great Awakening, even though it took place three thousand miles away from where she was then living, at a time when she was a small girl. The first was George Whitefield, who had been instrumental in triggering the revival in his American mission of 1739–41, and who later preached in Manchester to crowds that included Ann Lee. Here we can see an understandable causal sequence at work. The second thread is tangled and, apparently, haphazard. One of the leading families in Enfield, Connecticut, was that of the Meachams, and Joseph Meacham senior became a Baptist minister in the town not long after Edwards had preached his famous sermon there. A quarter of a century later, Meacham's son Joseph moved to eastern New York State and in 1776 was preaching at New Lebanon, about forty miles from Niskeyuna. And three years later the phenomenon known as the New Light Stir took place.

The Stir was basically another revival, on a smaller scale than the Great Awakening, in fact mainly confined to the Berkshire hills along the border of Massachusetts and New

York State. Like its more influential predecessor it was characterised by a belief that the end of history was imminent, but its participants also tended to have a specific faith in the Second Coming of Christ. The War of Independence, with its implication that an old order was ending and a new one being born, acted as a secular counterpoint to this spiritual expectation, and no doubt contributed to the combination of hope and fear that accompanied it. By the summer of 1779 the Stir was centred on the town of New Lebanon, and was being led by Joseph Meacham himself, along with the former Presbyterian minister of the town, the Rev. Samuel Johnson.

We can get a taste of the excitement of the Stir from the testimonies of some of those who participated in it. Richard Treat, a twenty-two-year-old newly married man, describes how the revival, rather like some sort of epidemic, 'broke out' in June 1779 with people seeing visions and prophesying that the millennium was nigh, 'even at the door'. Another of the New Lebanon participants, Amos Stower, talks of how 'rugged, stout-hearted young men, who came merely as spectators, fall like men wounded in battle, and screaming so that they might be heard at great distances'. By contrast, Samuel Johnson, a graduate from Yale, gives a much more sober and restrained account (even though, a couple of years later while he was on trial with Ann Lee, a plea of insanity would be offered on his behalf). A few years before, he tells us, he enquired of the most eminent divines around, 'how long it would be, according to their calculations, before Christ would make his second appearance', and having been told that the most reliable estimate was about twenty years, concluded it was time to prepare for it. Most of the revivalists had more immediate expectations, as we can see from Treat's account, though their confidence was by no means unalloyed. Treat himself suffered from a fear that he would not recognise the redeemer when he came, since this is what had happened during Christ's first appearance on Earth. Many others shared this anxiety, including Joseph Meacham, who warned that 'Christ would come like a thief in the night'.

This short-circuiting expectation, that Christ was about to reappear but that the very people who expected him would somehow miss him altogether, was an important factor in what was to happen the following year, as was another widespread belief amongst the enthusiasts of the New Light Stir: the need for celibacy. Meacham himself had come to the conclusion 'that a virgin life would be required', and though he hadn't dared to preach the doctrine openly, presumably because of the danger of causing confusion and disruption to married people like Samuel Johnson and Richard Treat, it turned out that 'the same belief was impressed on the minds of many others in the revival'. Treat tells us that as summer moved into autumn, and the Stir lost its impetus, marrying and giving in marriage began again, negative evidence that the institution had been seen as incompatible with the imminent salvation that had been promised – logically enough, since the very fact that marriage *is* an institution, one dedicated to the propagation of future life, makes it irrelevant if you believe time is about to come to an end.

As fervour dissipated, depression set in. Treat's own reaction to the retreat of the spirit anticipates the spiritual desolation of a character in one of the short stories that Nathaniel Hawthorne was to write in the following century, projecting his imagination back to the puritan outlook on life and the afterlife: 'The exercises of my mind were distressing beyond expression. I believed I had committed the unpardonable sin; for I thought I had sinned against so great a light that I could not be reclaimed. I continued in this deplorable state of mind through the winter.' This tendency to morbidness is a common feature of the revivalists. Another of them, Joseph Main, describes his wretched state of mind during the early part of his life, unable to do anything but retreat to the woods for one part of the time, and retire to his bed for the remainder of it, in both locations crying out to God, mourning and pining. Job Bishop gives a very vivid account of the despondent atmosphere that took hold during the winter of 1779–80: 'The meetings were still continued; but they seemed lifeless. Even the former leaders and speakers sat in silence, with their heads bowed down. If any rose up and attempted to speak or pray, they found their utterance taken from them, and they were obliged to resume their seats in dumb silence.'

All those assembled at New Lebanon experienced 'deep distress and agony of mind'. Meacham himself was gripped by this despair, saying he could not help the people because he could not help himself. Doubt and disillusion are obviously in ratio to the exhilaration of belief, creating an emotional zigzag that looks to the outsider rather like a communal form of clinical depression. All the revivalists could do, as their new light gave way to winter darkness, was encourage each other 'to wait with patience, to pray and not faint'.

What we have, in the early months of 1780, are two communities forty miles or so apart, the tiny group of Shakers at Niskeyuna waiting for converts, and the much larger group centred on New Lebanon waiting for the return of belief. It is rather like putting positive and negative polarities in proximity to each other, and watching for the spark to jump between them.

In April, two of the participants in the New Light Stir, Talmadge Bishop and Reuben White, set off westwards from New Lebanon in classic American fashion, to seek their fortune. What they found, when they stumbled into a clearing in the forests north of Albany, was Mother Ann. She exactly fulfilled the requirements that the millennial expectations of the previous year had created. She had been hidden from view, like a thief in the night; and had taken a form that they hadn't in the least anticipated – the female form. On the other hand, she represented exactly what they *had* expected: the unexpected.

Richard Treat was one of the first of the New Lebanon revivalists to seek out the Shakers after Bishop and White had reported back, and he leaves a vivid account of his experience, one that gives a remarkable insight into the way the Shaker conversion process worked. He set off on foot with a friend called Justus Webster. The weather was very wet, and the track muddy: as they approached through the woods in the late evening they heard singing. They were given a warm welcome, and seated by the fire to dry their clothes. The first words Treat ever heard Ann utter had an appropriately Christ-like resonance: 'James, go fetch some water and wash these men's feet.'

James Whittaker brought in a pitcher of water and began to do so. When Treat tried to object, James said, 'Make no words.'

Treat was in a morbid state of mind. After his feet were washed, he sat in another part of the room from his friend, waiting for his doom, as he put it, to be pronounced. He felt the Shakers were paying more attention to Justus than to him, which increased his sense of being disapproved of.

After a while a strange thing happened. One of the Shakers, John Partington, suddenly came up to him and made the sign of the cross on Treat's chest. As he did so, he said, 'Thou art neither cold nor hot: I would thou wert cold or hot. So because thou art lukewarm, and neither cold nor hot, I will spew thee out of my mouth.'

The violence of this language (quoted from Revelation iii, 15–16) with its hectoring repetitions, confirmed Treat's worst fears. 'There, thought I, that is just what I expected' – and he immediately fell to the floor in a faint. From our long-distance perspective the technique seems to resemble good policeman–bad policeman. Treat is welcomed in and has his feet washed; then is suddenly told he is to be 'spewed out' again.

When he came to, Treat heard Ann's voice from outside the room. She was saying to James Whittaker, 'Come James, let us go in; for that man prays.'

She came in with her elders, and said to William Lee, 'Take this man and hear him open his mind.' Treat duly went off and made a full confession, which gave him deep relief and satisfaction. After he had spent a few days with the Shakers, Ann sent him home, telling him that he had to right all the wrongs he had done in his whole life, making full restitution to anyone he had ever injured or defrauded in any way, and that he must take up the cross against sin and especially works of the flesh (which meant, in Shaker-speak, leading a celibate life).

Treat did as he was told. There is a certain comedy in his account of the reaction of those he had wronged when he approached them and insisted on recompensing them for his sins, however trivial and distant in time they may have been: 'But when I came to confess to the wicked wherein I had wronged them, and offered to make restitution, they were offended to hear me mention and offer restitution for such small trifles.' The use of the word 'wicked' catches the sudden switch that has taken place. His own confession of sins is a permanent closing of the account: he himself is no longer one of the wicked, but his fellow-citizens are. His wrongdoings to them are a technicality that they are prepared to overlook: but his strict accounting saves him, the sinner, and leaves his victims in the mire. He has subscribed to the absolute, while they are left floundering in the world of give-and-take. It is now Richard Treat who is spewing.

As far as the permanent closing of Treat's account is concerned, this is the specific claim of the Shaker confession procedure. In this respect it differs from the

Roman Catholic institution of confession, which is regular and repeated: a dynamic of sin and forgiveness that continues throughout life, while of course Protestantism in general, and fundamentalist Protestantism in particular, has its own tradition of unceasing struggle. What the Shakers offered was a rigorous confession as part of the conversion experience, with a line then being drawn under both the past and the person who experienced that past. Shaker life is to be experienced as sin-free. The New Light pilgrims who were soon coming to Niskeyuna in droves repeatedly questioned the Shakers on this issue, as well they might: '"Are you perfect? Do you live without sin?" They replied, "The power of God, revealed in this day, does enable souls to cease from sin; and we have received that power; we have actually left off committing sin, and we live in daily obedience to the will of God."' Ann of course had gone through the whole strenuous process herself. 'When I confessed my sins, I labored to remember the time when, and the place where, I committed them. And when I had confessed them, I cried to God to know if my confession was accepted; and by crying to God continually, I travelled out of my loss.'

Hannah Shipley was among the pilgrims from New Lebanon in the early summer of 1780. She performed an act of confession but told Ann that she had 'not lived up to the light which she had received'.

One of her companions, no doubt to cheer her up, told her, 'I believe you are a child of God.'

Ann squelched that facile praise, however, saying, 'Do not daub her with untempered morter. She has the right work upon her.' She then gave instructions for a full confession: 'You must begin at the top twigs, and rip them off, and continue cropping until you come at the root, and then you must dig that up, that it may never grow again.' She also offered the incentive that Hannah's weakly body would be healed as well as her soul, and so it was. A year or two later, at Shirley, Massachusetts, Ann would use another vegetable analogy when addressing a convert called Sarah Burl, telling her that her carnal nature was like an onion: she would 'strip off one covering and then find another and so on till she came to the core'.

Another of the pilgrims, Abijah Worster, had a tumultuous conversion, as did many others – one of those experiences that take us to the heart of Shakerism, where the force unleashed has a ferocity that nowadays we are more likely to associate with the world of gothic horror or science-fiction than with religion: 'God, in great condescension to my weakness, laid his blessed power upon me, and brought me instantly upon my knees, where I was shaken with such astonishing violence, that it seemed to shake the whole house, like an earthquake.' He then made his confession to James Whittaker 'and soon received that blessed protecting power against the power of evil'. This protection included complete deliverance not just from fleshly lust, but also (and this seems to have been a higher priority for him) from a tendency to have 'more than a common appetite for victuals', thus enabling him to go for the next thirty years without ever feeling hungry.

Nineteen-year-old John Farrington had a different problem. When he arrived Ann talked to him, as usual, about the necessity of confessing his sins. He eventually did so, rather cautiously, as one would perhaps expect from a teenager. Ann saw through him at once, and told him, 'You have done very well so far, but you have not confessed all.' She then led him out into the dooryard where they both sat down, and she began to explore his sins.

Farrington goes on: 'She then told me of a number of secret sins that I had committed, which I had not recollected.' He went home and said in amazement, '*I have seen a woman who was able to tell me all that I ever did in my life.*'

It's not hard to see how an experienced woman of forty-four, who had grown up in a household with eight siblings all crowded together, could make a pretty shrewd guess at the sort of sins that might have been buried in the recesses of a young man like John Farrington. The atmosphere in eighteenth-century New England villages was fairly inhibited and prudish. When, in 1750, a few years after his sermon on 'Sinners in the Hands of an Angry God', Jonathan Edwards was dismissed by his congregation in Northampton, Massachusetts, it was at least in part to do with a scandal involving the young people of the parish, who had managed to lay their hands on an instruction book for midwives, the nearest thing to pornography that was available, and had gleefully passed it from one to another. Edwards had named the culprits in church, which had so humiliated the parents that they determined to get rid of him. In that kind of repressed environment it's not surprising that John Farrington thought Ann had performed a miracle in winkling out his most secret vices.

Confession was a strenuous process, but the prize was a great one: perfection. When, early in the nineteenth century, Shaker theology was codified, the doctrine was explicitly stated: 'The opinion which prevails so extensively among mankind, that no man, not even a real Christian, is able to live without committing sin, is one of the most destructive errors that ever proceeded from the powers of darkness.'

The original sin, committed by Adam and Eve in the Garden of Eden, was to have sex outside the order of the 'times and seasons' of natural creation, to invent what we would call 'recreational sex'. The 'prince of darkness' infused into the animal sensations of the woman the lust of concupiscence, which she communicated to the man, and by which they were both 'overshadowed with darkness, and unseasonably led into the act of sexual coition; and thus they partook of the forbidden fruit'. Adam and Eve didn't mate functionally as the lower animals do, but did it for pleasure, and thus they brought humankind into a state of sin. What they were guilty of was 'the evident violation of the order of nature, in a total disregard to times and seasons, in the work of generation'.

This doctrine is a little confusing, because it would suggest that the way to redemption is through achieving once more a moderate and utilitarian approach to sexuality. But this is not the case. The flesh has to be 'crucified' because Christ, the second Adam, replaced the natural realm with the spiritual one: 'Jesus Christ, the second

Adam, the Lord from Heaven, is a quickening Spirit: he came not only to redeem mankind from that loss into which the first Adam had plunged them, but to raise them to a state far superior, even to eternal life, from which they could not fall.' Jesus's role was to make eternal life available as a possibility; and that is a state which would render even functional sex redundant. The question obviously arises of where Ann comes in this scheme of things, and this, as we shall see, was the issue broached by Joseph Meacham after he met her and the other Shakers in May 1780.

After a full confession, perfection is readily obtainable: 'So when a man comes up to all the requirements of God, he then stands perfectly justified in the sight of God, and is, in that sense, *a perfect man*, and walks before God with a perfect heart. Hence we may see that perfection, in this sense, (which is all that can be required,) instead of being unattainable, is perfectly easy.' The consequences of this easy achievement of perfection are profound, and potentially dangerous, in fact comparable to those produced by the antinomianism that caused colonial leaders such a headache in the seventeenth century and led to the expulsion of Anne Hutchinson, the chief proponent of the heresy, from Massachusetts in 1638. In the case of antinomianism the logic is of a slightly different sort: human beings are worthless and can only be saved by the intervention of the Almighty; if you are saved, you are saved, so it makes no difference whether you behave well or badly. But the social threat posed by reckless 'saved' people, or perfected ones, is the same: they have been given a blank cheque for their behaviour. Who can criticise the actions of a perfected being? The strong reactions of communities and of the representatives of law and order to the Shakers suggest that this danger was not lost on them, though as it happened the apparent anarchy of Shaker worship did not extend into other areas of their lives after the migration to America – they were always too practical, too streetwise as we might call it, to step out of line in other ways, apart from the vexed question of their pacifism.

It was this quest for perfection that sent potential converts in such numbers from New Lebanon to see the Shakers. When, a month after his first visit, Richard Treat again set off for Niskeyuna, this time accompanied by his wife, so many of the New Light revivalists had followed that road since he had previously trodden it that children came out of the log cabins and clapboard farm-houses scattered along their route to jeer at them and cry, 'Shaker! Shaker!' When they arrived, Richard found that a huge expansion in the community had taken place. His wife, like so many others, was duly converted.

What is fascinating from the large number of testimonies, more than thirty in all, that these converts have left behind is the way Ann and the other Shakers adapted their response according to the psychology of each candidate. This was conscious policy on Ann's part. A year or two later when she was in Harvard town in central Massachusetts, she sent one of her American followers, Abijah Worster, the very same who was now immune to the pangs of hunger, off to the town of Douglass on a mission, with this tactical advice: 'Some are of such a hard make, that nothing will reach them but severity. Others are more easy to work upon; and if you go and deal in severity with them, you will only destroy them. He that wins souls must be wise, Abijah.'

We have seen how Richard Treat was bullied, and John Farrington was given the third degree; each pilgrim who knocked on the door of the cabin in Niskeyuna was treated in a manner tuned precisely to his or her needs and deficiencies. Most of them, in fact, were impressed by their welcome. In the few years they had been working their land, the Shakers had got it into good order, which in itself acted as a confidence booster to country people. One of them, Daniel Moseley, said, 'I was brought up in New-England, among good farmers; but such neatness and good economy as was here displayed in the wilderness I never before saw.' Abigail Cook, another of the New Lebanon converts, describes going to visit Ann and the Shakers in early March 1781. 'Many people were there from different places, and their house was but small; and in order to accommodate all who came, they gave up their own beds and slept on the floor themselves, with but very little to lie on, or to cover them.' They would say to visitors: 'Come in, brethren and sisters, come in; we have but little room in our house; but we have a great deal of room in our hearts.'

Eliab Harlow at eighteen was even younger than John Farrington when he visited Niskeyuna from New Lebanon in the summer of 1780, but his experience was very different. Instead of getting the shock treatment, he was gently played, like a fish: 'In passing by me, as she walked the floor, she [Ann] turned to me and said, "Young man, you must wait with patience; your time is not come yet." This she repeated several times, which inspired me with a feeling of reverential love.' It wasn't until Harlow visited Ann and the elders while they were imprisoned in Albany later that year that he was able to make the required confession. The Rev. Samuel Johnson acknowledges Ann's perspicacity – or prescience as he thought of it – at their first meeting: 'The first words I recollect hearing from Mother Ann was, "James, take this man and let him open his mind."' Johnson points out that 'This was just what I desired; and by this I perceived that she knew the state of my mind.'

Yet another approach is shown in the case of Lucy Wight. Like so many of the New Lebanon cohort she was drawn to the Shakers, but found it difficult to make a full commitment to them because, like other gloomy young New Englanders, she was obsessed by her sinful nature. At an evening meeting she slid in behind the believers and sat on a bench. James Whittaker spotted her, however, and came up and told her she was like the Jews of old, who didn't recognise their Messiah because he was 'too mean for them'. This time the bad policeman plays his part first, provocatively challenging a young woman whose self-esteem was quite low enough to start with. Lucy Wight replied humbly that her problem was that she could see no way for herself to approach God. 'Then Mother and the Elders came and kneeled down before me; my head was bowed down into my lap, and I was unable to raise it up, or to help myself. Mother wept and cried for a few minutes, and then began to sing, and sung very melodiously. They then told me that there was a way of God for me, if I would confess and forsake my sins. This I fully believed, and in obedience to the faith I then received, I went immediately out and confessed my sins honestly before Mother: and I found her to be a Mother indeed.' (As one might guess, Lucy Wight had lost her own mother when she was young, just as Ann had lost her children.)

Thankful Barce's testimony reveals a more assured and confident personality, and once again Mother Ann was able to intuit it and produce the right approach: 'Her first salutation to me,' Thankful recalled, 'was in these words: "Being a daughter of Zion, how camst thou hither without a cap on thy head?"' Ann then sat in a chair and Thankful took her place at her side. Ann shut her eyes and began to sing, gracefully moving her hands in time with the 'heavenly melody of her voice'. Every now and then, one of her hands would brush against Thankful 'and at every touch . . . I instantly felt the power of God run through my whole body'.

There are all sorts of terms one can use for what is going on here: charisma, or sexual charge, or animal magnetism or, of course, as the Shakers themselves would call it, supernatural power. Many other converts, both in this period and later, experienced a similar excitement when they were touched by Ann Lee, or listened to her sing, or both. But perhaps it's best to conclude this series of case studies with two that strike rather different notes.

The first illustrates Ann's practical side and grasp of detail, while the second shows her earthy and robust quality, her ability to mix it with anyone, no matter how hostile or obdurate.

John Deming, having confessed his sins and been received into the faith, explained to Ann that he was in debt, his wife was chronically ill, and his five-year-old child had swallowed a large metal button some months previously and was not expected to live. Ann gave him assurances about his wife and his debts but didn't mention his child. She also gave him some very specific instructions: 'You must never cut your nails, nor scour your buckles, nor trim your beard, nor do any such thing on the Sabbath, unless in case of great necessity.' (It's intriguing to try to imagine what such a necessity might be.)

A few days later she came to him with a smile and told him it was time for him to go home and take care of his sick child. 'By this John perceived that Mother had not forgotten what he had said about the child' – and Ann had scored her victory. Given the cascades of would-be converts that were arriving by the day, it was vital that she left nothing, and nobody, unaccounted for, not even a button in an unseen infant's throat. John went home, and discovered his child's button had been dislodged about the very moment Ann had spoken to him. Shortly afterwards he was able to pay his debts, and to cap it all his wife recovered her health.

Hezekiah Hammond did his best to resist all the excitement that accompanied the American discovery of the Shakers, and kept his family away from Niskeyuna, though they wanted to go. Then one day he had a dream that compelled him to travel there, though he remained strongly opposed. After a day or two in residence he still hadn't changed his mind, and he sent for his horse in order to ride home. William Lee came into the room, and began to upbraid him for his lack of faith. Hezekiah was conscious that this was a last-ditch attempt to get him into the fold, and braced himself to resist William's approach. 'Having his horse-whip in his hand, he sat, twirling the lash upon the floor, and strove to fix his sense upon that, rather than upon Father William's discourse.'

Then Ann came in, and took the situation in hand. 'Put down that whip and hear the word of God, you idle old man!' she exclaimed. 'It is the Devil that makes you do that, to shut out the word of God.'

Hezekiah immediately dropped the whip and began to pay attention to what William was saying. 'Soon the power of God fell mightily upon Hezekiah; his arms were instantly brought up to his sides, and fixed, like a criminal pinioned for execution; his head was braced back, and his whole body bound, in such a manner, that he could neither move nor speak.'

After remaining for some time in this position, he regained the power of speech, though not much else, because all he actually said was: 'The hand of God is upon me – I cannot go home; I shall have to stay here. I wish you would go home and tell my family how it is with me: for the hand of God is upon me, and I cannot go.'

'"Now," said Mother, "you may confess your sins."'

*　　*　　*

As the New Light revivalists came back through the forests and across the Hudson River to New Lebanon to report on their experiences, Joseph Meacham realised that it was essential for him to meet the Shakers to discuss the nature of their beliefs. According to Shaker tradition, the date selected was 19 May 1780, a likely enough choice since it was the sixth anniversary of the day the *Mariah* had set sail from Liverpool. It was a date that was going to prove significant for another reason too, because at noon over much of Massachusetts and its neighbouring states, a strange and apparently supernatural phenomenon took place. It was the famous Dark Day of New England.

Imprisonment at Albany and Poughkeepsie.

6

The Dark Day

On Friday 19 May 1780, the Rev. Mr Cutler was enter-
taining some friends at his home in Ipswich-Hamlet,
near Boston. The sun had risen red that morning. This had
happened for several days previously, with the atmosphere
full of vapour and cloud. During the course of the morning
it began to rain. From the 'confusion of the clouds' the
Rev. Cutler anticipated a storm, but it didn't materialise
and the 'wind remained small'. At about eleven it started to
get noticeably dark, and by twelve o'clock the candles were
casting such a bright light that people's profiles could be
clearly seen on the walls of the room, as if it was night-time.

In an article in the *Boston Gazette*, written in response
to the paper's request for readers' experiences of the Dark
Day, he continues:

About one o'clock a glin of light which had continued 'till this
time in the east, shut in, and the darkness was greater than it
had been for any time before. – Between one and two o'clock,
the wind from the west freshened a little, and a glin appeared
in that quarter. – We dined about two the windows all open,
and two candles burning on the table. – In the time of the
greatest darkness some of the dunghill fowls went to their roost:

Cocks crowed in answer to one another as they commonly do in night: Woodcocks which are night birds, whistled as they do *only* in the dark: Froggs peeped – In short, there was an appearance of midnight at noon-day.

Some miles away in Rhode Island, John Howland had started the day studiously, reading Voltaire's biography of Charles XII of Sweden. At about nine o'clock it began to grow dark. At first he simply assumed this was caused by the weather becoming overcast, and he continued with his reading. Just as he got to the last page the darkness increased to such an extent that he had to throw some shavings on the fire in order to make out the concluding words. He then went out into the street, where crowds had gathered in amazement at the darkness, among them Dr James Manning, the president of Brown University. A 'powerful but profligate' man went up to Manning and asked him what he thought was going on. Manning's reply, which just might have been targeted at the enquirer's profligacy, nevertheless expressed the fears of many: 'I consider it, sir,' he said, 'as a prelude to that great and important day when the final consummation of all things is to take place.'

In Middlebrough, Massachusetts, the Rev. Isaac Backus noted in his diary that 'many in town and countery thought the day of judgment was come', adding, with a nice metaphorical reversal, that 'Elnathan Wood, Asael Shaw, Waelthy Pool, and others were brought out of soul darkness today'. In Garry, Massachusetts, a farmer called Issachar Bates, later to become a Shaker, while making his way through the darkness to a neighbour's house, saw people out 'wringing their hands and howling, "The day of judgement has come!!"' John Howland, meanwhile, managed to keep his presence of mind, perhaps having acquired stoicism from his reading of Voltaire. At noon he went home to a candle-lit dinner of fine roast veal and asparagus, though he was the only member of his family who was in the mood to eat anything.

In the afternoon, according to the Rev. Cutler, a brassy light came back, along with 'quick flashes or coruscations, not unlike the *Aurora borealis*'. Some witnesses speculated that the cause of this strange phenomenon was astronomical rather than meteorological. Olney Winsor, for example, claimed that though 'as the moon fulled the day past, it could not be a common eclipse of the Sun', there was nevertheless speculation that 'if she was eclipsed it must be by some plannet of whose course the Astronomers have no knowledge, none having mentioned it'. Cutler, meanwhile, seized on an explanation closer to home, one that is generally accepted nowadays. When he and his friends went out after their dinner they noticed the smell of burnt vegetation. People in a nearby tavern were much agitated by the strange appearance and smell of rainwater that they had collected in tubs. On inspection they saw a light scum, which proved to be from burnt leaves. Cutler concluded that the phenomenon was caused by the 'smoak from the woods which had been burning for many days', along with unusual winds. Samuel Williams, the professor of mathematics and philosophy at Harvard, studied the evidence and confirmed this conclusion, noting that during the previous three weeks various towns in northern New England had been clearing the land by burning off trees and vegetation. South-west winds, combined with cloudy skies, had produced an inversion and caused the effect, which, he noted, had been reported as far west as Albany in New York State. All he found were 'black ashes of burnt leaves without any sulphureous or other mixtures' – in other words, without any traces of hellfire and brimstone, despite the fact that, as Cutler noted, it had given 'distress to thousands, and alarmed the *brute creation*', including, of course, dunghill chickens, woodcocks and peeping frogs.

Whether Ann Lee and Joseph Meacham did actually meet on the Dark Day, as legend has it, or shortly before or after it, there is no doubt that the phenomenon helped to sharpen expectations that the final consummation of all things was approaching, and to hasten the droves of New Lighters on their way to their reception – hard or soft, according to the psychological profile of each candidate – at Niskeyuna. William Plumer, who was later to have a distinguished career as a lawyer and politician, visited the Shakers in 1782 and 1783, and met Ann Lee and the other leaders. He accepts that the Dark Day had been a turning point for them, though he doesn't mention the meeting between Ann and Joseph Meacham: 'This wilderness,' he says, having quoted the prophecy in the Book of Revelation, 'was a place near Albany, where she tarried with her adherents, then few in number, till the times were accomplished – which was on that memorable Dark Day, May 19, 1780, – that darkness being to her the signal from heaven to send forth her Elders "to preach the everlasting Gospel to them who dwell on the earth" '. Calvin Green, who was born to the Shaker converts Thankful Barce and Joseph Green on 10 October 1780, says that his birth was just four months and twenty-two days after James Whittaker delivered the first public address which opened the gospel of Shakerism in America. Counting back gets us to 19 May; for the Shakers it was undeniably a symbolic and significant date.

Whatever the actual sequence of events, Joseph Meacham and his colleague Calvin Harlow made their way to the Shaker settlement, to talk to Ann and the leaders. As they approached, Ann told James Whittaker, 'The first man in America is coming,' and gave him the task of discussing their faith with him. After talking for a while, James realised what he was up against, and returned to Ann and wept, 'sensing of what importance it was to gain him'. At the end of a day of this rigorous process, during which Meacham's 'labor was to measure his light with theirs', the Shakers succeeded in making a favourable impact. After he had returned home, however, Meacham thought of another major question he wished to ask, so sent Harlow back with it. The question got right to the heart of the issue of Ann's status. Meacham pointed out that St Paul had said it was a shame for women to speak in the churches. 'But you not only speak,' he pointed out, 'but seem to be an Elder in your church.'

Ann replied by making a comparison with the government of a family. The man is the senior partner, but when he is gone the woman takes charge. Jesus had inaugurated the 'spiritual Creation', and as a result was now living in it rather than in the material world. Ann meanwhile was here on earth, with the task of enabling humankind to gain access to the spiritual realm. As Anne Matthewson, one of the early American converts, put it, 'There are few in this day, who will pretend to deny the agency of the first woman in leading mankind into sin. Why should it be thought incredible that the agency of a woman should necessarily be first in leading the human race out of sin?'

It is a beautifully symmetrical structure. The first Eve brought down the first man, Adam, through introducing lust into the Garden, which caused the fallen state of humanity thereafter. The second Adam, Jesus, created the spiritual world, and Ann, in her wilderness garden of Niskeyuna, can be seen as both the second Eve and the female Christ, providing us with the opportunity of entering the domain Christ has established. As Shaker theology was later to have it:

And having received the Spirit of Christ, by the operation of which her soul was purified from the fallen nature of the flesh, she rose superior to it, and by her example and testimony, she actually led the way out of that nature and all its works, and was prepared to stand in a proper order to manifest the spirit of Christ in the female line. Hence the image and likeness of the Eternal Mother was formed in her, as the first-born Daughter, as really as the image and likeness of the Eternal Father was formed in the Lord Jesus, the first-born Son . . . As the substance of the first woman was taken from the body of the first man; so that Divine Spirit with which the second woman was endowed, and which constituted her the second Eve, was taken from the Spirit of the second Adam, the Lord Jesus Christ; therefore she was necessarily dependent on him, was subject to him, and always acknowledged him, as her head and lord.

From a modern point of view there is a tantalising double-bind in this celebration of the female principle. A woman has become an authentic expression of divinity; but at the same time, because she *is* a woman, that expression is subordinate to the male one.

Ann herself was aware of this paradox. In 1781 she talked to Eunice Goodrich about the failure of Christ's disciples to believe he had risen from the dead: 'They would not believe he had risen, because he appeared first to a woman! So great was their unbelief that the words of Mary appeared to them like idle tales!' But, she went on to assert, 'His appearing first to a woman, showed that his second appearing would be in a woman!'

Shaker doctrines were remarkably compatible with the beliefs of the Stir, chiming in with its millennialism, its celibacy, and above all its need for a revelation, for an encounter with otherness. Ann Lee, as a woman and an immigrant, filled the bill so perfectly that it's hardly surprising that the revivalists, Meacham among them, felt they had found their destiny and their salvation. More-over, after those desperate months when Meacham had confessed he could do nothing for the distress of his con-gregation, Ann's complete conviction and authority must have been like a balm. Shakerism was a hierarchical religion in its way – Ann was quoted as saying that 'A body without a head is a monster.' She was that head, with her senior English followers, her brother William, James Whittaker and John Hocknell, acting as her elders – a title which, with this new influx of followers, soon came into common usage, though in Shaker testimonies they would also be known as Father, just as Ann herself was Mother.

During the spring and summer of 1780, Niskeyuna was humming with activity. It's not clear how many converts were made during these months, but over thirty of them produced testimonies for an anthology published in 1827, half a century later. Allowing for death and apostasy, a figure of over a hundred would be a fair guess. Characteristically, the new converts would stay for some days, return to their communities, report back after a month or two with other candidates for conversion drawn from their families, recharge their batteries and go home again, thereby spreading the gospel further.

One of the most graphic accounts we have of their experience at Niskeyuna, and of the way worship took place in the community in 1780, comes from the hostile pen of Shakerism's arch-enemy, Valentine Rathbun. He was a Baptist minister from Pittsfield, Massachusetts, was caught up in the excitement of the revivalists' discovery of the Shakers, went along to Niskeyuna on 13 May, was converted, and stayed for several months. By December of the same year he had become so disillusioned that he wrote a pamphlet attacking the Shakers, the opening shot of a campaign that was to last many years.

On arrival, Rathbun tells us, the newcomer is met by

'many smiles'. The Shakers bid him welcome, 'and directly tell him they knew of his coming yesterday'. Certainly many of the believers testified to Ann's prescience about their arrival; Rathbun sees that as part of a cynical greeting strategy. The Shakers provide food for the newcomer and then sit down and 'sing odd tunes, and British marches, sometimes without words, and sometimes with a mixture of words, known and unknown'. They then begin shaking their heads, with 'their eyes shut and face up; then a woman about forty years old [Ann Lee herself; Rathbun doesn't want to dignify her with a name] sits and makes a sort of prayer, chiefly in an unknown tongue, (if I may so call it) then one of the men comes to the person, and pretends to interpret the woman's prayer; after which they tell the person he has come to the right place to be instructed; they enquire the person's name, and ever after call him by his Christian name; they use no compliments, but their language is yea and nay'.

That simplicity of language reflects the Shaker affinity with the Quakers, as does their plain dress code. 'If the person has long hair,' Rathbun says, 'he must have his hair cut short, telling him he wears the mark of the beast.' This severe attitude is confirmed by Plumer, who was told that 'if I was guilty of no other sin but wearing long hair, it would damn me to endless misery'. The point is to achieve a communal, almost a tribal, identity. Rathbun explains that if the novice does consent to have his hair cut, 'after it is done they come round him, and touch him with their fingers here and there'.

They then tell the candidate that the churches are all

anti-Christ and that no one has gone to heaven for twelve hundred years, not since the apostolic age. But those who died in the past go to 'a small hell' (the fact that this telling phrase is used, rather than some more technical expression like purgatory, gives us a sense of the home-made quality of Shakerism) and they can be finally redeemed. Anyone missing the present opportunity, however – shades of 'Sinners in the Hands of an Angry God' here – will be damned for ever: 'it is a gone case with him'. Sometimes while the Shakers are explaining all this, Rathbun writes, they are affected by a strange power which makes them convulse, like 'the operation of an electerising machine'.

Antagonism gives Rathbun's account a valuable clarity; he wants to ground his anger in the tissue of their actual behaviour, to itemise every maddening detail. As a result, by dint of trying to shut the door on the Shakers once and for all, he paradoxically succeeds in making them available to us over the span of centuries. His account of their mode of worship is as bizarre as it is fascinating.

They begin by sitting down, and shaking their heads, in a violent manner, turning their heads half round, so that their face looks over each shoulder, their eyes being shut; while they are thus shaking, one will begin to sing some odd tune, without words or rule; after a while another will strike in; and then another; and after a while they all fall in, and make a strange charm: – Some singing without words, and some with an unknown tongue or mutter, and some with a mixture of English; The mother, so called, minds to strike such notes as make a concord, and so form the charm. When they leave off, they drop off, one by one, as oddly as they come on; in the best part of their worship every one acts for himself, and almost every one different from the other; one will stand with his arms extended, acting over odd postures, which they call signs; another will be dancing, and sometimes hopping on one leg about the floor; another will fall to turning round, so swift that if it be a woman, her cloaths will be so filled with the wind, as they were kept out by a hoop; another will be prostrate on the floor; another will be talking with somebody; and some sitting by, smoaking their pipe; groaning moast dismally; some trembling extremely; others acting as though all their nerves were convulsed; others swinging their arms, with all vigor, as if they were turning a wheel, &c. Then all break off, and have a spell of smoaking, and sometimes great fits of laughter.

What is striking is the combination of opposites: the way that individualism becomes concert, as Ann's voice (everyone testifies to the beauty of her singing) weaves together the discordant sounds and makes a 'charm' of them; the way that the mood of the occasion modulates from despair to exuberance. The overall effect is richly anarchic: 'groaning, jumping, dancing, drum[m]ing, laughing, talking and fluttering, shooting and hissing, ... A perfect bedlam; and this they call the worship of God.' The tone here is rather different from the one Rathbun adopted in the first flush of enthusiasm, when he spoke to a barnful of interested residents of Pittsfield, Richmond and Hancock about the faith he had just discovered: 'They sing the song that no man can learn. I could not learn their song any more than I could track the birds in the air. They seemed like an innumerable company of Angels.'

Rathbun's apostasy no doubt explains this difference in attitude, though with such improvised worship there was inevitably quite a lot of inconsistency of performance. Sometimes William Lee rebuked his fellow-Shakers for walking about in their meetings in a careless manner, telling them, 'You ought to pass by each other like angels; but you appear to me like the troubled sea, whose waters cast up mire and dirt.' Ann herself rarely addressed meetings, leaving that task mainly to the oratorical skills of James Whittaker, but she instructed her followers to try to maintain harmony. Sometimes an individual's impulses or 'gifts' took him or her in a different direction from the 'leading gift' of a meeting; when that happened, Ann told them 'they should labor to get out of it as soon as they well could, and unite with the rest'.

Rathbun explains in his pamphlet that Shaker worship could sometimes be heard two miles away. Often they would run wild 'in the woods and elsewhere hooting and tooting like owls'. He makes the charge of nakedness, but, like William Haskett later, sees this behaviour as essentially innocent from a sexual point of view: 'Some of them have stripped naked in the woods, and thought they were angels, and invisible, and could go out among men and not be seen.' Isaac Backus repeated this charge two years later, and despite his own hostility again suggests a pure and Edenic motive: 'men and women . . . dance together entirely naked, to imitate the primitive state of perfection'. The point Rathbun is trying to make is that this behaviour is deluded and contemptible rather than provocative, and he repeats what must surely have been an old joke even in those days: some of them 'have lost their cloaths, and never found them again'. Similarly, while it is certainly true that the Shakers frequently claimed to see the dead (whether their own relatives or those of candidates for conversion), Rathbun's animus takes him over the top in his version of the phenomenon: 'Sometimes while eating at the table, they say their dead parents and brethren come on the table and set on a pye and they see them.' It is probably too much to buy into this vision of the Shaker dead coming back and seating themselves on a pie; generally, though, Rathbun's description corresponds sufficiently with those of the Shakers themselves, and with accounts of more neutral observers like William Plumer, to be accepted as accurate.

The behaviour of the Shakers at Niskeyuna, and the changes they effected in their converts, began to bring them both fame and notoriety. The experience of Elizabeth Johnson, wife of the Rev. Samuel, was typical. While he was away at Niskeyuna, being – as it turned out – converted into the faith, she naturally enough felt worried about him, and sent one of her Stockbridge neighbours, David Mudge, to New Lebanon to meet him on the way back. 'But when David came where he was, the power of God operated so mightily upon him that David durst not speak to him. However, he returned home with David; but was still under such powerful operations that the neighbours gathered in to see him. They felt much opposed to that power.' Nathan Tiffany, who was at the time living with his parents in Somers, Connecticut, became aware of the practice of a strange religion above Albany: 'It was said their leader was a witch; that they were enemies to our country; that their religion was witchcraft, and was dreadful and terrible beyond expression.' While the war was going on all around them, it is hardly surprising that a group of English immigrants who were attracting New Englanders to their sect in dozens should arouse suspicion, particularly since their pacifism could be construed as an attempt to disarm the militia and even the ordinary country people who were holding themselves in readiness for the fray.

Loyalists – those who supported the British during the war – received short shrift from the community. A family called Ingrahams, for example, had a comfortable farm in the Albany area, but the man of the house went off to join the Regulars, in support of the British cause. The Rebels took possession of the farm and confiscated the livestock, all but a handful of animals and a pet lamb belonging to the four-year-old son of the household. The wife was forced to pay rent for her own property. When her husband returned on 13 September 1783 he told them they must all leave the area at once. He read to his family from the local paper, where Loyalists were described as 'abominable wretches, robbers, murderers, and incendiaries. Let it be a crime abhorred by nature to have any communication with them . . . let them be avoided like persons contaminated by the most deadly contagion.' The family went off to Canada in one of the sloops provided for those who had supported the British and who were in effect being expelled from their homes.

Given that this sort of treatment could be meted out to local people, the Shakers were inevitably going to arouse suspicion and resentment. Rumours circulated that Ann Lee was a witch, a spy, a camp-follower. Her characteristic ebullience didn't make matters any easier. During the war there was a Loyalist soldiers' song called 'The World Turned Upside Down', which obviously expressed British bewilderment at the upheaval in America (it had been sung in England in the previous century, during another confusing time: the Civil War). One of the early converts, Talmadge Bishop, was about to return home. The surrounding country was full of agitation and alarm about this new and strange religion, so he asked Ann what he should tell people about it. '"Tell them," said Mother, "that we are the people who turn the world upside down."'

On 1 July 1780, David Darrow, Daniel Green and Joseph Potter were driving nine fat sheep from New Lebanon to Niskeyuna to help the community cope with the demand on their supplies. On their way, however, they were set upon by a mob and subsequently arrested. The sheep were taken away and the three men were sent before Mathew Adgate, the local Justice of the Peace. The charge was that they were attempting to convey the sheep to the British forces – in effect, committing treason. Adgate therefore had no choice but to send the men under guard to Albany to appear before the 'Commissioners for

Detecting and Defeating Conspiracies in the State of New York'.

Joseph Meacham had gone with Darrow to the sitting before Adgate, and now went back to Niskeyuna to report to Ann. She sent him and Hocknell on down to Albany to act as character witnesses. The hearing was on 7 July. Green and Potter explained that they had no intention of allowing the sheep to fall into the hands of the enemy, and the charges against them were dismissed. Darrow, however, denied the authority of the Commission, and added for good measure that his religion prevented him from taking up arms in defence of the country. (Ironically, before his conversion Darrow fought on the Rebel side in the war, rising to the rank of lieutenant.) Meacham and Hocknell testified that Darrow had indeed stated the case accurately, and added that they shared the same principles. For 'acknowledging a Concurrence of Sentiment with him', they were promptly arrested as well, and all three were imprisoned. Warrants were also made out for Jonah Case and Zadock Wright, accused of associating with 'a set of people who call themselves shaking Quakers', and also of dissuading people from carrying arms.

Shortly after this Mathew Adgate sent Joel Pratt and Hezekiah Hammond (the very same who a few weeks previously had concentrated on twirling his horse-whip in order to render himself immune from Shaker overtures) along to the Commissioners, and at a hearing on 17 July they also asserted that they would not carry arms. The Shakers' commitment to pacifism was absolute. By 1832 it was estimated that $23,633.54 was owed in pensions to soldiers who had converted to Shakerism; none of it was ever drawn, 'being the unhallowed wages of war'. The Commissioners on this occasion decided that the time had come to write to Mathew Adgate and advise him about how he should deal with the problem posed by the Shakers. The week after, on 24 July, the Commissioners resolved that following complaints by local residents, a warrant should be made out for 'John Partherton' (Partington), 'William Lees' and 'Ann Standerren' (Lee). Jacob Kidney, the splendidly named and titled Commissioners' Door Keeper (or court officer, as we would call him), was sent to apprehend them.

Kidney's arrival must have taken Ann back seven years, to her troubles with the law in Manchester. One of the Shakers described her coming into the room with tears running from her eyes and saying, 'The wicked are plotting against us; they mean to drive us away from this place; and it is unknown to me whether I shall ever see you again in this world.' Jacob Kidney used his initiative, and decided to arrest 'James Whiteacre' (Whittaker), Calvin Harlow and Mary Partington in addition to those for whom he had a warrant, on the grounds that it appeared 'that they had also been guilty of the like Practices'. Thankful Barce described the trauma of the moment when Ann was taken away: 'It was truly a mournful scene. She [Ann] prayed earnestly that she might be able to endure with patience all that should come upon them. She often prayed for her persecutors, when they came to abuse her, in these words, "Father, forgive them; for they know not what they do."'

The Court House and Prison in Albany, 1794.

Ann and the other Shakers were imprisoned in Albany jail. As it happened, though, she and her followers did not remain there for long. Their worship created its usual shattering volume of sound – Richard Treat says that when he visited them the mighty power of God infused their singing to such an extent 'that it really seemed to me as if the very foundation of the prison trembled'. To prevent damage or disruption the authorities concluded they should be removed to the old fort on the hill, some distance from the centre of population. This prison proved to be the very one Ann had visited during the depths of the night five years previously, when she had slipped out of the Hudson River sloop which had been taking her to see the land John Hocknell was proposing to lease at Niskeyuna.

Even here the Shakers were able to preach to the crowds through the 'grates of the prison', and indeed to make a number of conversions from their odd vantage point. Ann was able to meet interested parties in her 'apartment' in the fort. One of these, a Shaker called Mary Knapp, brought along her troublesome daughter Hannah, who was in a state of 'obstinate unbelief'. Ann told her she was a haughty creature, and ordered her to kneel. Then she instructed Mary to take her away and get her to confess her sins, which she continued to refuse to do, telling her mother 'that if there was no other way to be saved, she was sure of going to hell; because she never could join them'. A little later she compared Ann to a 'drunken squaw'. But the very force of her words triggered a reaction, and she fell under an 'immediate judgment' which led her to confess her sins to John Hocknell. This gave her no relief from guilt, however.

That evening the believers came to Ann's cell to worship, Mary and her daughter among them. While they were kneeling Hannah remembered what she had said about Ann and 'was compelled to cry out, as if it had been for her life'. She prayed Mother Ann would forgive her. Ann took her into her arms and said, 'God forgive you child!'

During this period Ann also clarified her position on the war. Zadock Wright had been arrested for his Shaker sympathies, as we have seen, and was imprisoned along with the others, but originally he had been a Loyalist and had fled from his home in Canterbury, Vermont, to Canada to avoid arrest. He had returned, however, to collect his family, and he may have found it less onerous to claim Shaker affiliations than out-and-out Loyalist ones. On his imprisonment his estate was confiscated. He visited Ann in her cell to tell her all his troubles. At the meeting she told him he would be delivered from his financial embarrassments, and also explained to him that the Revolution 'was the providential work of God, to open the way for the Gospel'. A year later his fortunes were restored, he resumed family life at Vermont, and was subsequently converted into the faith by two proselytising Shakers, Israel Chauncy and Ebenezer Cooley.

Not understanding that Ann, in her pacifist fashion, was actually a supporter of the Revolution, albeit for her own special reasons, the Commissioners, meeting on 26 August after the Shakers had been in prison just over a month, concluded that the best solution to the problem she posed would be to send her over the British lines to be reunited with her countrymen. To this end they ordered that she and Mary Partington should be sent down into the care of the Commissioners at Poughkeepsie, from where they would have only a short distance to convey her to the British troops in New York. A Shaker called John Bishop visited Ann in prison and was upset to hear that she was going to be taken away the next day. When Ann asked him why he was troubled he told her that he didn't know whether he would ever see her again in this world. She replied, 'You shall see me at your house, in New-Lebanon; for I know it of God.' This comforted him; and sure enough, as we shall see, Ann made her appearance at his house three years later.

The jail at Poughkeepsie had been burnt down as a revolutionary gesture at the outbreak of war, a symbolically satisfying action but hardly a practical one, since prisons are always useful, whichever side you're on. Instead an old farm-house called the Baltus Van Kleek house had been requisitioned for that purpose, and Ann was duly installed there along with Mary Partington, who by this stage had been cleared of any charges and was simply acting as her companion, with permission to leave their quarters when necessary and go to the grocer's to buy provisions. In due course the authorities thought better of their plan to send Ann back behind British lines. The difficulty of explaining to the enemy that you were sending them the female Christ had perhaps proved insuperable.

Meanwhile it was the turn of Samuel Johnson, minister at Stockbridge, Massachusetts, and, with Joseph Meacham, one of the leaders of the New Light Stir, to run afoul of the authorities. After the initial shock of seeing her husband in the full throes of his conversion, under the operations of God, his wife Elizabeth had been gradually

The Van Kleek house, near Poughkeepsie.

following along the same route, and they had gone together from their home in Stockbridge to New Lebanon to attend a Shaker meeting at the house of Dr Isaac Harlow. During worship a mob broke in and dragged Samuel off to appear before Mathew Adgate. He sent him under armed guard to Albany, where he arrived on 28

August and was remanded by the Commissioners to prison on the grounds that he was 'going about the Country & dissuading people from taking up Arms in defence of the American cause'.

Left on her own with three children, Elizabeth Johnson made her own way to Albany. There she found that Ann had been sent off to Poughkeepsie, that the elders and other Shakers were confined in the fort, but that Samuel, as a late-comer, was in the prison by the city hall. On 6 September the Commissioners considered Samuel's case, with Elizabeth appealing to them on behalf of her husband. John Johnson, Samuel's brother, also appeared before the board, carrying a letter from a Colonel William B. Whiting arguing that Samuel's current pacifist principles were so at odds with his previous warm support of the American cause that the only possible explanation was a sudden attack of insanity. His recommendation was that Samuel should be delivered into the care of his brother. John carried another letter from Adgate in support of this proposal, which was agreed to by the Commissioners, though they also cautioned Samuel against returning to the state of New York 'whilst he persists in inculcating such dangerous and destructive principles'.

After a few weeks in the Van Kleek building, Ann was released into house arrest in the home of James Boyd, a resident of Poughkeepsie who was a sympathiser. While they were living there, hostility developed 'among some of the lower class of people' and one night a number of them 'painted and habited after the manner of Indians' surrounded the house, and tried to throw papers containing gunpowder through the windows and into the fire. They were sharply reproved by Ann and Boyd, and went off, but returned in the night and dropped another gunpowder parcel down the chimney. Luckily it bounced out of the hearth and failed to explode.

The Shakers held in Albany were released in mid-November, each of them on a recognisance of £100 for good behaviour. William Lee promptly went to James Clinton and persuaded him to write a letter to his brother, the state governor, asking for Ann's release, which he did on 19 November. At the end of December James Whittaker reinforced the point by pleading Ann's case on his knees to Governor Clinton, who happened to be in Poughkeepsie, and he ordered her release.

After regaining their freedom Ann and her followers spent the remainder of the winter and the following spring at Niskeyuna, and, perhaps as a result of the notoriety they had received, many visitors poured in. Most of them were sympathetic or at least open-minded, but the Shakers were also afflicted with 'mockers and scoffers' who 'were ever ready to judge with an evil eye', and rumours of lewdness and drunkenness began to circulate.

While Ann was being held in the Van Kleek house at Poughkeepsie, she had been visited by a young man called Jonathan Slosson. He had confessed his sins and gained a measure of faith, but couldn't make a full commitment because he was in love with his cousin. After Ann's return to Niskeyuna, he visited her again, and an odd little incident took place, one that gives a vivid impression of Ann's brusque authority.

Shortly after he entered the house, Mother came into the room. Jonathan, with his back to the fire and the skirts of his coat drawn forward, asked, 'How does Mother do?'

She replied, 'If I am your Mother, young man, I'll teach you to turn your face to the fire, not your back: for heating your backside by the fire enrages lust. It shows ill breeding, and bad behavior, for people to stand heating their backsides by the fire.' Then she added, 'God will break in pieces the man and maid. If you want to marry, you may marry the Lord Jesus Christ.'

Another incident that occurred in the period after Ann's release from Poughkeepsie shows her in a similarly uncompromising mood, and also sheds light on the discipline of Shaker confession. A couple called Rufus and Zeruah Clark, having received testimony, arrived to undertake their full confession. What sin or sins Zeruah had committed we can only speculate, but she wanted very much to make her confession in private. This of course was unacceptable, and from the Shaker point of view unnecessary. William Lee said to Zeruah, after Ann had briefed him on the subject in an unknown tongue: 'We can see all the sins that you have ever committed, as plain as though they were written on your forehead.' He then told her she had to make her confession in the presence of her husband, and vice versa. Even though in the very act of becoming Shakers they were repudiating their sexual relationship, it is still cringe-making to imagine this scene being acted out between the couple. When it was over William 'warned them, in a very solemn manner, never to upbraid each other of the sins which they had then confessed to God, before his witnesses'.

It was invariably sex that brought Shakerism's grim and uncompromising side to the surface. If it wasn't an issue, conversion could be a cosy affair, as it was for Hannah Cogswell, a seventeen-year-old who joined the Shakers in January 1781 and who shared a room with Mother Ann for the next four and a half months, often sleeping in the same bed with her.

During this period Ann was in an evangelical mood, envisaging the ultimate spread of the gospel throughout the world. Shortly after returning from Poughkeepsie, she told her followers: 'You are called in relation to all the rest of mankind; and through your faith and obedience, they must receive the gospel ... The increase ... at the first, will be small; but the time will come when souls will embrace it by hundreds and by thousands: for this testimony will overcome all nations; it will increase until the covering is taken off; and then mankind will see the rottenness of Antichrist's foundation.' Interestingly, considering the adventures that they had already experienced and the greater ones to come, Ann here perceived the mission as an unobtrusive one: 'The work of God, in this day, is an inward, spiritual work; it is not so great, in outward appearance, as it was in past dispensations.' But just because there would be no loud fanfares, 'souls must be very cautious how they treat this gospel; for such as finally reject this testimony, will not have another day'.

In the spring of 1781, this evangelistic mood turned into a concrete intention. The woman in the Book of

Revelation was to spend 1,260 days in the wilderness; Ann, if one deducts her time in prison, had spent three or four hundred days longer than that – close enough, perhaps, but it was time to be on the move. For a year the Shakers had welcomed a stream of converts from New England via eastern New York, and Ann now decided on a missionary journey across the Hudson and into the region which had already given her so much support. It would enable her to reinforce the faith of those who had already become Shakers and subsequently returned to their home-towns. It would also enable her to spread the word to new potential converts.

She was to be gone for two years and three months. During that time she would establish American Shakerism on a solid foundation of faith. In one respect, however, her powers of prophecy had misled her. It would not be an unobtrusive and uneventful process. The mission would be fraught with danger and suffering from beginning to end, and her religious triumphs would be purchased at huge personal cost.

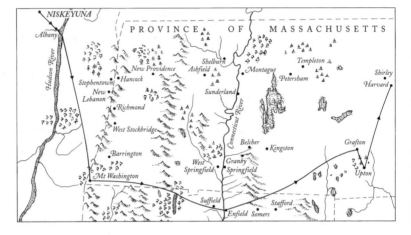

Ann's journey from Niskeyuna to Harvard, Mass.

7

The Journey to Harvard

Ann and her entourage were on the move, but of course the whole point of a mission is to leave behind firmly established groups of converts as you pass onwards, and Niskeyuna, the starting point of the journey, could be no exception. It was left in the care of John Hocknell, who had done so much to underwrite the community in the first place, and who certainly had the fervour to keep up the atmosphere of spiritual excitement. 'If you could see the glory of God that shines around you, as I do, and the angels that minister the power of God to you,' he told the Niskeyuna faithful at one of their meetings, 'your hair would rise on your heads, and your flesh would crawl upon your bones.'

The Shakers were as aware as Jonathan Edwards had been that God could be angry. A few years later one of the believers described James Whittaker coming into a room on tiptoe: as he went by, he said, 'I feel such fear of God that I fear to step my foot upon the floor.' Ann Lee herself, as the Lord's representative, could bring about a similar reaction. One of the New Lebanon converts, Rachel Spencer, remembered Ann as 'meek, modest, reserved and thoughtful', but went on to say: 'I really loved and feared her more than any person I ever saw.' She added: 'that which was carnal and ungodly in me would often tremble in her presence'. As we have seen, the activity of shaking has a wide-ranging significance, but in part it is an expression of fear: 'Thus the Lord promised, that he would *shake* the earth with terror' (Isaiah ii, 19, 21).

While John Hocknell took charge of the base, three of the English contingent, William Lee, James Whittaker and Mary Partington, along with the Americans Samuel Fitch, Margaret Leland and John Farrington, set off with Ann on her journey on 31 May 1781, the women trundling out of Niskeyuna in a wagon, accompanied by the men on horseback. They were heading east, through New York State, across the Hudson River, and into Massachusetts. The landscape through which they would travel had been settled for a century and a half, yet was wild and formidable compared with the patchwork fields of north Cheshire, the only countryside the English contingent had previously known. There was a mountainous ridge to cross first, part of the Appalachian chain, here known as the Berkshire hills, and beyond it a massive undulating area of forests, scattered farms and small townships, with log cabins like the one at Niskeyuna in clearings, and clapboard frame-houses clustered together in more cultivated areas to form little communities, mostly measurable in tens or hundreds of inhabitants. Tracks and paths could be muddy or rocky or even both, and the massive scale of American geography, and the consequent problems of communication, led to real and also psychological remoteness and provincialism, with communities possessing a strong sense of their own identity and a suspicion of strangers – particularly when the strangers were as strange as the Shakers, and there was a war going on.

Their route was determined by invitations from converts, and the need to reinforce their faith as well as helping in the spreading of the gospel to friends and family. But as with the original journey to America, there was a visionary element involved. Mother Ann had seen a destination for herself while still in England, a true spiritual home in America. This was not Niskeyuna, the location prophesied in the Book of Revelation, despite the fact that, wilderness though it was, it had proved to be a fertile seeding-ground. A further destination would provide the setting for the next stage of development, a place where the religion could be nurtured and consolidated. Ann was becoming ever more closely targeted on her destiny.

First of all, though, she had calls to make. She visited Jonathan Slosson, the man who had recklessly warmed his backside, and Benjamin Osborn at their homesteads on Tucconack Mountain (now known, in commemoration of the victor in the war which at this time was still raging, as Mount Washington), and stayed in the region about ten days, attracting large numbers of people, some sympathetic and others hostile. A certain Dr Hollibert tried to dispute with the elders, but was 'put to the blush' by James Whittaker, and, magnanimous in defeat, advised the mob to let them alone. The Shakers then continued on another seventy miles to the home-town of Joseph Meacham, in Enfield, Connecticut. A young girl called Elizabeth Wood was picking strawberries at the roadside outside the property belonging to David Meacham, Joseph's brother, when the party rolled up. She immediately opened the gate and followed them through to the house.

Ann got down from the wagon and asked, in her no-nonsense Mancunian, 'Where is the old man?', referring to Joseph Meacham's father, Joseph senior, who had visited her in prison at Albany and been converted in his turn to the faith that had been so enthusiastically adopted by his two sons. The old man duly came to the door and let them in. Ann took off her things and asked for some water to wash with and then, after they had eaten, she went off into one of the rooms where she could be alone.

What happened next gives some insight into the impact Shakerism had already had up and down New England. This was an environment saturated with religious enthusiasm, and the arrival of a new cult had crystallised emotions into eager anticipation or deep unease. Elizabeth followed Ann into the room, knelt down before her, and confessed that before she had even met her she had wished her 'shot with a piece of silver' for being a witch. Nearly a century had passed since the witch-hunt of Salem, but a spiritual shadow still lay over that sunny afternoon in the country, a girl picking strawberries and running to open a gate and let in new arrivals. Elizabeth's instant confession is also testimony to the authoritative and clarifying effect of Ann Lee's physical presence.

'What made you call me so,' said she, 'was it because you have heard others do so?'

Elizabeth told her she did not know.

'Well it was,' said she, 'and I can forgive you, and pray God to forgive you. Get up, child. Have you any parents?'

Elizabeth answered 'Yea.'

'You have a step-mother, have you not?'

'I have a mother-in-law,' Elizabeth replied.

There was a little discussion on this point, in which Ann made it clear that 'step-mother' was the appropriate term. Having brushed aside the charge of witchcraft she was defining an identity she herself found much more congenial, that of substitute mother. But it was necessary to invest that role too with a flavour of the supernatural. Ann talked at length about the woman in question, convincing Elizabeth that she could only know all this information by the gift of God, in much the same way in which a fairground fortune-teller amazes clients with her apparent knowledge of their lives and relationships.

During this visit Ann impressed other local people too. In an echo of her brother's remark to Zeruah Clark at Niskeyuna, she told Mary Tiffany (rather touchingly, in view of her own illiteracy), 'I see the travel of your soul written upon you in great capital letters, and I can read them as fast as I can speak.' Despite the usual testimony to the sweetness of her voice, for one impressionable man her singing 'sounded louder to him than any clap of thunder which he ever heard in his life'.

Many members of the small community resented the impact she had. The 'world', Elizabeth Wood tells us, became bitter, and watched to make sure that the party would leave town at the time they had said they would. In view of this reaction, Ann decided it would be wise to keep to their timetable, and after a week they proceeded east sixty miles to Grafton, where they stayed with John Maynor. They had now moved into an area of Massachusetts that possessed, as far as the Shakers were concerned, a very significant past and, as a result, a great potential for the future.

Nearly thirty years previously, the Congregational clergyman in Grafton, the Rev. Solomon Prentice, had been caught up in the excitement of the Great Awakening, the parent revival of the New Light Stir, along with his wife Sarah. Sarah was particularly vulnerable to the onset of religious enthusiasm because of the recent loss of her father, and she went through a long process of spiritual struggle, culminating in an ecstatic conversion during which she went into a trance, crying out, 'It's Lovely! It's Lovely!' Long after the revival had lost impetus, the couple remained fanatical, so much so that the Rev. Prentice was dismissed by his congregation in 1747. Given this degree of emotional intensity, it's not surprising that in the early 1750s Sarah fell under the influence of a cult-leader in her home-town of Charleston, Massachusetts. He was called Shadrack Ireland, and, like Ann Lee a little later, he was an artisan – a pipe-fitter by trade – originally drawn to religious proselytising as a result of hearing the preaching of the Methodist George Whitefield. In 1753 Ireland had a conversion experience which, he claimed, had left him immortal, and he now preached the doctrine of Perfectionism, through which his followers would have the opportunity of achieving the same desirable state. Indeed one of them, a resident of the town of Hopkinton by the name of Nat Smith, had 'proceeded to assume & declare himself to be the Most High God', and in an odd anticipation of the modern fashion for baseball hats 'wore a Cap with the Word God inscribed on its front'. Nat also possessed a great chair, which 'was a Holy Chair & none but himself must sit in it'. Interestingly, a splinter group of Whitefield's English followers also became Perfectionists, under the leadership of a certain George Bell. They too believed they were 'holy as the angels' and 'incapable of ever sinning again' (they also forecast the end of the world for 1763).

Sarah Prentice, too, had arrived at a state in which her 'Body would never achieve Corruption', and as a result of this transformation she had begun to sleep with Shadrack Ireland. Like the Shakers who were at this time formulating their doctrines in England, Ireland advocated sexual abstinence – with one important proviso, which was that having reached perfection he and his followers were able to have sex with each other, since their bodies were now free from sin and therefore true temples of the spirit. Any offspring produced by these pairings were dignified by the title of 'holy children'.

Solomon Prentice does not seem to have followed his wife into Ireland's cult, but the couple stayed together and by the early 1770s were settled back in Grafton. Sarah had long ago given up on Ireland as a spiritual husband, and was now living in total celibacy – for over twenty years, she told one enquirer, she had 'not so much as shook hands with any Mann', her earthly husband included. The Rev. Prentice had died in 1773, but his widow was still living in Grafton when Ann Lee and her company arrived in mid-June 1781.

We don't know of any direct contact between the two women, though John Maynor, with whom Ann Lee and her elders stayed, had been a Perfectionist, and it is clear that the Shakers were homing in on the remnants of Ireland's cult. The next staging-post was the town of Upton, Massachusetts, just eight miles down the road, where they stayed with Daniel Wood, who had also been one of Ireland's leading followers and who the year before had come to Niskeyuna and been converted to Shakerism (his sister, Margaret Leland, was part of Ann Lee's entourage); the stop after that was the township of Harvard, where Ireland had settled about twenty years previously and where, just the year before, he had inadvertently contradicted the most fundamental tenet of his own religion by suddenly dying.

Things had become hot for Shadrack Ireland in his home-town of Charleston in about 1760. Clearly his unconventional lifestyle brought opprobrium on his head, and eventually he decided it would be wise to do a disappearing trick, leaving his bodily wife Elizabeth behind and letting local followers spread the story that he had died. In fact he took up residence in Harvard, in central Massachusetts, where a few years later, in 1769, his disciples Isaac Willard, Zaccheus Stevens, David Hoar, Abel Jewett, Samuel and Jonathan Cooper, Ethan Phillips and

John Maynor built a house for him, allegedly erecting it in one night to outwit nosy neighbours – though if that was the case they did a remarkable job, since the building is still standing (now a pleasant family house in private hands) in the countryside north of Harvard town. Ireland himself played his part in the construction work; indeed, some accounts of him claim that he was also a carpenter by trade (the house, like most in New England, was of white-painted clapboard). A Shaker annalist, years later, offers rather grudging approval: 'Ireland did considerable work in the finishing of the Square House. The stair banister and railings are without doubt his work. He was a good workman, – a kind of cabinet maker or joiner. He began quite zealous, – had much of the Spirit for his day when he began, and probably meant to go pretty correct.'

The building has always been known as the Square House on account of the flattened design of its roof, though that has been replaced long since by one of the conventionally cambered variety. The secretiveness that went into the building is manifested in the design as well, with a cupola reached by a secret staircase providing a lookout, and a string connecting the kitchen with Ireland's study so that a bell could be rung to warn him if visitors approached. Clearly, the disruptive nature of Ireland's doctrines would have made him enemies, just as Ann Lee's did; and there is also a suggestion that he feared prosecution for blasphemy on account of an attack he had made on the sloth and self-indulgence of the Congregational clergy; nevertheless, one has the sense of a siege mentality evolving over the years, rather on the lines of

the one which in more recent times triggered the catastrophe at Waco. Ireland hardly ever left his study, and
when he did it was only to conduct services with his
followers on a nearby hill, from which he could still keep
a lookout over the surrounding countryside. For the purpose of secrecy his followers seldom used Ireland's name,
but referred to him as 'The Man'.

During the last months of his life The Man seems to
have had intimations of mortality. He told his followers
that he was not to be buried if he died, because like Christ
he would rise again on the third day or, more originally,
on the ninth. His soul, in other words, might leave his
body, but it would return in due course. In the summer
of 1780, while Ann Lee, a hundred and fifty miles away
at Niskeyuna, was being deluged with pilgrims from New
Lebanon, Ireland's predictions were finally put to the test.

There are two versions of his final moments. One sees
him displaying calm and fortitude, and above all a confidence that his spiritual destiny is being fulfilled. 'Sister
Nabay,' he said, using an affectionate nickname for Abigail
Cooper, one of his followers who lived in the Square
House with her own perfected family, 'the Lord hath
Done with me, and I have Completed all the work he
sent me to do; but Don't be Scared, for I am going; but
don't bury me, for the Time is very Short. God is Coming
to take the Church.' The other account shows him in a
different light: 'The night he died, he walked the floor in
great distress of mind & groaning with deep groans.'
Finally he exclaimed, 'I feel the wrath of God!' Abigail
Lougee, Ireland's current spiritual bride, rushed off to

fetch Abigail Cooper but by the time the two women returned with a light, he was dead.

Whatever Ireland's state of mind might have been at the moment of truth, his followers took him at his word. They barred the Square House against outsiders, and watched the body, still seated in its chair, day and night. Unfortunately it was the height of summer, and after a few days it became necessary to carry the corpse down into the cellar, where in due course it was placed in a coffin and then, in Edgar Allan Poe fashion, bricked up. Several months later all hope of resurrection was abandoned.

The disappointment felt by the Perfectionists is inevitably an occupational hazard in immortality circles: Charles Owen, in his book attacking the French Prophets, gives examples of people who made the same claim and then failed to deliver. In one such case the subject failed to rise again on the due date for the simple reason that he hadn't actually managed to die by then; another, Dr Thomas Emes, passed away in 1707, just before the millennium which he had prophesied was due to be inaugurated. It was accordingly announced that his resurrection would take place on 25 May the following year, which must have seemed to provide a reasonable margin at the time; when the day came round a huge crowd (estimated at twenty thousand people) assembled at the graveyard but the deceased doctor failed to reappear, much to the embarrassment of those in attendance.

Two of the Perfectionists, Abijah Worster and David Hoar, eventually broke through into Ireland's cellar tomb, and took his body out into a nearby field, just southerly from the wash-house (the precise recording of the location suggests a lingering wish that some good might still come of the tragedy). They buried him in a cornfield, and then, still in the grip of the paranoia that had taken hold of the cult, replanted all the corn afterwards so that the where-abouts of the body could not be determined.

This outcome must have been a dismal anticlimax. Just as the participants in the New Light Stir lost faith that their redeemer would ever come, so the Perfectionists in the Harvard area of Massachusetts had to come to terms with the fact that their leader had gone for good. In both cases the cure for spiritual woe, for many of those experiencing it, was provided by the Shakers.

A number of Ireland's followers, Abijah Worster and Daniel Wood among them, had made their way to Niske-yuna, and been converted along with the New Light contingent, with Abijah going through a tumultuous experience, as we saw in Chapter 5, which culminated in him being freed from the pangs of gluttony for the rest of his life. The religious background of the Perfectionists made them prone to throes of spiritual and physical contortion that were extreme even by Shaker standards. Worster himself described one such moment of posses-sion in graphic and appropriately disjointed language: 'As I was tossing – tumbling – rolling – jumping – throwing myself against the wall – the chimney – the floor – the chairs, in fact everything that did not keep out of the way I felt that my blood was boiling, and every bone in my body was being torn asunder my flesh pinched with hot irons, and every hair on my head were stinging reptiles.'

The experience was so traumatic that Abijah lay on the floor and waited to die. But then Ann appeared. She scrutinised him and exclaimed, 'Why, Abijah, there is some of the worst looking spirits on your shoulders I ever saw in my life.'

She then made some passes over him and he was relieved.

When the Perfectionist converts returned to their home territory they took this particularly tempestuous expression of Shaker commitment back with them. The two daughters of Abel Jewett were early converts, and went over to the Cooper family, who were still living in the Square House, to demonstrate their new faith. They 'set down on their feet put their hands under their knees & hopped or jumped across the room in that position'. This performance, athletic though it was, did not have the desired effect. 'But all their labor did not prevail on her [Beulah Cooper] or any of the family to embrace the testimony until Mother came.'

Nevertheless the Coopers, along with the other Perfectionists and their friends and neighbours, were being made aware that Mother was indeed going to come.

A twenty-two-year-old woman called Jemima Blanchard, whose family lived in Harvard and had been involved in Ireland's cult, was living in the household of Isaac Willard, one of Ireland's followers, probably helping with children and doing some housework. One evening she was visiting her own home when Daniel Wood arrived, and explained about the Shakers, telling Jemima and one of her brothers, Joseph, about their doctrine of confession and the way they were operated on by the power of God. He wanted to take Jemima off to meet them but she refused. Nevertheless, both she and Joseph began to feel afraid. 'Daniel said he did not know but they would come here and I feared it this was in the winter.'

The following spring there were reports that the Shakers were on their way, and Joseph told Jemima that he was going to sea in order to get away from them. He did exactly that, and Jemima never heard from him again during the whole of her long life. Jemima took less drastic avoiding action, taking the advice of friends to go to the town of Hollistown and take work with a family called Cutter. As Jemima later described it, 'We determined like Jonah, to flee from the presence of the Lord.'

It's clear that there was deep foreboding in the awaiting communities as Ann Lee made her progress across New England. Elizabeth Wood in Enfield, Connecticut, wanted to arm herself with a silver bullet, as we saw earlier, on the assumption that she was a witch. Jemima and Joseph Blanchard were perfectly prepared to concede that the Shakers might indeed be the chosen people of God – in fact, that was precisely why they took action to try to escape. Whether she was a witch or a redeemer Ann Lee could instil terror in people, just as the God of Isaiah had when he made tremble the earth. What connects the reaction of Elizabeth Wood with that of the Blanchard siblings is the awe experienced by all three at the prospect of a power beyond the natural order: it's almost a secondary consideration whether that power is benign or malignant. Their fear is of being overwhelmed.

Ann Lee rolled into Harvard in late June 1781. She stayed for the first night at the house of Zaccheus Stevens, another of Ireland's followers, in Still River, within the town boundary, and then moved over to the Willards', where Jemima had been working until she fled the town. As names recur we get a slightly misleading sense of a microscopic community. In fact the census of 1776 gives the population of Harvard as 1,315; it was a reasonably sized New England township, with a common (on which the militia now trained) at the base of a slope called Pin Hill, its Congregational church and its white-painted clapboard houses clustering around and fading into the farms and orchards of the surrounding countryside. Within that larger environment, however, there was a much smaller and more tightly knit network of ex-Irelandites and their allies who were already involved with the Shakers, or at the very least were receptive to them. Isaac Backus, the eighteenth-century Baptist minister and historian, who scorned both Perfectionists and Shakers, described Harvard as 'a place where the goodness of God and the folly of man have been remarkably discovered'. Isaac Willard himself was in his sixties. Thirty years previously he and his wife, along with two other couples, had caused trouble in the Congregational meeting-house. He was 'peculiar in his religious views and indulged in distempered fancies'.

While Ann was staying at the Willards' her attention was directed to the Square House, a couple of miles northeast of the centre of town. She told a group of people who came to see her soon after her arrival: 'God has a people in this place; he has heard their cries; they have had great light. Their leader got overcome; God has taken him away and sent me here. The wicked seek my life; as they did in England, so they do here; but heed it not; for God will establish his work here, and the wicked cannot overthrow it.' Clearly, she was aware of the potential for replacing Perfectionism with her own creed. There were important elements that connected the two doctrines: common property, pacifism and (to a degree) celibacy. Both cults depended on charismatic leadership, and one had lost its leader. The implication was obvious. So, as Ann's words made clear, was the danger. One night she had a vision of a large mob in black filling the road to the Square House, and trying to prevent her from going there. Then two angels made a route through the assembled company, which meant that God would open the way for her to go through.

It was now seven years since Ann had set out on her long journey, and she was in sight of her ultimate destination. Just because there were obvious strategic gains to be made in displacing Perfectionism, they do not invalidate the authenticity of her mystical vision. Because Shakerism is a total vision of the world, practical and spiritual motives are knitted together in a single system, in just the way, as we saw in an earlier chapter, that metaphors have a tendency to become literal. This is the house, and these are the people, Ann said, that she had seen in England. Looked at from the point of view of simple geography, there seems nothing to connect a teeming terrace in Toad Lane, Manchester, with a roomy wooden house set in the woods and meadows of the undulating Massachusetts countryside. But a coherent religious vision turns the two dwellings into poles of a single system, and makes the long journey between the two – three thousand miles, seven years, a leaky boat, poverty, imprisonment, triumph and hostility – into something of the equivalent of a spiritual epic. Though that story would not end with arrival at the Square House: on a quest like Ann Lee's, there can be no final resting-place.

In due course she set off with her followers for the Square House. There is no record of a mob in black trying to impede her progress, though there would be plenty of mobs in the future.

The door was answered by Abigail Cooper.

'Are you willing that we should come into your house?' William Lee asked her.

Abigail 'had gotten a little hint that they were trying to get in at the Square House to make their home there', and therefore replied, 'No, I don't know as I am.'

William was insistent. 'Well, I suppose you'll let us come in, will you?'

'I suppose I must,' Abigail conceded, and let them in.

Once inside, the Shakers sat down and began to talk to Abigail. They told her they were going on to another house for the moment and that when they came back 'We had thought of tarrying with you for a while.'

Abigail was obviously uncomfortable with this prospect, so they changed tack, asking her if she was content with her religion and whether it saved her from sin. Ann said, 'All we want is to help souls to God.'

Abigail's reply was that she had seen a great deal of false religion, and did not want to see any more. 'If you have any new religion you can keep it to yourselves, I do not want it.' As a parting shot she added, 'I do not care about seeing you; you are English people.' It's worth remembering that Harvard was close to Lexington and Concord, and not far from Boston, the heartland of Rebel patriotism in the war.

As the Shakers left, they asked Abigail if she loved them. She told them she didn't. Rather threateningly, William answered, 'We will make you love us before we leave the place.'

He then did something quite extraordinary, an action which sheds great light on Shaker techniques of psychological manipulation. He gave Abigail an apple.

Abigail later recalled that she did not want it, but took it all the same, and 'laid it on the manteltree piece'. She then got on with her housework, but as she swept the floor her eyes kept being drawn to the apple she had been given, and she took it into her hand. When she did so her feelings about the Shakers went into reverse. 'I knew they had something good, because I felt such love to them. I longed to have them return, & when they did I was thankful to take them in. And I found Mother's words to be true.'

There is something of the fairy-tale in this account of the magic apple; there is also a clear reference to the story of the Garden of Eden, and it should always be remembered that the Shaker project was to reverse the cause and effect of that event. But above all the anecdote gives a sense of the hypnotic quality of Shakerism, the way in which it would change an individual's perspective. As Jemima Blanchard feared, it was a religion that could overwhelm your will.

The Shakers duly took over the Square House and, in due course, most of the Perfectionists along with it. Ann took a characteristically uncompromising tone when dealing with their doctrine of the immortality of the body, addressing the more elderly Ireland followers on one occasion in the following terms:

You are now old people, and yet you think you shall never die! One is dropping away here, and another there, among you; yet you lay it to some secret cause – to something which they have done. That is to say, if they had been faithful, it would not have been so. Look at yourselves; you carry about you all the marks of mortality that are on other people. Your skins are wrinkled; your hair is turning white and falling from your heads; your eye-sight is failing; you are losing your teeth, and your bodies are growing decrepit. How inconsistent it is for you to think you shall never die! These natural bodies must all die and turn to dust.

Shadrack Ireland's presence was felt in the Square House for some time. One day, Ann announced to her brother William: 'Shadrack Ireland has been here to see me; and I made labors with him; but he would not believe; therefore he went to hell; and the souls in hell were frightened at him, because his torment was so much greater than theirs. But he will never come out until some of his people find their redemption.' Ann often had vivid and

Dantesque visions of souls in the afterlife, on one occasion telling Samuel Fitch that she had seen spirits in the regions of darkness who had wept so much they had worn gutters in their cheeks. As we have already seen, the Shakers believed that spiritual development and ultimate salvation were still possible in the afterlife for those who had not had the advantage of the conversion experience Ann and her elders could offer. But the very proximity of some of Ireland's doctrines to Shaker belief made the areas of difference seem dangerous and threatening, and thereby ensured that his particular 'little hell' was exceptionally painful. Moreover his malign spiritual influence was still being experienced in the world, and until that could be rectified he would have to pick up the tab in the afterlife.

The material nature of his spirituality, his doctrine that the body itself could be perfected, gave an ironic appropriateness to a lingering afterlife in the mortal realm. Sometimes Ireland's ghostly presence could be detected while the Shakers were at worship. 'There being quite a heft of death and darkness in meeting, Mother Ann came out of the chamber, and told the people to labor for the power of God, "for," said Mother Ann, "there are the darkest spirits here that I ever sensed, – Shadrack Ireland is here, – he began in the spirit and ended in almost total darkness of the flesh."'

The legacy of Shadrack Ireland persisted on a more practical level also, though in this respect it would be more appropriate to talk of the lack of a legacy. The assumption of his followers was that the Square House was their joint property, since many of them had been involved in its erection, and in any case they held possessions in common. David Hoar, however, seemed to resent Ann's take-over of the building and the religion, and took it upon himself to inform Ireland's heirs of the status of the property. They made a claim for it, and eventually the Shakers had to buy the Square House from them for the sum of $500.

But these legal and financial problems were the least of their worries. Abigail Cooper had let them into the Square House, and they were determined to use it as their base. But many of the Harvard inhabitants were equally determined that they should not, and the next two years were to be dominated by struggle and violence.

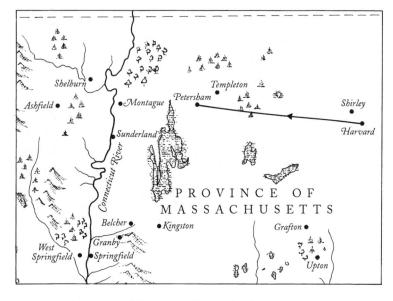

Mission to Petersham.

8

The Experience of Jemima Blanchard

While the Shakers were settling in at the Square House, Jemima Blanchard continued to work for the Cutters at Hollistown. Meanwhile her sister Phebe had been converted. Jemima herself was by no means out of range of their influence. One evening Daniel Wood appeared, wanting to talk to her. As luck would have it, she was away from the Cutter house at the time, visiting friends. Amos Cutter sent word for her to remain where she was overnight in order to keep out of his clutches. Daniel Wood remained at the Cutters' for most of the next day in hopes that Jemima would return, but eventually had to leave disappointed.

What made this game of cat-and-mouse particularly tense was the ambivalence of Jemima's own feelings. When she returned to the Cutters', having dodged Daniel, she began to put pressure on Cutter himself to go and visit the Shakers in order to report back on what was going on. Cutter's wife (as Jemima always called her) was just as curious, and backed Jemima up; finally he agreed to go.

Perhaps in defiance of his own expectations Cutter was impressed by what he saw at the Square House. He was a preacher himself, and had been caught up in the New Light Stir, so the atmosphere of religious enthusiasm was congenial to him. William Lee told him that God was at work within him, and that if he should gain conviction at any time in the future he must come back to see them. Cutter promised he would if the occasion arose, and on his ride back to Hollistown felt so moved by the whole experience that he got off his horse and lay upon the ground. It is almost as though the New Englanders of this period had a capacity that for most of us is now largely defunct, an organ capable of registering acute spiritual excitement.

Cutter's account confirmed Jemima's intuition that the Shakers had the true faith, and she persuaded him to take her and his wife into Harvard so that they could have a closer look at what was going on.

Her account of what happened next, the most detailed and illuminating of all the early conversion experiences, was recounted by Jemima to Roxalana Grosvenor more than half a century later, when Jemima was an old, blind Shaker sister. The first stop for the reconnoitring party was at Zaccheus Stevens's house, where she saw two local people, Eleazer Rand and Tabitha Green. Their countenances were 'solemn and heavenly', but that wasn't all. The visitors were invited to join the little gathering for supper. The Cutters duly kneeled with the others to say grace, but Jemima didn't dare to participate. While she looked on at the praying people she saw with wonder that the power of God was visible on the faces of the believers and even on their clothing. 'It looked perfectly white and run in veins.' They had been mysteriously transmogrified by conversion to Shakerism.

There is a strange anticipatory resonance of the works of Stephen King in Jemima's description, as though these inhabitants of a small town in rural New England had been taken over by alien forces from outer space. That, in a sense, is precisely what had happened. The God whom Jemima was encountering through the persons of the Shaker converts was not a cosy, comforting presence, but the embodiment of otherness, a force operating outside and above the human realm. While the Shakers ridiculed Shadrack Ireland for his belief that the human body could be perfected through faith, they nevertheless held that the spiritual and physical dimensions could intersect, either in the process of shaking or, as here, in the substantial manifestation of what, in other faiths, would be the intangible gift of grace. James Whittaker, describing an early mystical experience of his own, uses terminology that vies with Jemima's in its physicality, and indeed in its sexual overtones: 'One day, as I was walking with Mother, I felt the heavens open, and such flows of the heavenly manifestations and givings of God fell upon me, in so marvellous a manner, that my soul was filled with inexpressible glory; and I felt such an overflowing of love . . . that I cried out, *As the Lord liveth, and as my soul liveth, I will never leave thee nor forsake thee.*' This sexually charged mysticism has its precedents in Quakerism, at least according to a seventeenth-century apostate by the name of George Keith, who claimed that they believed their religious enthusiasm turned into a physical substance, 'a certain efflux or effluvium of animal volatile spirits ... that flow from their bodies by the command of their will into the bodies of ... new proselytes'.

Jemima, along with the Cutters, spent the night at her father's house. The next day she set off by herself to see what she could discover.

As she passed by Jeremiah Willard's house she came across his two-year-old son Oliver, who ran out to her. She picked him up. When he was in her arms he looked her in the face and then began shaking his head so violently that she feared his neck would break. From another point of view this would just be a symptom of the 'terrible twos'; for Jemima it was a manifestation of miniaturised Shakerism. She promptly put him down again, whereupon he grabbed hold of her clothes and pulled her into the house, where she 'found them all Beleivers'. 'They spoke kindly to me,' she explains, 'yet they seemed so solemn and so strange that I soon came out.' There's a note in a different hand in the manuscript, giving the fate of little Oliver. The diminutive Shaker died the following year. 'Being in great distress in his sickness his friends would pity him but he would reply, "Pain ain't hell."'

Jemima went to the house of Isaac Willard, Jeremiah's father, where she had worked until fleeing to Hollistown. Here she 'found the same change in the appearance of the people'. The strange milky substance that seemed to run over the skin and clothes of converts was particularly evident on the younger ones. Friends and neighbours seemed to have been mysteriously transformed into smiling but somehow sinister aliens, who nevertheless did not put a foot out of line. A massive change had taken place and yet there was no objective evidence to prove it. Seventy years or so later the poet Emily Dickinson, writing in Amherst, not many miles west of Harvard, was to find words for this sort of spiritual revolution: 'A Wind that rose/ Though not a Leaf/ In any Forest stirred.' Nathan Tiffany, who lived with his parents in Somers, Connecticut, near Enfield and under the Baptist ministry of Joseph Meacham senior, put his finger on the enigma when he described the return of their pastor – 'the old man', as Ann Lee familiarly called him – who had gone to visit his son during his imprisonment at Albany and who had been converted in turn: 'He appeared to have something in him which he did not possess before.'

At this point Jemima decided she had to go to the Square House to see for herself the origin of this something that her friends and acquaintances had not possessed before.

She arrived at the house and was let into the hall. As she was passing through it, two young women of her acquaintance came out of the kitchen where they were working and greeted her lovingly. These were Deliverance and Beulah Cooper, the very same who had resisted the squat-jumping exhibition of the Jewett girls the previous year, but who had since been converted. They asked Jemima to come with them into the kitchen, where she found Ann Lee washing herself.

It is the perfect Shaker mixture of the eerie and the ordinary. Ann is the agent of mysterious and disturbing changes and at the same time presents herself as a homely woman giving herself a scrub at the kitchen sink. She turned to look at Jemima 'with such a pleasant and heavenly countenance that it absorbed my whole soul so that I scarcely knew what my companions said to me'.

Ann quickly put on her cap (Jemima noticed she wore it with twisted strings rather than tape or ribbons, 'yet she looked very neat') and her handkerchief, and then came over and took Jemima by the arm. She asked: 'Wilt thou be a daughter of Zion and be searched with candles?'

Not surprisingly, Jemima didn't know what to reply, so said nothing. Ann then took her to meeting (that's to say, to the Shaker service) where Jemima had the sense of being constantly watched by her penetrating eyes. Later in the day when they were passing through the kitchen on the way to another meeting, Ann sat down and suddenly pulled Jemima into her lap and hugged her, saying, 'How is it that you are the buntling, when Phebe is the youngest?'

Jemima was always her mother's pet; this affectionate question confirmed her sense that Ann knew all about her. One remembers John Farrington's amazement at Niskeyuna: '*I have seen a woman who was able to tell me all that I ever did in my life.*' In this case, though, we are in the cosy realm of family endearments. Everything about the quick-change act Ann performed in the kitchen of the Square House for Jemima's benefit, her bewildering switches from the domestic to the hypnotic, suggests that she was able to an extraordinary degree to combine qualities of two of the roles that most embody, in the absence of modern career structures, the possibility of female power:

witch and mother (femme fatale, at least in the usual sense of the phrase, not being an available option).

Jemima had merely been an observer, not a participant, at the Shaker meetings; perhaps surprisingly, given the extreme behaviour that often took place, the Shakers seemed to have no problem in allowing outsiders to watch them at worship. But now the Cooper sisters announced that they had prepared dinner, and that it was the custom of all those who were going to eat to kneel down and pray together. As in Zaccheus Stevens's house, Jemima felt she had to refuse.

In a religion without a sacramental system mealtime prayers may have had a particular significance for new converts, as well as for those trying to resist conversion. Zipporah Cory, a young woman from New Providence, Massachusetts, who became a Shaker in 1782, returned to the family home of the Quaker preacher with whom she worked determined to keep her conversion a secret. But before she had taken leave of the Shakers she had been instructed by John Hocknell to pray before and after eating, as well as at other times. Because she felt she couldn't kneel before the family for fear of giving herself away, she went without her supper and breakfast. Not surprisingly the family 'discovered an alteration in me, and thought I was sick'. Soon afterwards, the power of God came upon her while she was working at her spinning wheel, and brought her to her knees, which of course gave the game away.

Jemima's father had arrived at the Square House by this time. Like his daughter he was hovering on the edge of the religion; in due course he was converted, only to repudiate his faith subsequently and then to be reconverted on his deathbed. He urged her to conform, but Jemima refused; she was particularly influenced by the fact that many of the 'world' were looking on with expressions of contempt and scorn on their faces.

At this juncture Ann herself intervened. She came up to Jemima and said, 'It is becoming in all people to send their thanks to God.'

Unable to answer the point, Jemima finally knelt in a grudging way that showed she was only doing it for manners' sake. Nevertheless she had now begun retreating from her position as interested outsider. The next concession came with Ann's suggestion that she and Cutter's wife should stay overnight. This hadn't been Jemima's intention, but she gave in so she could meet up with old acquaintances.

The following morning the two women met Ann in the hall. One has a sense of her always being in wait round the next corner, though it must be remembered that, in relation to the numbers it served, the Square House wasn't a particularly large building. Ann was very loving, and invited them to stay for breakfast. Cutter's wife countered by telling her they had to be on their way as soon as possible.

Ann moved, as she seemed to be able to do effortlessly, from a tone of affection to one of authority. 'Why do you want to get this young woman away?' she asked her. 'You cannot help her soul to God. All we want is to help her soul to God, and you cannot do this for you have not found him yourself.'

Cutter's wife took offence at the rebuke and went off, telling Jemima to come along soon. She replied that she would be at her father's house for breakfast.

Ann then went upstairs, leaving Jemima alone. She in turn went into the kitchen to say goodbye to her friends there. Discretion being the better part of valour, she left her compliments for Ann, and slipped out of the house, 'feeling released' that she had got away.

Her release was short-lived. She had only gone a few yards when she distinctly heard Ann's footsteps coming back down the stairs and entering the kitchen. Then her voice: 'Where is that young woman?'

'She is gone,' the Cooper girls replied.

'Gone? What did you let her go for? Go and call her back. Tell her she did not bid me farewell and it was I that invited her to stay and she has not treated me with good manners.'

Jemima stopped, 'as it were involuntarily'. One can picture her frozen in mid-stride, her back to the conversation, listening as her fate, for the remaining sixty-six years of her long life, was irrevocably sealed. She turned. In her blind old age she could still see the tableau: Ann standing on the doorstep, the young women approaching with their message.

They arrived, they said their piece, Jemima went back with them to excuse herself. She was by nature a bashful person, her mother's 'buntling', and no match for Ann. She hated the idea of treating anyone with ill manners, especially such a beautiful and God-like woman. Her excuses came out in a rush: she could not stay, she liked them very much but could not be *like* them, at least at present, her family were now waiting for her to join them for breakfast, she could not stay any longer, perhaps she would come again.

'Oh-oh, nay, you do not mean to come again,' Ann told her.

Jemima could not reply, as this was her very thought.

Ann grasped her by the arm. Jemima shook her off, but Ann grabbed the other one and propelled her towards the house. When they reached the door Jemima 'resisted going in as much as I could civilly'. It is poignant how this struggle for a soul is choreographed to the tune of polite behaviour. In, inevitably, she went.

Once inside she kept up her struggle to leave, but Ann would have 'another and another word to say'. She praised the Shakers, reminded Jemima how she liked them, how much they had done for her. At the end of every sentence Jemima tried to go. Finally Ann sprang the trap. 'Don't you want the people of God to pray for you?' she asked.

'I do,' Jemima replied.

In an instant Ann's arms were around her waist, and they were both on their knees. 'I shook,' Jemima recalled, 'so that the windows clattered but I did not know what it was for some minutes.'

It was another explosive conversion. It is hard to visualise a spiritual force that manifests itself with enough violence to shake a house's windows in their frames, but this gothic effect was a regular phenomenon. One Sunday while the Shakers were sitting silent at meeting in the Square

House, James Whittaker suddenly extended both his hands upwards and cried, 'Heavens! Heavens! Heavens!' Straight away, we are told, 'the house was shaken, and the casements clattered, as though they had been shaken by a mighty earthquake'.

While Jemima knelt, Ann turned in triumph to Whittaker. 'James, did I not tell you that the time had come that we must go into the highways and hedges and compel them to come in.' In the light of the strong-arm tactics that had been applied, quite literally, to Jemima Blanchard, there is something chilling about that word 'compel', and one begins to understand why so many of the townspeople of Harvard and other places would offer violent resistance to the march of Shakerism in the next two years or so. As for Jemima: 'After this I thought no more of going home being exercised almost constantly by the power of God for many days.'

The Cutters had grown fond of Jemima. They stayed at her father's house for about a week, hoping she would return. Then they made their way to the Square House. Jemima was 'laboring' (which could mean doing physical work but is also Shaker language for wrestling with the spirit) by the east door, and Cutter's wife grabbed her by her dress and told her Cutter was standing by the fence and had to speak to her. The two women made their way round to the south door, where they were spotted by the believers. Some of them at once came over and hurried Jemima into the house while the remainder 'raised a war' and drove the Cutters off.

After this vain attempt to spring her, Jemima remained at the house, attending meetings and doing 'exercises in the gifts of God' more or less non-stop, except for occasionally lending a hand in the kitchen. In her memoirs she marvels at the efficiency of the catering arrangements, coping with one to two hundred people at dinner-time. Ann was obviously able to run a tight ship with her experience of working as a hospital cook, and had an eye to economy also, gathering up the 'driblets' from people's plates on to one dish and making her own meal of them. She felt that these rural New Englanders were profligate with food in comparison with the frugal ways learned in Toad Lane. 'The American people are so full fed they have not learned to pick their bones & clean up their plates as we English people have,' she explained on one occasion, turning down some warm victuals that the kitchen sisters had prepared for her: 'I have made a good meal of what was left on the table.' She also took care of Jemima herself, noticing that, American though she was, she had only a small appetite and needed to be encouraged to eat.

Believers were flocking in, and Ann kept her sharp eyes on them all. She had a supernatural sensitivity to their needs and motivations. 'In all the time I was with Mother I never saw a gift pass by unnoticed by her,' Jemima recalled. Jemima describes what is obviously a mystical process in language that has a magic, and a charm, of its own: 'I have often observed her when she heard the first sound of a gift; I could often perceive a sound in her eye. She would listen and very soon make her way to the place from whence it came; and although sometimes it would seem to die away, it would always revive and increase until it had the desired effect.'

There were also more pedestrian considerations to take on board. With so many believers there was a danger that in the throes of their exercises they might crash through the floorboards and end up in the cellar, particularly as one of their modes of worship, called 'heavy dancing', involved a 'perpetual springing from the house floor about four inches up and down'. Accordingly, a party of brothers was despatched to the woods to cut timber for props. Eventually children under fourteen were sent away from the house under the guardianship of suitable persons – one must never lose sight of the way in which Shakerism broke up families – and half the young sisters were taken out of the house to perform their worship in the fresh air, so the strain on the building was lessened.

As time went on Jemima grew restive. She wanted to do more work with her hands; after a month she began to feel homesick – not, as it happened (she was now a Shaker, after all) for her family house but for Isaac Willard's, where she had lived and worked before fleeing to the Cutters'. She spoke to Ann, and was told that the elders would 'labor upon it'. While the Square House was clearly the spiritual centre of Shakerism at this time, just as Niskeyuna was the home base, there was no concept during Ann Lee's lifetime of the sort of dedicated communities of Shakers that were founded later, and which established the religion's modern reputation as America's foremost utopian experiment. Nevertheless the early

Shakers built up a network of believers' houses, and the comings and goings of the brothers and sisters were controlled. Susannah Barret's experience after being converted at Harvard was probably typical. She attended a meeting at Elijah Wilds's house in the satellite township of Shirley, and afterwards was just about to go home when one of the Shakers asked her if she had 'liberty' – that is to say, a pass-out, or ticket-of-leave. She replied stoutly that she had attended without liberty so didn't see why she should need it to return home. Nevertheless, the issue must have preyed on her mind, because later on she asked Ann Lee directly if there was any harm in going home without liberty. Ann replied, 'Not a bit', but then used the etiquette argument she had marshalled to such effect against Jemima, adding that she would have liked to have the opportunity of saying farewell.

In Jemima's case the outcome was that she was allowed to leave and go to Jeremiah Willard's place, home of the precocious Oliver. She had to come back to attend meetings at the Square House every night, however. When on one occasion she stayed over at Jeremiah's, Ann rebuked him about it, telling him that it must not happen again because of the danger that one of Jemima's brothers would come along and spirit her away.

The following winter her warning came true. A brother of Jemima's appeared at Jeremiah's house and told her that their mother was ill. There was a discussion amongst the believers present, and it was decided Jemima had better go along with him.

When she arrived she discovered it was a ruse. Her

mother was perfectly well, doing her knitting, and Cutter was waiting for her.

Cutter made his case. He told her that his wife wouldn't rest until he made another try at getting her back. They were a well-to-do couple and he reminded Jemima that she could regard their property as hers if she stayed with them. Jemima's family, especially her mother, supported him.

What makes Jemima's testimony so fascinating is her ability to remember how Shakerism seemed from the out-side looking in at the menacingly smiling faces of the converts, and in the same narrative to describe how it felt to be on the inside looking out, at the upset and pleading faces of those left behind. The childless Cutters are offering to treat her like their daughter. She shows not a smidgen of compassion or gratitude: she is the adherent of a religion that has replaced such ties. 'I stood against them all,' she says proudly. Bashful though she naturally was, she discovered a gift to speak to Cutter, and did so to such effect that he sat with his face in his hands, and could not say a word in reply. Her own mother told her off for being saucy.

Afterwards Jemima heard from Cutter that he had lost his property and become 'real poor'; a 'judgement', as far as she was concerned, 'as their was no apparent cause for it'.

The Shakers relished hearing about the misfortunes of their enemies, and by trying to talk Jemima out of her beliefs, Cutter had become one of them. He was now 'wicked' in just the way kind Abraham Standerin had proved to be, when he set his will against Ann Lee's.

* * *

As soon as the Shakers had settled into the Square House, opposition began. Nothing organised at first, but there were individual examples of 'slandering, mocking, scoffing, stoning, pilfering, cheating, defrauding and the like'. Ann herself probably didn't help matters by informing the local community that their hearts were like 'a cage of unclean birds'. In nearby Acton the Reverend Moses Adams gave the Marlborough Association of Clergy 'an account of the strange conduct and temper of a number of people who were come to Harvard who were called Shakers, and under the guidance of an "elect lady"'. There was an uneasy atmosphere and Ann got headaches, which she put down to the heat, scorching in a Massachusetts August compared to the damp, mild summers of her native Manchester, and she would sit for a while on the cellar steps of the Square House to cool down. She didn't want to get bogged down with small problems and Dilly Cooper (as Deliverance was known) later recalled that when people troubled her with trivialities she would say, 'Let it pass let it pass, and labor for the gifts of God.'

James Whittaker had his own retreat. He had taken over a room in the Square House in order to continue his trade of weaving, though now it was just a hobby. He would buy a web on the beam and weave it out up there, on one occasion making gowns for both Ann Lee and Mary Partington. Beulah Cooper would often join him, since she liked to work at her spinning wheel. Whittaker was better educated than the rest of Ann's English elders, though not, according to one ex-Shaker, 'above the middle walks in life'. He had quick, dark eyes and a habit of looking people squarely in the face, though his manner was normally polite and mild. He was also capable of a more ironic outlook than most of the Shakers could achieve, and sometimes displayed playfulness which bordered on mockery of his own status and power within the sect. Once, the elders were about to go on a visit, and so as not to bother their hosts they asked for something to eat before they left. At short notice all the kitchen sisters could produce was buttered potatoes, the second day in succession on which they had provided the meal. As it happened, James was particularly addicted to that simple dish. Nevertheless, he looked at it solemnly, and asked, 'What, potatoes and butter for two days going, will that do for me?' On another occasion he dismissed a meeting at Elijah Wilds's house and then, just as the believers were leaving the room, resumed his singing. The faithful promptly came back into the room and began dancing joyfully once more. James stopped singing, dismissed them again, then played the same trick. When the faithful were in full swing and having 'a real good time', James looked about him in astonishment, as if he couldn't work out where they had all sprung from. He did this repeatedly, until the believers were coming back by reflex, and in the end he could only dismiss them properly by leaving the meeting himself.

These episodes remind one of a certain sort of sardonic schoolteacher who likes to play little tricks at the expense of his pupils, though it must be remembered that there was plenty of scope in Shaker meetings for the display of good humour. High spirits could even spread to William

Lee, normally a much more emotional and brooding presence. The first time Susannah Barret attended a meeting
at Elijah Wilds's house (probably the very occasion which
culminated in that awkward discussion about the need for
liberty), she discovered that 'Father William was full of
the spirit of life and heavenly joy so much so that he
played and laughed around the brethren, and was very
cheerful, I thought to myself, what! Is that the way to
worship God, to dance and play so?'

The sceptical side of James Whittaker's nature found
the 'wild and strange' behaviour of the ex-Irelandites very
amusing. 'He used to talk to her [Beulah] about Daniel
Wood's followers and would laugh and be quite pleased
at her relation of them.' No doubt Beulah told him about
the antics of the Jewett girls, including the time when
Sarah Jewett was so uplifted by the power of God while
out riding that clear daylight could be seen between her
bottom and the horse's back until she was nearly out of
sight.

Clearly, an odd little intimacy developed between
James and Beulah. She knitted him a pair of long stock-
ings. He told her in his teasing way that he was 'not
particular all he wanted was that they should exactly fit
him'. Of course a relationship between a male Shaker
elder and a female convert could go only so far. On one
occasion Beulah tried to go that step further. She was
twenty-five and no doubt subject to the normal range of
sexual needs and impulses. The fact that James Whittaker
was the most attractive and approachable of the male
leaders probably triggered her desire to confess her

temptations, but if, subconsciously, she had hopes that this would intensify the rapport between them, she was in for a shock. He 'stamped upon the floor and told her never to let him hear anything of the kind from her again'. Innocently she assumed that what, to an outsider, would appear a revealing overreaction was in fact simply a way of inculcating a moral lesson, and as a result she found herself able to 'gird up her loins' – with more literalness, presumably, than that figure normally allows – and subsequently 'resist temptation'. She mentions that when any of the young women tried to touch James he would recoil, and tell them that 'when we get to heaven you may hug and kiss me as much as you have a mind to'. There's something twitchy about this avoidance of contact, and a certain wistfulness about the deferment of caresses to the afterlife, which lead one to take with a certain amount of salt his claim that he had 'no more lust than an infant' (we're a century before Freud's discovery of the sexuality of children).

Complicated, ironic and oversensitive, James Whittaker was also the best public speaker among the Shakers, and could hold the attention whatever the subject might be. He had been the elder deputed by Ann to negotiate with Joseph Meacham, and now, as the summer wore on, it was becoming evident that his powers of persuasion and diplomatic skill would once more be called into play, as the harassment of the Shakers developed, by late August, into more serious antagonism from the surrounding community.

Rumours had circulated in Harvard from the time the

Shakers arrived. Some people said they had appeared like an invading army, with seventy wagons and six hundred rifles. More modestly, a certain David Whitney claimed he had heard tell of a 'curious chest of firearms' at the Square House. A town meeting was held in Harvard on 31 August 1781: 'To hear and consider a petition of a number of Inhabitants of Harvard and see if the Town will, agreeable to said petition, consult and determine on some means to remove the people called Shaking Quakers who are collected together in this Town'. For the duration of the war the community had its own Committee of Correspondence and Safety in parallel with the one in Albany that had imprisoned the Shakers the previous year, and its members, under the leadership of their chairman Asa Houghton, were requested by the town meeting to go to the Square House, in company with the local militia under the captaincy of Ephraim Davis, and inform the Shakers of allegations which had been made to the effect that they were English spies and were secreting weapons.

The deputation arrived and duly levelled these charges. James listened to them at the door of the Square House and replied in his most reasonable manner: 'I understand that you have heard that we have weapons of war here, and are apprehensive that we are enemies of the country; . . . we are a harmless, inoffensive people; we do not want to injure any man either in person or property; we want no man's silver or gold; but only their souls to God; this is all we want of anyone. But if you believe these reports, you may have free liberty to search the house, or barn, or any of these buildings round.'

This response satisfied some members of the party, but Asa Houghton nevertheless gave them an ultimatum to leave town. Whittaker's line hardened a little: 'We came here peaceably, and we can say, as was said of Saint Paul, we dwell in our own hired house.'

The confrontation continued till late afternoon when most of the delegation left, though some stayed until evening out of curiosity, and Whittaker addressed them on the necessity of confession and reforming. An 'ungodly ruffian' heckled, but was rebuked by William Lee. He tended to act as the Shakers' strong-arm man, and could be quite a threatening presence. On one occasion a young man laughed at him while he was addressing a crowd. William 'sparkled with rage', lifted him from the ground with one hand round his neck, and said: 'When I was in England, I was a sergeant in the King's lifeguard, and could then use my fists; but now, since I have received the gospel, I must patiently bear all abuse, and suffer my shins to be kicked by every little boy; but I will have you know that the power of God will defend our cause.' Between James's skill at exposition and William's impressive physical presence the Shakers carried the day; indeed, some of the deputation were 'pricked to the heart' and started out on the road to conversion themselves.

After this stand-off an uneasy truce came into play, enabling Ann and the other leaders to remain at Harvard through the autumn and the early part of the winter, helping the new converts to settle into the discipline and exercises of their faith. This could be a difficult and strenuous process. On one occasion Jemima Blanchard had a vision of hell and thought she was 'on the brink in imminent danger of falling'. It's easy to understand why Jonathan Edwards's sermon on 'Sinners in the Hands of an Angry God', in which he pictured members of his congregation dangling vertiginously over the inferno, had had such an impact forty years previously. Even an unassuming person like Jemima could picture herself teetering above indescribable horror. While people went about their daily business in these quiet rural settings they were also enacting heroic and terrible dramas in a spiritual landscape that was in fact more real to them than the external one. Jemima 'crept around the room on her knees uttering the most heartrending cries. Mother stooped to her, and in her agony, wringing her hands, she got hold of Mother's apron. She knew not what it was or that Mother was near her, but it felt like a comfort & support to her, so she kept winding it up around her hands. Mother followed her around the room some time in that position and then took off her apron and let her have it.'

Perhaps nowhere do we get a more memorable picture of Ann Lee in action than in this image of her being tugged by her apron around the room as the normally retiring Jemima worked through her hysterics. The final gesture, when Ann gives Jemima her apron to use as a security blanket, is just as touching. The imagery of Christianity is being feminised, with domestic garments taking the place of the traditional clerical garb. Later on, when she looked back at this episode, Jemima decided her terror had been an anticipation of her sister Phebe's subsequent apostasy.

There were gentler moments, of course. On one occasion when things had been hectic and a lot of company had been staying at the Square House, Beulah Cooper and Tabitha Green noticed that the kitchen cupboards had got very dirty, so they set to and gave them a scrub. 'When they had got everything cleaned up nice Mother came and looked all around opened the cupboard doors and snuffed saying "How sweet you smell"', then hugged and kissed them both. Ann was a great advocate of cleanliness and good order: 'There is no dirt in heaven,' as she put it.

During those first months at Harvard the Shakers were almost victims of their own success, because as the year went on they began to run out of provisions. Ann called one of the faithful, Jonathan Slosson, to her room. She compared their ability to sustain themselves with the miracle of loaves and fishes, which for good reason was one of the Shakers' favourite gospel stories and which would be invoked over and over again during the next two years. With characteristic practicality she warned Jonathan that this happy arrangement could not be relied on indefinitely. Jonathan suggested he should go to townships with Shaker communities to the west of the state and over the line into New York – Hancock, Richmond and New Lebanon, all of them more than a hundred miles away – and request supplies. He then went off on his foraging expedition with one Reuben Harrison, and in due course brought back ample stores of flour and cheese. On their return Ann and the other leaders wept in gratitude.

By December it was clear that despite the local tensions,

the Harvard Shaker community was well established, and it was time to continue the mission to save souls. Ann and her entourage set out once more, heading for Petersham, about forty miles to the west, where she would shortly experience one of the most terrifying and traumatic ordeals of her life.

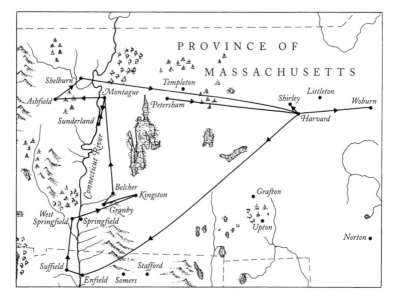

To Ashfield and back.

9

Black Guards

Ann and her entourage arrived at Petersham in snowy mid-winter. They had not been to the town before and wanted to see some of their converts who lived there. It was evening when they arrived at Thomas Shattuck's, where they found the family waiting for them. The Shakers were experts at making an entrance. Ann said, 'It is good to watch, and you should always watch.' William chimed in: 'Ye watched, for ye knew not which hour we would come.'

The gospels come through to us as texts in which all speech and actions have clarity and significance; somewhere, inaccessibly behind the language, there is the contingent reality of actual people with their awkward, improvised behaviour. The Shakers, though, came from a tradition that laid emphasis on the biblical story as an oral transmission, and Ann Lee was herself illiterate. They would not therefore have possessed our modern sense of the gulf that lies between language and the world; and perhaps as a result, they seem to have had an extraordinary ability to live life in the gospel mode, so that in their case the word implies not a record after the event but the moment-by-moment experience of encountering reality.

They were helped, of course, by the fact that the puritan tradition of New England encouraged the inhabitants to see their own lives in allegorical terms.

Ann's party went on to David Hammond's to spend the night. The next day was the Sabbath, and James preached from the epistle of his namesake: 'Cleanse your hands, ye sinners' (iv, 8–9). Ann rarely seems to have led meetings, though of course she attended. Far from diminishing her status this would have the effect of adding to her mystique and emphasising her authority. Many outsiders ('people of the world') had come to the Hammond house out of curiosity, but they behaved with civility.

On the evening of the following day there was another meeting, again at David Hammond's, and again led by James. Once more numbers of outsiders had come as spectators. The meeting-room was partitioned off within a larger one where the 'world' were to sit, but as so many had turned up, James said that those who wished could come into the inner room with the believers. It was an intimate arrangement. Ann and Elizabeth Shattuck were sitting on a bed, with other Shaker sisters nearby. James was standing with a candle in his hand and had just begun to read from the Bible when there was a sudden cry: 'Knock out the lights!'

The room had been infiltrated. All the candles were knocked out except for the one James was holding. In the panicky darkness, three men rushed through from the outer room. Their faces were disguised with black paint – appropriately enough, since they were members of the self-styled Black Guard Committee, 'lewd fellows' from the middle of the town. They grabbed hold of Ann and tried to drag her away, tearing a strip out of the new gown she was wearing (perhaps the very one woven for her by James). Elizabeth Shattuck and several other sisters 'immediately clinched hold of her and held her'. Luckily, the passageway was narrow, and Elizabeth anything but, so she kept Ann safely corked in her place, no matter how hard the Black Guards pulled at her. Suddenly they retreated, having taken fright at the prospect of being recognised.

James asked the rest of the 'world' to return quietly to their homes.

When they had gone, Ann prophesied that the attackers would soon try again. In fear, the Shakers began to 'labor' to keep evil away. Eventually they decided they ought to try to get some rest. The other brethren and sisters left for their homes, leaving Ann and her elders with the Hammonds.

Before she went to bed, Ann looked out of the window, and saw black shapes moving around the side of the house. There was a sudden flurry of activity. The Shakers hid the candles and began securing all the doors and windows, while Ann herself, knowing it was her they were after, ran out of the room to find somewhere to hide. Then the outer door burst open and about thirty men rushed in, shouting and swearing.

They knocked down David Hammond and beat him, then did the same to 'his woman', Mary (the Shakers not recognising the married state), despite the fact she had a child in her arms. James Whittaker was felled, and even the powerful William was hurt. The Black Guards then pulled logs out of the fireplace and blew them into flame to give them light for searching the house.

They found Ann in a bedroom. They manhandled her so that she lost her cap and handkerchief, and then, just like their opposite numbers in Manchester, pulled her downstairs by her feet so that her skirts rode up, dragged her out of the house, and threw her into a horse-drawn sleigh that was waiting outside.

As they galloped off, William Lee and David Hammond managed to grasp hold of the back of the sleigh and hang on, despite being beaten by whips. Meanwhile Ann was being molested by the three men in the sleigh, who committed 'acts of inhumanity and indecency which even savages would be ashamed of'. They tore off her clothes under the 'pretence to find out whether she was a woman or not'.

The Shakers could be perceived as threatening these little Massachusetts communities in many different ways. They were English, and therefore possible spies. They broke up families, and forbade sexual relations. But above all they were led by a woman. This had been at the forefront of Joseph Meacham's mind when he'd made his query about St Paul's injunction against women preachers. On a much more primitive level it preyed on the minds of the Black Guards, as they pretended to find it incomprehensible that a person in her position could be a woman at all, and accordingly violated her sexually in revenge for her female presumption and as a way of defusing any threat of witchcraft.

Eventually, after travelling three miles through the freezing night, the sleigh pulled up outside Samuel Peckham's tavern and the Black Guards trooped in with their prize and began to drink. Apparently the whole thing had been carefully orchestrated, since Peckham was the local captain of militia, and had promised the men as much rum as they could handle if they brought Ann in. At this point, however, the atmosphere began to change. Peckham's wife treated Ann with kindness, and this in itself may have helped them to see her as a human being and to feel some shame about their actions. David Hammond and William Lee also tried to reason with them. Perhaps more to the point, they began to feel nervous about the legal repercussions of the assault and kidnapping they had just committed. Eventually they said they would release Ann in exchange for a promise not to prosecute. This was agreed. As they walked out to the sleigh once more, one of the men gave Ann his handkerchief to wear on her head, and another lent her his overcoat. They drove back to the Hammond house, and Ann entered singing a song of praise. The Black Guards asked forgiveness, and she replied: 'I can freely forgive you. I hold nothing against you and I pray God to forgive you.'

Meanwhile James Whittaker had been too badly injured in the attack to follow the sleigh to Peckham's tavern. When he was able to get to his feet he picked up Ann's cap and handkerchief from the floor where they had fallen in the struggle and put them in his pocket. Then he went to Thomas Shattuck's house and asked if he and his brother Abel could 'settle the matter and get Mother'. He then went out to their barn and lay on the hay till day-break. When he awoke his upper lip was 'swelled out almost even with the end of his nose and his under jaw was much swollen'. After he came out of the barn he took Ann's cap and handkerchief from his pocket, looked at them sadly, and said, 'That is the last handful I can get of Mother.'

It must have been an enormous relief when he arrived at the Hammond house and found Ann was back. She told him all that had happened to her. When her cap and fillet (the ribbon used to secure her cap on her head) had been torn off a clump of her hair had been pulled out as well. James confided in turn that he thought his jaw was broken – as we shall see later, he had a slight tendency to assume the worst about his injuries – but he could pray for their attackers nonetheless.

'Father, forgive them,' he said, kneeling, 'for they know not what they do.'

It was clear it would be unwise for the Shakers to stay long in Petersham. Not long after the kidnapping, rumours about witchcraft began to resurface, and in January 1782 Ann and her elders made their way back to Harvard.

At the Square House their problems soon returned. During the course of January a senior officer, General James Sullivan, along with two other bigwigs, arrived to request the male Shakers to take the oath of allegiance. Inevitably, they refused.

'These men will never do you any hurt,' Ann told him, 'for they are well-wishers to the country. They will do all the good to the country that they are able to do.'

'I want men to go and fight for the country,' the general explained, not in a mood to beat about the bush.

'You never will kill the devil with a sword,' she replied.

The general had to be content, but more military intrusion occurred late in the month, when Captain Phineas Farnsworth appeared outside the Square House with a large number of militia. There was a touch of Falstaff's army about his company, however: they poised and shouldered clubs in hopes of giving the Shakers the impression they were muskets.

Farnsworth was allowed upstairs to talk to Ann, who gave a characteristically combative performance. He told her she had to leave town.

'I will be gone tomorrow, if it's God's will,' she replied.

He fell into the ambiguity, agreeing that she would not be molested given that she was going the next day.

'Yea,' she replied, 'I expect to go tomorrow, if it is God's will.' One can almost see the captain nodding his approval. 'But,' she went on, 'I will return again the next day, if it is God's will, for all you.'

Having given a promise to lift the threat of violence, Farnsworth was stuck with it. He took his leave and went downstairs, no doubt seething at being outmanoeuvred.

In the meantime problems had arisen down below. William Lee had ordered the volatile Daniel Wood to guard the partition that separated off the sisters' apartment. The militia wished to search it for weapons, which would have been a gross breach of their privacy and, inevitably, a sexual provocation. Eventually 'a violent spirited, stout man' grabbed Daniel with some violence and hurled him through the locked door, making blood pour down his head and chest.

At that moment Captain Farnsworth appeared on the stairs. He asked who was responsible for Daniel Wood's state. On being told it was one of his own men he withdrew them all.

The next day Ann left town, as promised. The day after that she returned, as she had also promised. She had proved a point, but it was a Pyrrhic victory, and the atmosphere continued to be hostile. It may not have been helped by a tragic incident that happened in late February.

A certain Elias Sawyer and his wife from the town of Ashfield, more than a hundred miles to the west of the state, had become Shakers, and on 22 February 1782 they arrived in Harvard. She was particularly enthusiastic, and danced with the Shakers till late in the evening. Then, 'being hot and sweaty', she left the meeting and went out in the night air to make her way to another Shaker household where she was staying. As a result she 'catcht a bad cold and was seized with the billows colic'; undeterred, she danced the next night as well. Then she became seriously ill, and died on the night of 25–26 February.

Mrs Sawyer's fate would have been one more item for the rumour mill, and the Shaker leadership in Harvard began to feel that their usefulness was 'nearly hedged up' for the time being. Nevertheless, Ann clearly feared that the converts might feel she was letting them down. 'I could freely lay down my life for you,' she told them, 'if it could be any gain to you.' As it was, however, 'I am called of God to preserve my life, and take care of myself for your sakes.' The believers wept at the prospect of her departure.

Ann, along with her elders and her companion Mary Partington, left the Square House that day and stayed the night at Zaccheus Stevens's. The following morning they headed for Enfield, Connecticut.

Their exit was in the nick of time. A mob came after them that same morning. Not finding any sign of Ann at the Square House, they placed a barrel in front of the door. They then forced each of the believers in turn to stand on it, and interrogated them. No one told them anything, however.

The crowd next went to Isaac Willard's property, where Jemima Blanchard used to work. A future Shaker leader, Lucy Wright (not to be confused with Lucy Wight, whose conversion was described in Chapter 5), and Elizur Goodrich, her former husband, were secreted in the house.

Lucy was born in 1760 in the town of Pittsfield, Massachusetts, the stamping ground of Valentine Rathbun, and in 1779 had married Elizur, one of twelve brothers and one sister from a prominent western Massachusetts family (one of Elizur's brothers, Ezekiel, married Rathbun's daughter Eunice). Elizur was a merchant, and the young couple settled in Richmond. It was hardly a conventional arrangement, but proved to be one perfectly adapted to Shaker conversion. Elizur claimed 'Lucy was so beautiful and amiable that he could not bear to spoil her with the flesh', and 'hence they lived uncommonly continent'. The chaste young couple were both caught up in the excitement of the New Light Stir and along with many others made their pilgrimage to Niskeyuna in the early summer of 1780. Elizur promptly became a Shaker convert (as did his brother Ezekiel and sister-in-law Eunice). He confided to Ann that he doubted whether Lucy would convert in her turn because she came from 'lofty high-minded people'. Ann seems to have intuited Lucy's potential for leadership from the start, responding pro-phetically: 'We must gain Lucy if possible; if we gain her, it will be equal to gaining a Nation.' Sure enough, Lucy was also converted a little later. They dissolved their mar-riage (perhaps to their joint relief, given their lack of sexual appetite) and Lucy resumed her maiden name.

Lucy Wright represented home-grown leadership potential, like Joseph Meacham. The hierarchical struc-ture of Shakerism during this period was tartly explained by Amos Taylor, one of the enemies of the religion: 'Their discipline is founded on the supposed perfection of one of their leaders: the Mother, it is said, obeys God through Christ; European elders obey her; American labourers obey them.' The elders were aware that this state of affairs could not, and should not, persist indefinitely. Later in her mission Ann would send Lucy off to Niskeyuna to act as leader of the sisters there, counterbalancing John Hocknell and thus anticipating her future role as Mother of the Shakers in tandem with Father Joseph Meacham, after whose death she took sole charge of the movement for many years until her own death in 1821. For the present, Lucy was waiting in the wings: to be more precise, she and Elizur were concealed in an upper room in Isaac Willard's house, with a hostile crowd at the door.

Some of the mob pushed their way in and began searching the house. They went up the stairs and got as far as the door of the room where Elizur and Lucy were in hiding. Then Isaac Willard called their bluff, telling them he would get the law on them, and managed to put sufficient forcefulness in the threat to convince them to withdraw.

Meanwhile Ann and the elders arrived at Enfield, Connecticut, in mid-March 1782, and stayed at David Meacham's house once more. A woman called Tryphena Perkins lived in Enfield. She apparently made a 'great profession of Christianity' but Ann would have none of it, and one day, while in the hearing of a number of people, she rebuked her for her wickedness and said, 'You are a filthy whore.'

Not surprisingly, Tryphena took enormous offence, and complained vociferously about being abused. The altercation gave Ann's enemies a welcome opportunity to prove that she was a false prophet and to threaten prosecution for defamation of character. In normal circumstances it would be difficult if not impossible to establish definitively the rights and wrongs of such name-calling, but in this particular case Tryphena's allies felt they had something approaching hard evidence. 'They said they could prove to a certainty that Tryphena was not formed like other women; and therefore could not possibly be guilty of the charge of whoredom. She was ... of necessity, a pure virgin.'

Ann lost the argument, faced with some apparently intractable anatomy. She eventually had a moral victory, however. It turned out that despite these technical difficulties lust had had its way. 'But behold,' the Shaker annals gleefully announce, 'she was soon found with child, by a married man!' A footnote adds that the ensuing birth was a Caesarean, and that the incision wouldn't heal and 'ever afterwards caused a very loathsome stench'. The Shakers, as even the gentle Jemima proved, had a capacity for gloating over their enemies' misfortunes.

Incidents like Ann's indictment of Tryphena Perkins could have done nothing to increase the Shakers' popularity in Enfield. After they had been at David Meacham's for about a week some two hundred people assembled outside the house. They were led by Jonathan Bush, the local captain of militia, his lieutenant, who happened to be his brother Eli Bush, and a local man called Isaac Terry. The mob formed a ring around the house, and began to shout for the 'Old Elect lady' to come out. The Rev. Moses Adams of Harvard had called Ann 'the elect lady' when he had addressed the Marlborough Association of Clergy the previous year. The reference was to the enigmatic address to the 'elect lady' in the second epistle of John – 'The elder unto the elect lady and her children, whom I love in the truth; and not I only, but also all they that have known the truth' – but it's a loaded phrase, bringing in its wake the whole puritan doctrine of election by which God is seen as having chosen his saints in heaven from the beginning of time, before they ever began their lives on earth. Since God knows everything, he must know who the saved will be; but of course the implications for a doctrine of free will are serious, and led to a huge output of knotty theological argument over the centuries on the part of puritan divines. The issue was not all that pertinent to the Shakers, who believed that any individual could be perfected if confession was undertaken with sufficient rigour and the Shaker life was led with due sincerity. It is true that in his attack on the Shakers Valentine Rathbun pointed to what he obviously felt was a crucial inconsistency in this respect. 'Three of the males, and two females, profess to be perfect,' he explains, while at the same time Ann herself is the 'mother of all the elect'. There is in fact no contradiction, since where she led others could follow, and at that stage four of them, it was felt, had incontrovertibly done so (presumably James Whittaker, William Lee, John Hocknell and Mary Partington).

It is significant that the mob called Ann 'old'. She was forty-six, but she was not leading an easy life, and this was not a period when people hung on to their youth.

Ann walked out of the house and into the circle of people. She asked, 'What do you want of me?'

A man stepped up and said, 'We want to know if you are the head of the church.' It was the old question, the one that had puzzled Joseph Meacham; the one that was implicit in the Black Guards' sexual assault.

Ann, of course, was ready for it. 'Christ is the head of the church,' she replied.

After a number of similarly tricky questions successfully navigated, the crowd let her alone. Nevertheless Ann and the elders were ordered to leave town within the hour.

James Whittaker addressed the mob, telling them sarcastically that since 'they had judged themselves unworthy of the Gospel' he and the other leaders would go elsewhere. Why waste pearls on swine, in other words. Before they left, Eliphalet Comstock reported that Mother Ann again appeared in front of the crowd, and 'sounded the gospel trumpet with singing. Her voice was very powerful, and her singing truly melodious. Some who were with that company, received faith from her which continued with them ever after.'

After she had got into the wagon one of the rabble stepped up and pulled out the lynchpin, which would have caused the wheels to fall off, but a Shaker spotted what was going on and replaced it, so they were able to leave safely.

They set off towards Lovejoy's ferry across the Connecticut River about eight miles away, followed by the mob. The brethren and sisters sang the praises of God as they went, 'while their wicked persecutors, who understood none of these things, followed on, in gloomy silence'. As they drew near the river the atmosphere began to get ugly again, but then a young American officer rode up and saved the day, rather as the mysterious nobleman had done in England years before. This one had a name, however: he was Lieutenant Elijah James, of Colonel Sheldon's regiment of Dragoons. He escorted Ann on to the ferry, assuring her she had nothing to fear, and left only after seeing her safely across the river. God had sent the young man for her protection, Ann said later. As the ferry left the shore one of the crowd shouted that Ann and the elders were never to enter Enfield again, and if they did they might expect 'tarring, feathering, ducking, &c'.

There was no reprieve when Lovejoy landed them in Suffield, on the opposite bank. Another rabble was waiting for them, and there was a counterbalancing loudmouth venting forth, one Ebenezer Burbanks this time, who specialised in hooting and singing in a fashion that parodied the way William's thunderous voice had carried to them across the water.

Ann and the elders journeyed to West Springfield, crossed the river again, and arrived at Kingston. From here David Meacham, who had been travelling with them, went back home to Enfield to fetch another wagon to make their journey easier, while they waited for his return over the weekend at Scott's tavern. Then they went on to visit other Shakers in Granby and Belcher. After this they went up the river to Montague, where a weaver called Peter Bishop lived with his family. They had become believers the previous summer and were the only ones in town, so they faced a lot of hostility. This had affected business, but Abigail Bishop used all the flour she had left to make Mother Ann a cake. Ann said: 'I pray that the morsel of meal may be like the widow's barrel, and the cruse of oil that did not fail in time of famine.' After a night at the Bishops' they set off back down the river to Sunderland, crossed over, and arrived at Asa Bacon's in Ashfield at the end of March 1782.

Meanwhile, back at the Bishop household, a man came to the house who was in debt to them and repaid them in grain. Abigail Bishop noticed 'that he heaped every measure, and pressed it down till it run over', thus fulfilling Ann's prayer.

Ashfield in western Massachusetts was a poor rural community that like so many similar places in the region had been caught up in the New Light Stir. Israel Chauncy and his sister had gone to Niskeyuna and been converted, and having brought the faith with them into the town, had made further converts in turn. This had had the usual divisive effect, and as Ann and her elders approached the place, a Committee of Safety had been set up 'to warn the Straglin Quaquars to Depart the town immediately'. Despite this the Shakers received a degree of protection from the civic authorities in Ashfield which they did not experience elsewhere, and in due course the place became an important refuge for them.

Ann and the elders kept a low profile in Ashfield. She kept a tight rein on her followers as usual, however. Lucy Bishop, who had come with the party from her family home in Montague, made the mistake of cutting her nails on a Sunday. Ann had strong views on this subject, as was apparent in Niskeyuna when she instructed John Deming, the man whose baby had swallowed a large button, not to cut his nails, scour his buckles or trim his beard on the Sabbath except in cases of emergency. Lucy got the full treatment from her: 'It is wicked. Walk on your knees to Elder James, and ask him to teach you to pray.' Ann's advice to a sick believer was more upbeat, though there was a headmistressy edge to its psychological perception: 'You must not be so down in your feelings; you must walk sharp; and if you think that you can do as well as you can, you must take faith, and labor to do better: this is the way for you to gain strength.' That little, energetic imperative, 'you must walk sharp', provides one of those moments when one has a sense of Ann's actual voice speaking. Another believer shared Abijah Worster's problem of being too fond of his food, and told Ann he was 'buffeted about eating'. While she had a tendency to dine off the 'driblets' on people's plates, she by no means advocated self-denial in respect of meals. Jemima Blanchard reports that when one of the brothers went without his victuals for the sake of mortifying his flesh, he received the third degree from Ann who asked him where he had 'got his gift' – in other words, what had put that idea into his head? Ann's message – and perhaps she was remembering here her own spiritual struggles in Manchester when she was reduced to skin and bones – was to eat as much as the body required. She had the same advice for the Ashfield man with the opposite problem, adding 'and then do the will of God; be not buffeted'.

In May 1782, just before returning to Harvard, Ann went five miles on foot with Mary Partington and some of her elders to visit two brothers, Jonathan and Aaron Wood, at Shelburn. Again we get a glimpse of her as she must have appeared to so many believers, a loving, reassuring, maternal presence: she walked into the Woods' house announcing, 'Now Mother is come.'

Interestingly, Aaron Wood had been the village ne'er-do-well, 'one of the most slack lazy men in creation', according to one witness. Conversion had been the making of him, however, and he'd become particularly famous for his gift of running after his own outstretched arm, an important Shaker activity as we have seen, and the means by which John Hocknell had discovered Niskeyuna. It wasn't, in fact, a gift that always stood Aaron in good stead. On one occasion a young boy from the area, who had been entrusted with the task of delivering corn to the local miller, failed to arrive on time. Aaron's pointing finger led the concerned locals to the spot where the boy's horse was waiting by the river, still loaded up with corn. The boy was nowhere to be seen, though, and Aaron and his fellow-villagers came to the conclusion that he had drowned crossing the water. Ever practical, the miller took the corn off to grind it anyway, an action that brings to mind Robert Frost's exploration of New England stoicism, the poem 'Out, Out – ', in which a young boy dies after a buzz-saw accident, and the watchers 'since they/ Were not the one dead, turned to their affairs'. There was a different outcome at Shelburn, however, because the boy in question turned up a little later, having gone off on another errand, and was bemused to discover that his corn was already being ground and that the villagers had given him up for lost.

It was a bad moment for Aaron Wood. His arm had misled him, homing in on the horse rather than the rider. Aaron 'felt rather blanked that the spirit had deceived or the vision was not rightly understood'. He must have concluded that he hadn't in fact been sufficiently receptive to his arm's dictates, because the setback only made him the more determined to be assiduous in following wherever it should lead; and it was this enthusiasm, which

also expressed itself in singing and in very energetic dancing, that made him beloved by Ann.

By now, Ann guessed that things had cooled off at Harvard, so she and the elders soon afterwards made their
way back, arriving around 20 May, and for the next three
months she continued her mission there, and in the nearby
townships of Woburn and Shirley. There was, as always,
a great deal of pastoral work to be done, particularly given
the almost neurotic self-searching of some of the converts.
One of the Wilds family of Shirley, Susanna, remembered
that before her conversion she had spoken against the
gospel. She brooded about this blasphemy and in due
course succumbed to despair. Ann came to see her, and
said, 'It is wicked to distrust the mercy of God; for he has
called you to be saved, and not be lost.' Ann's opening
words must have made Susanna's heart sink even further:
the calm reassurance that instantly followed released her
from her morbid sense of guilt.

It may have been at about this time that another
Susannah from Shirley, Susannah Barret in this case, the
young woman who left a meeting at Elijah Wilds's house
without a liberty, had a crisis of her own. She had a baby,
and in common Shaker fashion the child had been farmed
out to another household of believers in order to break
the family bond. This would become a formal procedure
when communities were established after Ann's death,
but even at this stage it was considered wise to foster
children of converts if at all possible. Calvin Green, for
example, was born to the Shaker converts Thankful Barce

and Joseph Green on 10 October 1780. On conversion his parents were separated. Joseph went to Harvard and Shirley to practise his trade of shoemaker there while Thankful, who was a schoolteacher, weaver and tailor, went wherever her skills were most needed. Little Calvin, meanwhile, was hived off to families of believers in New Lebanon and Hancock, though his mother, who obviously had some earning power, was expected to provide for him until he was seven.

Susannah became increasingly preoccupied with her absent child and eventually could contain her sadness no longer. Touchingly, she waited until she was in a meeting where the believers had a 'gift of sorrow'. In the midst of general lamentation she felt her own specific misery would pass unnoticed, tears in the rain, and allowed herself to cry for her baby. The human cost of Shakerism, its assault upon some of the deepest human relationships, those between husbands and wives and parents and children, is not always given full weight in modern nostalgia for the Shaker way of life. Ann, alert as ever, noticed there was a personal dimension to Susannah's sorrow and asked her what was the matter. When Susannah told her, Ann obviously realised that this was the moment for a concession. Later in 1782 she would be sending Abijah Worster off on his mission to convert the people of Douglass to Shakerism, and would give him the instructions quoted earlier, to be hard or soft according to the temperament of those with whom he was dealing; she was perfectly capable of following that advice herself. She also had memories of her own tragic experience of motherhood. She called the fostering household to her, and told them to give Susannah the opportunity of taking care of her child, 'for you know not the feelings of an affectionate mother'.

This flexibility would only go so far, of course, and while she was ministering to the population of Shirley, Ann encountered a would-be convert who made a spectacular miscalculation in his approach to her, obviously under the impression she was advocating some kind of touchy-feely Christianity. Having made a great profession of Christian love, and stating that he wished to have that love acknowledged by her, the man, 'in a fondling manner, attempted to put his head to her bosom'. Two centuries later it can still make one's hair curl to picture it.

Ann promptly marched him off to another room and passed him over to James Whittaker.

'"Here," said she, "is a man, that is full of religious devils, such as crucified Christ, the worst devils to cast out that are to be found in the world, and I leave him to be undeceived if he will."'

While at Woburn she received another approach from a 'man of the world' who wanted personal treatment, in this case perhaps with a view to making fun of her later. He, too, was told he must listen to James Whittaker.

The man replied, 'I do not want to hear him; I desire to hear that woman.'

Ann looked out of the window. 'I hear the heavens open,' she announced, 'and I see the glories of God.'

Suddenly out of his depth at finding himself the bystander at an epiphany, the man turned pale, 'and he said no more'.

Sometime around 10 July 1782, the young lawyer William Plumer visited the Harvard Shakers and attended one of their meetings. His detailed account, given in a letter to Lydia Coombs of Newburyport, is the most extended description we have of Shaker worship during this period by a neutral observer (though it closely corresponds with Rathbun's hostile account). Because it gives a glimpse of Shaker behaviour at this specific moment in time, Plumer's description is worth quoting at some length:

Before and after their eating, going to and returning from their beds, each of them falls to his knees, shaking, trembling, groaning, praying, and praising ... they generally assemble every evening, and frequently continue their exercises until after midnight. I went with them one evening to their meeting, and though they had cautioned me against being surprised at their worship, yet their conduct was so wild and extravagant that it was some time before I could believe my own senses. About thirty of them assembled in a large room in a private house, – the women in one end and the men in the other, – for dancing. Some were past sixty years old. Some had their eyes fixed upwards, continually reaching out and drawing in their arms, and lifting up first one foot and then the other, about four inches from the floor. Near the centre of the room stood two young women, one of them very handsome, who whirled round and round for the space of fifteen minutes, nearly as fast as the rim of a spinning wheel in quick motion. The violent whirl produced so much wind as kept her clothes as round and straight as though fastened to a hoop. As soon as she left whirling she entered the dance, and danced gracefully.

Sometimes one would pronounce with a loud voice, 'Ho, ho,' or 'Love, love,' – and then the whole assembly vehemently clapped hands for a minute or two. At other times some were shaking and trembling, others singing words out of the psalms in whining, canting tones (but not in rhyme), while others were speaking in what they called 'the unknown tongue,' – to me an unintelligible jargon, mere gibberish and perfect nonsense. At other times the whole assembly would shout as with one accord. This exercise continued about an hour; then they all retired to the sides of the room for a few minutes. Then the young woman who was the principal whirler walked into the middle of the room and began to dance. All the men and women soon joined her – dancing, singing, shaking and trembling, as at first. This continued near an hour.

After this there was a sermon, more than half of which, Plumer tells us, was delivered in the 'strong, persuasive language of the Scriptures'. The impressive speaker was not named but was almost certainly James Whittaker.

Then the assembly renewed their former exercises for more than an hour. This done, several of the young people, both men and women, began to shake and tremble in a most terrible manner. The first I perceived was their heads moving slowly from one shoulder to the other – the longer they moved, the quicker and more violently they shook. The motion proceeded from the head to the hands, arms, and whole body, with such power as if limb would rend from limb. The house trembled as if there were an earthquake. After this several young women embraced and saluted each other; two men embraced and saluted each other; a third clasped his arms around both, a fourth around them, and so on, until a dozen men were in that position, embracing and saluting.

Plumer adds: 'I did not notice any man salute or embrace a woman, or any woman a man.' He goes on to say, rather touchingly – at least to those of us who would find Shaker sexual taboos somewhat oppressive and arid – that despite all this gender separation he had seen a young Shaker man and woman sneak a kiss on the way to meeting.

In the meantime, resentment was building among the ordinary townsfolk of Harvard, Shirley and Woburn – partly, no doubt, because of the strangeness of Shaker worship – and the usual stale rumours about caches of weapons and skulduggery with the enemy were circulating. The brothers and sisters did their best to defuse this behaviour by trying to establish themselves as polite and inoffensive neighbours. 'The world used to notice the grateful and respectful manners of Mother and the Elders, how they would show respect and gratitude for the smallest favors,' Jemima Blanchard recalled. 'For instance, if any one picked up a pocket handkerchief for them, or the like, they would turn around and thank the person, in a very respectful manner.'

There may well have been something slightly menacing about these good manners, as indeed Jemima herself felt when she was smiled at by all her converted friends, before her own experience of making the Square House windows rattle. William Plumer quickly penetrated the surface pleasantness shown him on his visit: 'They are very kind and attentive to strangers so long as they have any prospect of converting them to their faith; but as soon as a man contradicts or asks questions hard to answer, they become sullen – pronounce him "damned" and avoid his company.' A young woman called Polly Swain was once on the receiving end of a particularly severe example of this sudden switch of mood, when she found herself being berated by two young Shakers called Elenor Pierce and Martha Prescott for her 'lust and pride'. The zealous believers actually began to push Polly about, until eventually she struggled out of their grasp and ran home. Abijah Worster complained about this aggressive behaviour to Ann while one of the culprits, Martha, was in the room. Ann shushed him: '"Well well," said Mother, "say nothing."' When Martha had left the room, Ann said that she and Elenor were full of zeal: 'If that was struck at they would go back to the world and be lost. Better it is that ten souls go to hell that never heard the gospel than one that had.' So much for Polly Swain. The logic behind Ann's attitude was that Polly could still be redeemed in the afterlife since she hadn't yet been converted, whereas if Martha and Elenor lost their faith they would not be given another chance.

In late July 1782, a notice of a town meeting to be held on Harvard Common was sent out to the inhabitants of Harvard and the nearby communities, and large numbers of people gathered. Phineas Fairbanks, deacon of the Congregational church, supplied two barrels of cider 'to stimulate the zeal' of the crowd. Less mischievous church officials convened another meeting in Harvard at the same time, and they persuaded the people to let them speak with the Shakers. A committee of four, led by Zabdiel Adams, popularly known as the Bishop of Lunenburg and a cousin of the Revolutionary leader John Adams, went to the Square House.

Adams demanded to know if he could ask the Shakers a few questions. The townsfolk believed that arms were concealed in the house, he said. As usual James Whittaker was deputed to speak for the Shakers. He made it clear he knew this charge was a mere pretext, saying heavy-handedly, 'There is liberty to search the house, if you can do it and not wrong your consciences – I say there is liberty to search the house all over, if you can do it and not wrong your consciences; but don't you wrong your consciences.'

Adams asked William Lee, who undoubtedly looked the most militant man in the group of senior brethren, 'Are you willing to take up arms against Britain?'

William's reply was slightly evasive: 'I never killed a creature with a gun in my life.'

Adams persisted: 'But are you friends to America?

This time James answered, equally ambiguously: 'Yea, we are friends to all the souls of men.'

It is quite clear from the reported dialogue that the Shakers were experts at taking the sting out of awkward questions. But their interrogators could show forensic talents of their own. 'But supposing one of your people should go into the war,' Adams asked, 'and should live to return home again, would he not have it to confess, as a sin?'

Again James refused to take the bait: 'Yea, surely, if he himself believes it to be a sin; but we don't bind men's consciences.'

Adams then turned his attention to a local man, Aaron Jewett, uncle of the redoubtable Jewett girls. He made a likely target because formerly he had been an officer in the war. 'When you confessed your sins,' Adams asked him, 'did you not confess your going into the army as a sin?'

But Aaron wasn't to be bested, either. 'I was so far from confessing it as a sin,' he replied, 'that I never once thought of it.'

The interrogation carried on for a while on much the same lines, James Whittaker reiterating 'that they had nothing to do with the war, one way nor the other', but also affirming: 'We will fight your enemy, and the enemy of all mankind; that is, the Devil.'

In the end the questioning must have petered out, because James began to sing, and the other Shakers joined in. He then invited the ministers to dine with them. They declined, and left. As they walked away, Isaiah Parker, the minister of the Baptist church in Harvard, asked Zabdiel Adams what he thought of the Shakers. 'I think the people better let them alone,' Adams replied. 'That Whittaker is a sharp man.'

Parker probably had mixed feelings about the encounter. He was exercised about losing members of his own congregation to the Shakers. So many were leaving to join them that there was a fear 'that our candlestick would be removed out of its place', and not long after this encounter, on 4 September to be exact, a day of fasting was decreed. This seems to have had the desired effect: forty-nine persons were baptised between 22 September and 24 November. But while he would have seen the Shakers as a threat, Parker himself knew what it was to experience persecution. The new Massachusetts constitution of 1780, established as an affirmation of independence from British law, had made it illegal to set one religion above another, and yet the Baptists had been required to pay taxes to the Congregational church of Harvard, and when they refused, Parker and two of his church officers had spent some months in prison.

Though the clerical delegates who had spoken to the Shakers recommended that they should be left alone, the crowd, fuelled by Phineas Fairbanks's alcoholic cider, were not so readily placated. They were finally dispersed by a bluff from the town's officers, who called for pencils and paper as though they were about to take down people's names with a view to subsequent prosecution. This 'gave them a start' and sent them on their way.

Tension continued to increase over the next few weeks. All over Massachusetts and upstate New York, Shakers were getting in their harvests, and when they had finished their attention turned to what had become the spiritual centre of their religion, the Square House at Harvard. In early August believers began to roll in from as far afield as Hancock and New Lebanon, a hundred miles and more away.

It may have been at about this time, and as a result of the uneasy atmosphere that was building up, that Lucy

Wright joined the ranks of believers who suffered from an eating problem. In her case she developed a weakness of the stomach 'to such a degree, that whenever she took her food, it occasioned a distress which extended even to her fingers' ends'. She decided the only remedy was to give up eating altogether, with a logic rather reminiscent of the story of the poor man who stopped feeding his donkey and complained that just when the beast had got used to going without, it died. In due course Lucy decided to confide in William Lee about her condition. To her surprise he immediately burst into tears, and said, 'I am just so myself.' As we have seen, William was known to be fast on the trigger as far as the waterworks were concerned. He had a tendency to weep with gratitude for the smallest of life's blessings, for water to wash in, and food to eat. However, the Shaker leaders were held in such high regard that even when they reacted inappropriately to the confidences of believers the desirable outcome could still somehow be triggered as a side effect. James Whittaker's hysterical reaction to Beulah Cooper's confidences about her susceptibility to sexual temptation was one example; similarly, William's lachrymose reaction to Lucy's problem had the cathartic effect of immediately and permanently rescuing her from her condition.

In August Ann had another vision of a hostile mob like the one she had previously had when two angels had guided her to the Square House. This time, God told her she must leave Harvard once again. On 16 August 1782, Ann said a sorrowful farewell and gave everyone her blessing: 'Brethren and Sisters, be comfortable; my spirit shall be with you.' Then she set out on her way. William and James, her senior elders, went with her, but Mary Partington stayed at Harvard, and soon found herself in the thick of a drama which was to culminate in the worst episode of persecution the Shakers were to suffer during this whole missionary period.

Another triangular journey to Ashfield.

10

Exasperating the Devil

Events moved rapidly to a crisis point. On 18 August 1782, two days after Ann had left Harvard, there was a huge exuberant service at the Square House, with 'singing, dancing, leaping, shouting, clapping of hands, and such other exercises as they were led into by the spirit'. It is ironic that one of the causes of hostility from the Harvard community was the Shakers' pacifism, since they were quite prepared to testify to their faith with a certain amount of aggression, as Jemima Blanchard confirmed: 'Mother used to say, "The Kingdom of Heaven suffers violence, and the violent take it by force; you must press into the kingdom and be zealous. Come to the help of the Lord against the mighty, and trample these enemies under your feet."' Their zealousness at their meeting on 18 August was so great that 'though joyful to the believers, [it] was terrible to the wicked; for the sound thereof was heard at the distance of several miles'.

The meeting, or more accurately, series of meetings, lasted all day and into the evening. Angry mobs marched on the Square House. Some of the Shakers went off to the homes of fellow-believers to spend the night but many remained in the Square House, which was surrounded by hundreds of people as darkness fell. The noise of the besiegers caused some of the Shakers inside to think they were being surrounded by Indians – ironically, given that the comparison was often made in the opposite direction.

Early the following morning one of the aged brethren opened the door to see what was happening, and before he could close it again some of the mob had pushed past him, looking for Ann. They became furious when they discovered she had eluded them again. Lucy Wright tried to placate them, but they threatened to push her head-first down the stairs. In this crisis Lucy began to show a talent for strategy which was to be of huge benefit to Shakerism in her later years.

The intruders had left the house again to join the rest outside and continue the siege. Lucy decided she had to get out and fetch help but her horse was stabled at Shirley, so she worked out a ruse. She and Mary Partington picked up pails, slipped out of the house, and walked calmly through the mob as if they were simply on the way to the barn to milk the cows (farming duties being an overriding imperative even in the middle of religious warfare). When they got to the barn and the crowd was safely behind them, they dumped their pails and fled over the fields to Solomon Cooper's house, from where they were able to spread a warning about the trouble that was brewing. Reinforcements among the local Shakers made their way to the Square House, pushed through the mob (now esti-mated at four hundred people) that was milling about outside it, and joined their fellow-believers inside.

There was a false peace for a while, with silence on

The Square House in about 1900, when a cambered
roof had replaced the original one.

both sides. John Hocknell, who had been given responsibility for affairs back at Niskeyuna, was visiting at this
period along with James Shepherd, and in the absence of
the leading triumvirate of Ann, William and James he now
found himself in charge. He told the Shakers to assemble
in one large room, which was soon completely full except
for a narrow gap separating the men from the women. He
then began to lead the prayers. This was probably a tactical
mistake – unless it was a deliberate provocation – since
it seems to have provided the spark that set the crowd
alight, and some of them broke down the barred doors
and came in again. They got to Richard Treat first (the
convert who had gone through such a strenuous induction
at Niskeyuna when he was accused of being neither hot

nor cold, and told he was going to be spewed out). The intruders grabbed his collar so violently they almost pulled it from his shirt. Then they seized other Shakers by the throat, hair and limbs, and began dragging them outside to deliver to their fellows. Some of the Shakers knelt round the elders to protect them. One of them, Elizabeth Jewett, was kicked in the side by one of the mob and received several broken ribs.

John Hocknell himself managed to struggle outside, where, slightly ingloriously, he leapt a fence and hid in a garden. He knelt down under some peach trees and cried to God to know what he should do. One can imagine his impotent anxiety, with all hell breaking loose next door. The consolation for the Shakers was that in the midst of all their trials God was closer to their experience and more attentive to their needs than is the case with most faiths. He duly came to John's aid and once again gave him the gift of a miraculous arm, just as he had seven years before, when he guided him to the wilderness of Niskeyuna. This time John found his hand stretching out towards the east, in the direction of Woburn, twenty miles away, where Ann had gone. 'He immediately followed its [his arm's] direction, which led him to Mother, and he informed her of those things.' Not that that could have done much practical good, given the time the journey must have taken, but it would presumably have made him feel better.

Meanwhile Phineas Farnsworth the militia captain, Jonathan Pollard his lieutenant, and some other local men, Isaiah Whitney, and Jonathan and Asa Houghton, had taken over leadership of the vigilantes. Farnsworth was obviously in a very different mood from how he'd been when negotiating with Ann – the explanation being, in all probability, that he felt he had been outwitted on that occasion. He and the other leaders instructed the local Shakers to go to their homes, and told the ones from out of town (known by their Harvard comrades as the 'distant Shakers') that they had an hour to down their breakfast and get ready to leave Harvard. This was very short notice given there were a hundred distant Shakers, and some of them came from over a hundred miles away.

After an hour the distant Shakers were formed into a procession and marched off. The local Shakers insisted on going with them. Some of the mob were on horseback, but only the Shaker women were allowed to ride, even though many of the men had their horses with them. Half the vigilantes escorted the vanguard, the remainder the rear. The Shakers were beaten with cudgels and whips to make them walk faster.

After a little while Isaiah Whitney beat Dyer Fitch around the face for praying out loud. Then, as they were crossing Jeremiah Willard's pasture, Abijah Worster hurried up to join them, embraced James Shepherd, and was promptly hit over the head with a goad staff by Asa Houghton for doing so. Abijah obviously had a local reputation, having been one of the Irelandites, and as an enthusiastic and proactive Shaker had no doubt made enemies for himself in the local community. He had been a fifer at the siege of Boston, though (presumably as a result of his conversion to Shakerism) was later listed in the muster rolls as a deserter – a sure way of alienating himself from his fellow-townspeople. He was put under guard and ordered to proceed along with the rest.

After three miles the procession was halted on a level stretch of ground by Still River. 'Now,' the vigilante leaders reportedly said, 'we will have a little diversion.'

What followed reveals the way in which a small-town fear of outsiders turns into a realisation that the advantage lies with the home team, and leads in turn to the torturer's mentality, a sadistic delight in teasing victims by the methodical infliction of pain and humiliation, as cats do with their prey.

The order was given to whip James Shepherd, who was the only original English Shaker in the procession, and therefore the best available embodiment of the leadership – and of its alienness. So they formed into a ring round him and sent one of their number into the bushes to cut switches. He returned and passed them around. Each member of the mob was deputed to give James a certain number of strokes. He was made to strip to the waist. He then knelt down, saying to his fellow-believers, 'Be of good cheer; for it is your Heavenly Father's good pleasure to give you the Kingdom.'

This incensed Isaiah Whitney, who gave him several lashes with his horsewhip without waiting for orders. Eleazer Rand and Jonathan Slosson appeared at just this moment, and Eleazer leapt on James's back to protect him. The vigilantes didn't pause in their whipping but simply distributed the blows between James and Eleazer, while some of them pulled at Eleazer in an effort to dislodge him. Eleazer, who was a small man, managed to ride James piggyback for some distance before the two were separated. 'Others of the brethren followed Eleazer's example, to cover James and each other from the blows, till they were all in a huddle.'

Eleazer, meanwhile, in his distress kept saying, 'O Lord?' One of the mob called (inappropriately) Priest shook him severely and told him to be quiet, but Eleazer replied, 'I won't hold my tongue – I will pray.' Priest repeatedly punched him on the neck, repeating the command and receiving the same answer, until he had propelled him along some distance. Finally he picked him up and hurled him against a stone wall.

When Priest rejoined the others Jonathan Houghton asked, 'Did you stop the little dog from praying?'

Priest replied, 'No, nor I could not, unless I had killed him.'

A Shaker called William Morey was so disgusted at the treatment meted out to Eleazer that he sharply reproved the ringleaders. But this only enraged them further, and Phineas Farnsworth hit him on the side of the face with such force that William lost several teeth. This didn't stop him from continuing to fulminate against the mistreatment the Shakers were suffering, but because of his injury he was not able 'to speak plain'.

Farnsworth now gave orders to resume the march and it continued for another six miles in all, until the border between Harvard and the neighbouring community of Bolton was reached. The local Shakers had been kept to the rear of the procession which was so long that, as the vanguard reached the town line, they found themselves standing outside Zaccheus Stevens's house. A number of the Shaker sisters were inside, and one of them, Hannah Prescott, came to the door weeping and said, 'Brethren, don't go back.'

The local Shakers replied that they would keep with their distant brethren as long as their persecutors did too.

'Do; I would die with them rather than leave them with that wicked mob,' Hannah replied.

The local Shakers then tried to push forward to join their distant brethren and sisters at the line. The rabble leaders responded by cutting them off with a strong guard and told them they were forbidden to go any further.

The Harvard Shakers now invoked law and order in their response, crying out: 'Are you highway robbers? We have as good a right to the highway as you have, and we will not trust our distant brethren with you; we will go as far with them as you do.'

It was a ploy that had worked for the Shakers on a number of occasions, but not this time. 'If you attempt it,' Farnsworth told them, 'we will spill your blood in the sand.'

They called his bluff and began to struggle forward. Farnsworth was as good as his word, however, and began to lay about them with his club, with other members of the guarding party following suit. Eleazer Rand, battered though he was, found himself on the receiving end again, getting struck by a club so hard his arm was broken. Then, according to the Shaker account, an odd and fortuitous event took place: Farnsworth's club flew backwards out of his hands. This so terrified his henchmen that they fled, leaving the Harvard Shakers free to catch up with the distant ones.

This may be a bit of embroidery after the event, but if it did happen – and it could be that Farnsworth had simply lost his grip on the club – the reaction perhaps identifies one component of the ruthless behaviour the militia and the mob were exhibiting: the possibility that they shared the Shakers' own capacity to identify miracles and divine intervention in their lives, so that they resented the Shakers precisely because their system of belief was challengingly close to their own.

The Shakers were then driven on through Bolton towards the next town of Lancaster. The abuses continued: 'whipping with horse-whips, pounding, beating and bruising with clubs, collaring, pushing off from bridges, into the water and mud, scaring the sisters' horses with a view to frighten the riders'. Jonathan Bridges, one of the distant Shakers, was unable to keep up with the pace and began to drop behind. To keep him going he was whipped almost every step for the best part of a quarter of a mile. Older Shakers who tried to mount horses were badly beaten, and one was hit across the back with a fence rail.

At Lancaster the vigilante leaders told the distant Shakers never to return to Harvard. 'But,' they added ominously, 'we have further work to do with the Harvard Shakers.'

The distant Shakers then gathered under a large elm tree and ate some bread and cheese that the Harvard contingent had given them. They thanked God that he had found them worthy of persecution. The implicit irony of the prayer enraged the mob further and, some on horseback, others on foot, they rushed in amongst the believers and began beating them again. One of the sisters had her head pulled back so far she began to turn black.

Finally the assault died away and it became time for the parting of the ways. The distant Shakers took 'an affectionate leave' of their Harvard colleagues and continued on their way, though not before they had received a last whipping from a large, rough-looking man who blocked the road as they departed. Richard Treat said that these were the most painful blows he received in the whole day. No doubt for many of them the denial of their civil rights and their freedom of movement was even more painful, and they might have reflected on the irony that a war to establish American freedom and self-determination was going on in the background even while they were being subjected to such a crude exhibition of persecution and bullying.

The Harvard Shakers, of course, weren't off the hook yet: they had to return home with their oppressors, receiving more ill treatment as they went. Jonathan Houghton, one of the ringleaders, wound the lash of his whip round his hand and assaulted the Shakers with the loaded whip-stalk, concentrating particularly on an elderly brother called Jonathan Clark. On arrival in Harvard the mob halted the procession outside Lieutenant Pollard's house and the decision was made to give Abijah Worster twenty lashes for 'going about breaking up churches and families'.

He was tied to a tree and Jonathan Houghton gave him ten lashes, but then a respected local man, James Haskell, rode up.

Shocked by what he saw, he took off his coat and cried, 'Here! Here! If there are any more stripes to be given, let me take the rest.'

This intervention finally shamed the vigilantes, who began to disperse. Abijah was untied and left the scene singing, though his sufferings had made others, even non-Shakers, weep.

Many of the citizens were in fact disgusted at what had gone on. One of them, Solomon Sanderson, rebuked Jonathan Pollard for the crowd's behaviour. Pollard tried to justify it, then hit Sanderson with his horse-whip. Sanderson, who was on foot, pulled him off his horse and would have given him a beating if he'd not been pulled off by others. Many other bystanders who had witnessed the persecution were similarly incensed. Years later, the Shaker survivors of that day made an interesting admission:

It ought also to be remarked, that the conduct and testimony of the Believers, while on the road, had a tendency to exasperate the Devil, and excite his emissaries to greater acts of cruelty than they probably would have committed had the Believers remained silent. But the Believers were, mostly, very young in the faith; many of them had believed but a few months, and were full of zeal and power; and being divested of all fear of man, they would sing and praise God on the road, that they were counted worthy to suffer persecution for the Gospel's sake.

They were only too keen, in other words, to 'press into the kingdom', and experienced a certain relish in martyrdom.

It is not possible to know how Ann reacted to news of the events of 19 August, when it was brought to her by John Hocknell and other messengers. Her own courage was not in doubt, as she had proved many times already, and was going to prove many times again in the year that remained of her mission. Even though she was aware of being the main target of hostility, and had made a careful tactical decision that the interests of the Shakers would be best served if she kept out of reach, she must have felt a pang at the suffering her followers had experienced. Certainly the glimpses we have of her in the next few weeks show her in uncompromising form.

After a short stay at Woburn Ann passed through Norton, visited Rehoboth for a week or so, and then returned to Norton, where she stayed at the house of William Morey, the man who had lost several teeth when he tried to come to the rescue of Eleazer Rand. She told William and his sister Hezekiah (it's a name that seems to have been given to both sexes) about a vision she'd had of their deceased parents, again shedding light on the architecture of the afterlife for those who died without the opportunity of receiving her ministry: 'I saw your father, about a week ago, in blackness and darkness, and before we left the house, he desired the prayers of the Church; and I saw your natural mother, with her mouth wide open in prayer to God for him. Since that time, he has appeared to me again, and has risen from the dead, and come into the first heavens; and is travelling on to the second and third heavens.' There is something unnerving about that glimpse of the 'natural mother' (natural as opposed to Ann herself, mother in spirit) caught in mid-utterance with her mouth open: one can imagine the Morey siblings dropping to their knees to join her shade in prayer for their father in his epic progress from one heaven to the next.

The next port of call for Ann and her elders was Stonington, Connecticut, where they stayed for several weeks at the Birch household. Here Ann pronounced on the morals of a young woman living with the family in the same uncompromising manner she'd used on the hapless Tryphena Perkins.

Lois Birch immediately came to the woman's defence, telling Ann she believed the person in question to be 'very honest and chaste'.

'Are you a Christian,' Ann replied, 'and think that girl is chaste and honest? You are deceived – She lives in whoredom with married men, young men, black men and boys.'

Lois found this declaration impossible to believe and as a result nearly lost faith in Ann altogether. But the girl in question soon after came forward and confessed the very things which Ann had laid to her charge. The pendulum then swung the other way, with Lois deciding that for certain Ann 'had the revelation of God, and was able to see what creatures had in them'.

Other members of the community were less impressed. Simeon Brown, the son of an elder in the local Baptist

church, began to persecute the Shakers with encouragement from his father, and a man called Henry Iner gave
Ann and her elders an ultimatum to depart within twenty-
four hours. Conveniently, they felt a corresponding 'gift
to depart' on their own behalf, and therefore did so, proceeding to Preston and then Windham, where Ann made
another, less targeted, assault on the evils of lust, declaring
against the flesh 'with such plainness, that the assembly
was greatly struck' – not surprisingly, since some of them
had apparently been following a doctrine of wife-sharing.
She then sent home a number of Shakers who had come
from outlying parts to be with her, while she and the
elders continued on to Stafford, where they stayed at Ezekiel Slate's.

What is clear from these journeys is that Shakerism
had already built up a substantial infrastructure in New
England. Despite the establishment of the settlement at
Niskeyuna and the use of the Square House at Harvard
as a base, there was no widespread attempt to organise
the sort of communities that we associate with the later
development of the religion; nevertheless teams of evangelists were sent out to remote towns and villages – Joseph
Meacham seems to have done a lot of this proselytising
– and in the communities where conversions had taken
place believers kept open house for each other, with large
congregations gathering for worship in fields or in and
around individual dwellings.

The next stop for Ann and her entourage was to be
Enfield, where they would be staying at David Meacham's. To get there they would have to pass through the

town of Somers. News of this intention reached some of the inhabitants who were opposed to the Shakers, and they planned an ambush. Meacham, getting wind of the plot, rode over to warn Ann about it. She was determined not to be intimidated, however, and set out on the journey, taking Mary Partington in her carriage with her and escorted only by Meacham and Calvin Harlow, Harlow on horseback at the front, and Meacham riding in the rear.

When they got to Somers they suddenly gathered speed, and rode through the town so fast the vigilantes were taken off-guard. Under the leadership of the captain of the Somers militia, Charles Kibbee, thirty or forty of the conspirators pursued Ann to David Meacham's house.

Ann got there just ahead of her pursuers. She and Mary rushed out of the carriage into the house, and hid in a back room on the ground floor. Cunningly the Meachams and other Shakers present positioned themselves at the bottom of the stairs, as if the two women had gone up them to hide. The mob burst in and began to beat them in an attempt to break through the cordon and search the upper part of the house.

It may be that Ann felt that this time she couldn't keep her distance while her followers were suffering on her behalf. She pushed her way into the thick of the crowd, 'spred her arms & said stand away & let me come, speaking with authority'.

Her bravado paid off. The crowd automatically moved back to let her pass through, and she made her way up the stairs. But then the penny dropped and a man called out, 'There she is! We will have her!' David Meacham immediately leapt on to the stairs to protect her but the man darted through his legs in his bid to get upstairs. Elizabeth Wood later recalled that 'David caught him by the neck & held him fast & spanked him about right. It sounded pretty smart as the chap had on a pair of leather breeches.'

The sudden moment of comedy abruptly changed the crowd's mood: 'The rest of the company was more pleased than mad, they hawhawed and laughed heartily and began to disperse.'

Unfortunately Mary Partington chose that moment to appear from the ground floor hiding-place in her turn. Her appearance immediately refocused the will of the assembled mob. They decided *she* must be 'the Old Elect lady sure enough', dragged her to a horse and hoisted her on to it. Then one of them got on behind her to hold her on. David Meacham stopped spanking the man on the stairs, rushed out and hauled Mary off the horse. The mob then 'collard David & pulled his ears till the blood ran down his shirt sleeves'.

Luckily the town constable, John Booth, appeared at this point, and threatened legal action against the rabble for riotous conduct. But they wouldn't disperse, threatening instead to burn the house down before morning. Booth therefore returned first thing next day with two magistrates, who took down in writing particulars of the violence and the names of the rioters. Shortly afterwards, the elders arrived from Stafford.

It's worth noting, particularly in view of certain events that were to take place the following year, that small-town authorities could show themselves willing, on this and other occasions, to defend Shaker rights. The offenders were summoned before the county court in Hartford, and given the choice of settling the matter to David Meacham's satisfaction, or standing trial. They therefore approached Meacham to ask him for his conditions. He told them that he didn't want any financial compensation: all he required was that they should make public confession of their misdeeds in their own churches. That was too humiliating a prospect for people who lacked the Shaker experience of rigorous confession, so they elected to stand trial and in due course received fines sufficiently punitive, apparently, to put a stop to all 'mobs and riots against the Believers, in the State of Connecticut'. David Meacham later recorded that three of the ringleaders from Enfield, and two from Somers, came to a sticky end, though one of them called Hambleton at least asked forgiveness before he died.

Meanwhile Ann and the elders had crossed the Connecticut River and gone to Joseph Bennet's house in New Providence, where they stayed for a few days. Ann had an intriguing little conversation with Joseph. She asked him which of the two elders, her brother William or James Whittaker, he thought had the greatest gift. There is obviously a possibility that she was engaged in assessing grass-roots opinion about a possible successor as leader.

'I think,' Joseph replied, 'that Elder William has the greatest gift of sorrow.'

'So he has,' agreed Ann, adding, perhaps a little tartly, 'James plants and William waters.'

Allowing for the fact that the Shakers' use of figurative language tended to be far less self-conscious and ironic than is normally the case nowadays, there still seems to be an edge to her remark, as if Joseph's carefully delimited reply to her question had confirmed her own sense that the lachrymose William did not quite have what it takes to be a strong and creative leader. The very intensity of the bond between them may have made Ann feel that there would be an unhealthy kind of nepotism involved in promotion for him. Shakerism involved the discarding of family relationships in favour of spiritual ones: the kind of gleeful redirection of affection inherent in William's claim that his sister had become his mother perhaps had inappropriate overtones. There is no doubt that the two siblings had unusually intense feelings for each other. Deborah Williams reported that once, when separated from Ann, William yearningly proclaimed: 'I would go to my Mother I had no God till I had a Mother, how could I be born without a Mother, what reason I have to bless God for my Mother.'

During this stay at New Providence Ann and the elders ran into a couple of bouts of tricky questioning.

'Your children don't talk as *you* do,' a Baptist deacon pointed out, 'why don't they talk so?'

Presumably by 'children' he was referring to the ordinary believers, and making the point that they either failed to communicate or else gave unorthodox versions of Shakerism to enquirers. Given the home-made quality of the theology even among Shaker leaders, one can imagine all sorts of strange and contradictory superstitions finding a place in the faith of the rank and file. It may be, though, that the deacon had simply encountered some of that sullenness Plumer commented on during his visit to Harvard a few months previously.

In reply Ann simply restated her authority: 'You must not expect children to be parents.'

Amos Taylor's complaint about the hierarchical structure of Shakerism was published in a pamphlet that very year. While it was true that adherents could achieve perfection through their inaugural confession, there was simultaneously a sense that leadership was essential, that Ann and her elders had a vital pastoral role to play. Those with greater spiritual experience were in a position to provide the necessary guidance to those who had only just set out on their pilgrimage. And, of course, the longest-serving Shakers, and thereby the most senior ones, happened to be the British contingent.

Ann obviously came to the conclusion that despite the deacon's apparent affability there was a hostile subtext to his remark, because shortly afterwards she turned on him, bringing 'some of his hidden works of darkness to the light'.

A certain Colonel Smith tried to out-argue the leadership, too.

'Is not there a woman who is head of the church?' he asked.

One can almost hear Ann sigh; she had heard it so often before. 'No; Christ is head of the Church.'

Smith reverted to gender question number two: 'But there is a woman here that teaches, is there not? We must not suffer a woman to teach.'

It was William this time who answered: 'We do not suffer man or woman to teach, except they have the spirit of Christ in them, and Christ teaches through them, and then either man or woman may teach.'

The Shakers were very consistent in their attitude to gender, although that attitude did involve paradoxes. Clearly their belief that a female messiah counterbalanced the male one was radical and provocative, guaranteed to give pause to the likes of Joseph Meacham and to thoroughly upset the likes of Colonel Smith. At the same time this very gender balance suggests a Christ-spirit, and indeed a Godhead, who is beyond or above gender. And while they were pioneering in their attitude that the genders were (nearly) equal in value and ability, the price the Shakers paid for this egalitarianism was a repudiation of sex itself.

William's riposte was enough for Colonel Smith, anyhow: feeling himself bested, he took his leave of the Shakers. Shortly afterwards came news of less cerebral opposition: another mob was forming, and once again Ann felt a providential 'gift to depart'.

Their destination now was Asa Bacon's house in Ashfield, where they arrived on 1 November 1782. If Niskeyuna was their base, and Harvard their spiritual home, Ashfield was now their refuge, and they stayed here until the following spring, building the first meeting-house specifically constructed for Shaker worship, a one-room hall measuring thirty by thirty-six feet with a chimney at one end, which was used for spiritual labours day and night. There was a shift system for eating, with a large round table accommodating the diners while their brethren and sisters continued to sing and dance behind them. The excitement generated by this arrangement triggered William Lee's emotional volatility – on one occasion, full of thankfulness for the love of God, he sobbed his way through a whole meal, deeply impressing the young believers who were eating with him. Provisions were brought in from Shakers far and wide, though as usual there was talk of multitudes being satisfactorily fed on almost nothing. That winter there were very vivid displays of Northern lights, which were interpreted by some as being a confirmation of Christ's Second Coming.

The Shakers worshipped enthusiastically – one meeting was audible, it was claimed, seven miles away – and John Farrington counted sixty sleighs and six hundred visitors on another mid-winter occasion. But Ann could operate on a more private and intimate level as well. A man called Peter Dodge came to the house where she was staying. He was in a state of spiritual despair, and sat himself on some stairs in the back corner of the kitchen, out of sight of everybody. Ann soon materialised in that mysterious way of hers.

'Mother,' Peter told her, 'I am full of evil.'

'Nay,' she replied, 'you are not *full* of evil: for if you were *full of evil*, there could be no room in you to receive any *good*.' Never one for facile reassurance, she went on: 'You have indeed a great deal of evil in you; but this conviction you feel is *good*.' Then, in a touching gesture, Ann reached out, took hold of one of his fingers, and led him to the new meeting-house. 'The moment she took hold of my finger,' Peter later recalled, 'I felt the power of God, from her hand, run through my whole body.'

Ann was in visionary mode during this period. Lydia Matthewson confided to her that her husband Philip's father, Thomas Matthewson, had died without knowledge of the things of God. Shortly afterwards Ann found herself flying into the depths of hell: 'I felt the power of God come upon me, which moved my hands up and down like the motion of wings; and soon I felt as if I had wings on both hands' – the woman clothed with the sun in the Book of Revelation is given two wings, 'of a great eagle' – 'and I saw them, and they appeared as bright as gold. And I let my hands go as the power directed, and these wings parted the darkness to where souls lay, in the ditch of hell, & I saw their lost state.' At that very moment, while Ann hovered in the ditch of hell, James Whittaker was preaching in the brand-new meeting-house. Ann remained aware of this, and saw that his words were reaching Thomas Matthewson and some of the other denizens of hell. She then came out of her vision and went into the meeting-house herself. There she found Philip Matthewson 'lying on the floor, apparently like a dying man. His father's state had fallen upon him.'

'I took him by the hand,' Ann explained to Lydia, 'and told him to rise up, and he obeyed; but it was some time before he was fully released from that state which had fallen upon him.' The surrogacy had been a success, however: 'His father united with the testimony of the gospel.'

On at least one other occasion during the Ashfield period Ann had a similar vision: 'I had great wings; and, with the ends of my wings, I uncovered the dead, who lay on the banks of the gulf.'

Another time the journey was the other way, with the dead invading the realm of the living. David Slosson was on the receiving end of what must have been an extremely unnerving experience. He was just about to go home after visiting the Shakers at Ashfield, and was brought into Ann's room to say his goodbyes. He was placed in a chair before her, with the elders also present. He had the sensation of being in the presence of God but at the same time felt very oppressed.

After a short silence, Ann said: 'David, you know not what you feel. I see the dead around you, whose visages are ghastly and very awful. Their faces almost touch thine. If you did but see what I see, you would be surprized.' She then went into religious labours and afterwards once more looked David full in the face, this time with an expression of joy and love, and said, 'Child be not discouraged; for I see the glory of God in thy right eye, as bright as the sun; its form is like the new moon. Be of good comfort, and be not cast down; for the dead gather to thee for the gospel, which thou hast received.'

It is clear from such incidents that ministering to the dead was as important to Ann and her followers as attending to the living. They were living at the crucial moment in the history of the world, in the last act of the human drama. Christ, in the form of Jesus, had made heaven available. Now Christ in the form of Ann Lee and her followers was providing access to that heaven. The spiritual geography had already been established; it was Ann's mission to enable the souls of people, both living and dead, to make the journey across it.

It wasn't simply Ann who led the believers into such difficult territory. The enthusiastic Aaron Wood took it upon himself to conduct a series of exorcisms, estimated at a hundred in all, during the winter in Ashfield. We have an extraordinarily vivid account of these services from a young member of the Matthewson family, Angell, who was about twelve during this period, and who wrote reminiscences of it in a series of letters to his brother when he was grown up and had left the Shakers. Part of the charm of these manuscripts rests in the fact that Angell was perhaps the worst speller who ever lived. He tells his brother that James Whittaker claimed schools were irrelevant 'as he that precched Christ never would lack a toung'. James himself was accounted a learned man – 'of the greatist education' – according to Angell, certainly as compared with the ordinary Shakers who 'ware a set of yanky farmers'. James's apparent anti-intellectualism was shared by Joseph Meacham, who burned his own extensive library, and testifies to two Shaker assumptions: firstly that they could obtain direct access to truth from the Almighty – 'mother was continualey in open vision of god', as Matthewson claimed – and secondly, that there was no earthly future to be educated for. Just as the institution of marriage was irrelevant to souls who were being collected into heaven, so the institution of schooling could serve no purpose to those whose sights were set on the afterlife – the outcome being that Angell could write exuberantly and humorously without being able to spell to save his life.

One of Aaron Wood's exorcism subjects, according to Angell, was Elias Sawyer, the Shaker who had lost his wife, or, in Shaker terms, his former wife, after she caught 'billows colic' following an energetic Shaker meeting at Harvard. Whether it was his bereavement that had caused Elias to manifest signs of possession, or some other reason, he was diagnosed by Aaron as a candidate for exorcism and the treatment was drastic indeed.

Men danced on one side of the meeting-house room, women on the other. Aaron stood in the middle. He would 'snarl grim[ly] and hollow [holler] "You devil!"' Then he would grab hold of his subject, and pull and push him. In the case of Elias he grasped him under his arms and span him around so fast his 'feet came up about 3 feet from the floor in this form he turned round about 40 times'. Another victim, Israel Chauncy, the Ashfield man who, with his sister, had brought Shakerism to the town, found himself being spun for three hours, an unbearably long time for both parties involved, and Angell had to assure his brother 'I am not riting to you Romantic fiction nor idle tails'. Ann herself attended this ritual.

The exorcisms were accompanied by 'yelling yawing snarling pushing halling [hailing, or possibly hauling] elbowing singing danceing,' he wrote, adding that 'the worst drunken club you ever see could not cut up a higher dash of ill behaviour'. The sessions must have hovered uneasily between the terrifying and the comic. While they went on the other Shakers shouted 'Howu howu you devil you – get out devil devil git out' until at last the devil had been cast out. It's not difficult to see how such strange and extreme behaviour should feed rumours that Ann Lee 'casteth out devils by Beelzebub'.

Aaron produced the same level of energy in normal meetings, where 'his close [clothes] would go wet with swet', but other believers showed a comparable level of commitment. We have seen how both Rathbun and Plumer described the skirts of spinning Shaker women as looking as if they had hoops in them; Angell's sharp eye produces a far more graphic image: when they were spinning the women's skirts would become 'full of wind to form a shape like a tea cup bottom up – in this exersise they would swet almost equil to Aaron'.

Ann made frequent appearances at the services held in the Ashfield meeting-house, but as elsewhere she kept a relatively low profile during the course of them, appropriately enough, given her status: 'Every trew believer believs that christ has made his second operance [appearance] in the world clothed in flesh & blood in the form of a woman by name ann lee.' Jemima Blanchard also made the point that Ann didn't join in the violent antics of the other Shakers. While William and James would labour with great power and zeal, Ann would content herself with singing in a low voice and gently motioning her hands. Nevertheless, she could be assertive when necessary. Angell says that he had 'sevril times heered her speak to the people mostly by way of reproof & chastisment it was handed out in harsh tirms with language that would have bin destitute of dilicasy in aney other woman but as hur divine benidiction was so great it was believed by hur folowers to be by the gift & power of god'. On one occasion during this Ashfield period, James Whittaker was obviously not holding the attention of believers as much as he should have. Ann came into the meeting and told them all off: 'When the word of God is spoken to you,' she pointed out, 'some of you are hawking and spitting, and some of you are shuffling about.' That was the devil's doing, to keep them from hearing God's word. In a lovely image she told them they needed the fallow ground of their hearts broken up, so that they could be receptive. 'When the word of God is spoken to me,' she told them, 'I stand as though my body were dead.'

This uncompromising tendency in Ann surfaced as she thought about the predicament of Joseph Bennet and his family at New Providence, where she had stayed shortly before coming to Ashfield. Fifteen or twenty of their cattle had died, and as she reflected on the problem she came to the conclusion that it must be caused by 'sin in the family'. Accordingly she sent one of her elders to investigate further.

When he arrived he went into labours with the Bennets and the upshot was that a young man was singled out and accused of defiling himself with the cattle. He confessed his sin, and the livestock malaise disappeared. At the very beginning of her American ministry, Ann had addressed the problem of bestiality: 'If you commit sin with beasts, your souls will be transformed into the shape of beasts in hell.' She warned against keeping dogs in the house, because children were liable to catch their evil spirits, and claimed that even cats were unclean animals.

As winter turned to spring the usual tensions began to develop between the Shakers and the surrounding communities. The catalyst in this case seems to have been Daniel Bacon, Asa's brother, who had fallen away from the Shaker faith, though his wife remained a believer. His disaffection became evident one day in March, when he brought his wife and child to the meeting-house by sleigh. He had no intention of going to the meeting himself, and 'without going into the house, he put them out of the sleigh, in a very rough and churlish manner, into the mud, before the house, and immediately drove off and left them'.

He had in effect dumped his family on the Shakers. Ann immediately realised that he was deliberately trying to cause trouble: 'This is a snare,' she said. 'He has done this to get occasion; she is his wife, and I will not keep her here so.'

Ann's refusal to fall into this particular trap didn't stop Daniel from trying to stir up mischief. Because the Ashfield community was unusually tolerant, he went a little further afield, to the neighbouring town of Shelburn, where he managed to gather together fifty or sixty indignant citizens. In response, the Ashfield residents appointed a committee to deal with the crisis, consisting of their militia captain, Thomas Stocking, and two other respectable townspeople. They were deputed to confer with Ann and her elders.

When Ann opened the door to Stocking's knock she

was not her usual ebullient self. On a number of occasions in the time remaining to her she shows fatigue and demoralisation in the face of the unending conflict her ministry brought on her. 'I am a poor weak woman,' she told him, 'and I have suffered so much by mobs, that it seems to me that I could not endure any more.'

Stocking gallantly replied, 'You need not be afraid, Ma'am; we have come not to hurt you; but to defend you.'

Stocking advised Ann and her entourage to move into the centre of Ashfield, and stay at Philip Philips's house. She politely refused, but gave him and the other men dinner. Afterwards the committee adjourned to Smith's tavern half a mile away, and met the vigilante leaders, who said they wished to check on scandalous rumours about her, and in particular to investigate the charge that she was a British spy dressed in women's clothes. The committee agreed to call Ann and let her answer for herself.

Some of the mob nevertheless insisted on going on to Asa Bacon's. They found Ephraim Welch standing in the doorway.

'Where is that woman you call mother?' they demanded.

'I suppose she is in the house,' Ephraim replied warily. 'What do you want of her?'

'We hear that she ran away from her own country – that she has been cropped and branded, and had her tongue bored through for blasphemy; and we want to see for ourselves.'

Ephraim went to fetch Ann. When the crowd told her what they wanted, 'she turned up her cap and showed her ears, and said, "See if my ears have been cropped; and see if my forehead has been branded." Then showing her tongue, she said, "See if my tongue has been bored."'

After the examination was over, Ann asked, 'What do you think now?'

One of the ringleaders replied, 'I think they tell damned lies about you.'

Ann then sent them on their way. Shortly afterwards, though, the committee appeared and advised the Shakers to go to Smith's tavern, and negotiate with the mob there; otherwise they were likely to return to Asa Bacon's.

Ann and her elders agreed and set out by horse-drawn sleigh.

At Smith's tavern the interrogation was conducted by the mob leaders, chief of whom was Colonel David Wells of Shelburn. When she had answered all their other charges, they insisted on having it confirmed that she was a woman. The tavern keeper's wife and another woman were appointed jury on this point, which at least showed more decency than the Black Guards at Petersham had possessed, though one senses similar contempt and prurience in the motives of Wells and his fellow-investigators.

The women examined Ann and duly confirmed she was indeed a woman.

Foiled in this respect, the persecutors then switched to other accusations, alleging that the Shakers had bought up all the hay in the town so that a poor man was not able to get any for his cow, and likewise with the grain, depriving the Ashfield population of flour.

It must be borne in mind that these inquisitors were

inhabitants of a rival town, and their charges stung the pride of the Ashfield committee, who chose to answer them themselves, saying that the Ashfield citizens had a surplus of hay and had profited from selling some of it to the Shakers; if anybody could produce the so-called poor man (and cow) in question they would be provided with hay; but no such man was found. As for the grain, the Shakers themselves had brought supplies with them, and sold some to the locals. The committee dismissed the charges and insisted the Shakers should not be harmed, nor the town disturbed.

Ann at this point took it upon herself to reprove the colonel, attacking him for listening to scandal, and cleverly emphasising the slight to Ashfield. 'Is not the authority of the town able to see to the affairs of their own town?' she asked.

The colonel, stung with this reproof, lost any veneer of civility and resorted to crude bullying: 'If you don't hold your tongue, I'll cane you.'

'"Do you pretend to be a gentleman," said Mother, "and are you going to cane a poor weak woman! What a shame it is!"'

This silenced the colonel. James Whittaker then gave a ringing address to all present, saying he was prepared to die for the gospel.

It was a moral victory for the Shakers. The mob leaders slunk off discomfited, and hitherto resentful locals like the tavern-keeper Smith and his family became more sympathetic.

A couple of weeks later, Daniel Bacon made a last attack

on the Shakers with a gang of twelve or fourteen individuals, standing outside his brother's house and railing at those within. John Hocknell came out and tried to reason with him. Daniel responded by beating him over the shoulders with the butt end of his whip.

The degree of violence he, and others, felt and demonstrated on this and similar occasions cannot be excused, but it does need to be put in context. While it is true that Ann had sent Daniel Bacon's wife and child back to him, the fact remained that they were alienated spiritually, and a full married life was at an end. It was not every man who could walk out alone into an unknown future, as Abraham Standerin, Ann's own husband, had done. And of course, although New England had been settled for a century and a half, there was still a frontier atmosphere in its small towns, and a tendency to resort to violence against strangers who seemed to pose a threat was unquestionably exacerbated by the war.

Daniel's violence proved counterproductive, in any case. Some of the crowd recoiled from the spectacle of him beating John Hocknell, and they soon dispersed. Nevertheless, Daniel shortly had the satisfaction of seeing the leading Shakers depart from Ashfield. Ann came to the conclusion that enough time had elapsed to enable them to return to Harvard. Ashfield might be a more welcoming community, but Harvard was the town she had seen in her vision in England, and the Square House was her spiritual home.

Before she left, Ann sent out three teams of missionaries to spread the word in the remoter corners of New England.

They were Joseph Meacham and Samuel Fitch, Calvin Harlow and Joel Pratt, and Ebenezer Cooley and Israel Chauncy. This evangelism played an important part in establishing a Shaker network in even the smallest and most isolated communities, though it is much less well documented than the central mission of Ann and her elders. She held a meeting to mark their departure, gathering all the children from six to twelve, including young Angell Matthewson, and getting them to join hands to make a ring. Then she sang to the assembly with 'much glee and politeness'. After this the six missionaries saddled up and rode off to preach. Their remit, according to Angell, was to 'tell people to labor for a gift of god to hiss at the devil'. Shortly afterwards, Ann herself left for what turned out to be her last visit to Harvard.

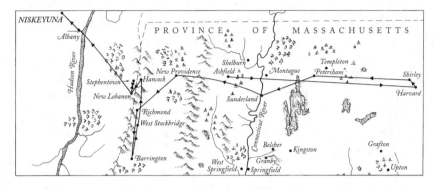

Final phase of Ann's mission to New England.

11

The Journey Back

Another episode with the simplicity and power of a folk tale.

A woman called Sarah Turner married a deaf and dumb man named Jude Carter. Shortly afterwards, like her brothers Nathaniel and Joseph Turner, Sarah became a Shaker. Her husband seemed 'friendly and pliable' towards the faith, and she induced him by signs to make some confession of his sins.

While they were staying at Elijah Wilds's house in Shirley, Sarah tried to persuade Jude to cut his hair in the short Shaker style and to sell his silver shoe buckles and buy something more functional and less vain. Jude signed back that he thought people would laugh if he had his hair cropped, and that other people wore large buckles as well as he. But on a shopping trip to Boston market Sarah persuaded him to sell the buckles.

On the way back the couple stopped over at Nathan Kendall's house in Woburn. The Kendalls were a rich family comprising Nathan and Sarah Kendall, and their children Nathan, Paul, Sarah, Rebecca, Jane, Eunice and Hannah. These were people who had known what it was to be stylish: 'As they were wealthy they of course ran

271

high in the fashions of a lost world', in the words of one contemporary. According to Jemima Blanchard, in the early 1780s New England women tended to wear their dresses short. After their conversion the Kendalls had stripped themselves of their finery and begun to dress modestly, the girls attracting Ann Lee's attention, and approval, by making themselves dresses that were longer than the norm. It was the right environment for applying pressure to Jude, and while they were here Sarah Turner managed to persuade him to get his hair cut. He fought something of a rearguard action, insisting that it wasn't going to be as severe as the usual Shaker style. Luckily he saw a man with a short haircut he liked the look of, and agreed to have his cut similarly.

So far so good, but the real problem occurred at bed-time, as in Shaker marriages it inevitably must. Jude made a strenuous attempt to sleep with his wife – to no avail, of course.

The next day he set off for Harvard by himself in a very upset state. As he went he complained by means of sign language to everyone he saw – and it must have been a strange and poignant display of semiotics – that the Shakers had 'robbed him of his silver buckles, cut off his hair, and got away his wife'.

This was enough to activate the mob once more. Ann foresaw what was to come. After a couple of weeks of relative peace, she had said to James Whittaker: 'There is going to be a great persecution; for I saw a man come and look in at the window, and he was as black as a negro.' This image, in conjunction with Ann's claim that Lois

Birch had slept with negroes, might suggest racist hostility on her part; the other side of the coin is a vision she had of the afterlife: 'I have seen the poor negroes, who are so much despised, redeemed from their loss, with crowns on their heads.'

It may have been at about this point that Ann found the opportunity to affirm the status of one of the more active American believers, Eleazer Rand, who had conducted himself so bravely the year before in quite literally leaping to the defence of James Whittaker. While she was at Zaccheus Stevens's house, she discovered some of the townspeople ridiculing Eleazer because of his smallness. 'They viewed him,' the Shaker annals explain ponderously, 'as a contemptible stripling.' Mother Ann turned on the sneerers, calling them 'a wicked generation of adulterers!' and prophesying darkly in the following terms: 'Take care what you say to a child of God! Touch not the anointed of God! He will have the keys of the Kingdom for the people in this place – He will be able to bind and to loose – he will be able to shut you out yet!' There may be an element of hindsight in these attributed remarks, since Rand was to become joint leader of the Harvard–Shirley Shaker community in 1791, but it is quite likely that Ann at this stage was aware of the need to pass power into American hands, and was confronting the unpalatable fact that her presence, and that of the other English elders, in this place was having a counterproductive effect, creating nationalist tensions and inhibiting the development of the most buoyant of the Shaker communities.

On 1 June 1783, at about eight o'clock in the evening,

Ann and the elders were worshipping at Elijah Wilds's house in Shirley when a mass of people led by Phineas Farnsworth, James Pollard, Elisha Fullam and Asa Houghton circled the building and blocked all the entrances. David Meacham was meanwhile 'in labors' with some of the believers in a shop nearby. He tried to break through into the Wildses' house but couldn't, so had to content himself with lecturing the mob until he was violently restrained. Meanwhile, one of the sisters trapped inside, Molly Randall, took a leaf out of Lucy Wright's book and persuaded the ringleaders to let her out so she could go home to her baby. It was a genuine excuse, but didn't prevent her from stopping en route to alert the town's Grand Juryman, Thomas Buckmore, as to what was going on.

The siege lasted through the night. The next morning the mob tried to persuade Ann and the other senior Shakers to step outside. They refused to obey but as a concession agreed to let the four vigilante leaders in. Ann told Eunice Wilds to prepare breakfast for them, though the gesture was strategic rather than hospitable. 'We must feed our enemies,' Ann told Eunice, 'and so heap coals of fire on their heads.' While the leaders were eating, Elijah Wilds cut up bread and cheese and carried it out to the rest of the besiegers in pans, along with cider to wash the food down.

Hoping to profit by these conciliatory manoeuvres, James Whittaker tried to address the crowd, asking, 'Have we hurt or injured your persons or property? If we have, make us sensible of it, and we will make you satisfaction.'

Elijah Wilds's house in Shirley.

Sadly, the ploy didn't work. He was seized by the arm and collar by members of the crowd while his fellow-Shakers pulled him by his other arm, so that he cried out, 'Lord have mercy! You will pull me in pieces!' He was nearly strangled before his assailants' hands were unclenched by another Shaker, one of the formerly well dressed Kendall clan, Nathan junior.

Thomas Buckmore then arrived, along with a peace officer named James Parker. They called for order and this seemed to 'strike a damp' upon the mob, but it continued to agitate and grow. The leaders were still demanding that Ann and the elders be handed over. Ann, meanwhile, was hiding in a narrow closet beside the chimney in the hallway of Elijah Wilds's house, with a chest of drawers positioned in front of it to hide its door. This refuge was thereafter known by the Shakers as 'Mother Ann's Closet', until the demolition of the house in 1902. Those searching for her supposed she had escaped through a window into the swamps.

Some of the Shakers had in fact managed to get out of the house. They knelt in the street outside to pray, inevitably provoking those vigilantes who had horses available to ride straight at them. Finally the crowd agreed to accept James Whittaker and William Lee as hostages in lieu of Ann. If the two elders went with them back to Harvard, they promised not to mistreat them. Just in case, David Meacham, Calvin Harlow and some other brethren decided to go along too.

When everyone arrived at Harvard, this gentlemanly agreement promptly collapsed. The Shakers who had come to guarantee fair play were driven back to Shirley, with the exception of David Meacham and Calvin Harlow themselves. David's horse was seized by the bridle but he leapt from it, telling his antagonists he had a right to the highway, and that if they tried to stop him he and Calvin would have the law on them.

At least this episode had the effect of distracting

attention from James Whittaker and William Lee, who used the opportunity to ride off to Jeremiah Willard's house. They hurried inside while Jeremiah sat in the front doorway to stop their pursuers from entering. But the mob grabbed him by the feet and pulled him down the porch stairs, his head thumping against each of the steps in turn. They then broke into his house and dragged the elders out.

The assailants now decided to whip James and William. They threw David Meacham and Calvin Harlow on the ground and held them fast in order to stop them causing trouble, then tied James to a tree. Isaiah Whitney began beating him with a stick cut from the bushes, and soon James's back was 'all in a gore of blood, and the flesh bruised to a jelly'. Then they began on William. He chose to kneel to take his whipping, so he wasn't tied. This gave James the chance to emulate the courage shown by Eleazer Rand to James Shepherd the previous year – he leapt on William's back to protect *him*. Seeing this brave gesture, Bethiah Willard, who had followed from Jeremiah's, leapt on James's back in turn. She was severely beaten and scarred for the rest of her life, receiving one stroke in her face that turned both her eyes entirely black.

Calvin Harlow, who was still pinned to the ground, cried out: 'See how you have abused that woman; you have exposed yourselves to the law.' This time, perhaps, his point was taken because shortly afterwards the crowd dispersed.

While this was going on, back in the garden of Elijah Wilds's house, seven miles away, Mother Ann told

Hannah Kendall, 'The Elders are in great tribulation; for I hear Elder William's soul cry to Heaven.'

After the mob had dispersed Father James knelt down and sang a song. He and William then made their way back to the Willard house, collected their horses and returned to Shirley.

When they arrived, Ann asked, 'Did they abuse you, James?'

'I will show you, Mother,' James replied. He knelt before her and showed her his wounds. According to Elijah Wilds, he cried heartily and said, as he had done after the Black Guard attack, 'Father, forgive them, for they know not what they do.' He then turned to Ivory Wilds: 'Ivory, I could take as many more for you if it would do you any good.'

Then the elders knelt and prayed.

'James, this is the life of the gospel,' Ann told him.

In the nineteenth century a stone monument was put up to mark the spot where James's suffering took place: 'On this spot a Shaker was whip[p]ed by a mob for religious views in 1783', and the local Shakers paid tribute by placing stones round its base. According to Shaker legend, the tree to which James was tied shortly afterwards withered and died.

The leaders of the Harvard persecution, the 'Shaker drivers' as they came to be called, were to pay for their misdeeds in the fullness of time. Phineas Farnsworth suffered financial reversals, and had to move to a little house in Shirley; years later, when the Harvard Shaker community was established and prosperous, he was reduced to borrowing money from the very people he had mistreated. Similar problems befell the Houghton brothers. Even worse, and this would have vindicated the Shakers' dim view of marriage, Asa Houghton came into conflict with his wife, and their son had to intervene to stop them killing one another.

The life of the gospel it may have been, but this episode finally convinced Ann that her presence in the Harvard community was a catalyst for trouble, and early in July she and her elders began the long, slow journey back towards Niskeyuna, stopping at many of the other New England Shaker communities as they went. On this trek the twenty-four-year-old Hannah Kendall seems to have taken Mary Partington's place as Ann's personal companion. As they set out Hannah offered Ann a silk handkerchief to wear over her small cotton check one, perhaps as a last echo of the Kendall family's high fashion days. Ann wasn't seduced, however, replying that it was for 'young folks' to wear silk.

Jemima Blanchard went with them on the first leg of the journey. She rode horseback, much to Mother Ann's perturbation, since as an Englishwoman she wasn't used to women riding. When they were met by Hannah Simonds of Petersham, who was on horseback behind her husband, Ann got her to ride Jemima's horse instead, putting Jemima behind Samuel Fitch, believing a married woman riding alone was in less danger of molestation.

Their first port of call was David Hammond's house in Petersham, where the Black Guard attack had taken place.

They were quite a gathering: Ann, her elders, and believers from Harvard and other places who had chosen to travel with them. After they had been there for three days, a crowd returning from a funeral gathered outside and tried to get in. Hammond and others stood in the hall to bar them while James read from the guarantee of freedom of worship in the Bill of Rights, no doubt emphasising the irony that a Briton needed to remind Americans of the liberties which they had been fighting his own countrymen to protect.

Then Ann came downstairs and rebuked the mob, telling them of the abuse she and the elders had previously suffered in this place. She let some of them in and showed them a narrow chimney passage in an apartment at the rear of the house, telling them: 'They thrust me through there; it seemed as though they would press my soul out of my body; I was never so abused in all my life.'

The protesters withdrew for a while but sadly the history lesson did not arrest history's tendency to repeat itself and at dusk many of them returned 'with redoubled rage', breaking the windows of David Hammond's house with stones and assaulting some of the Shakers. A few of them got into the house, but then Mother Ann came to a bedroom window to face the fifty-odd people below. 'She was exceedingly powerful, and it seemed she intended they should understand that she did not stand in fear of them,' witnesses later claimed. On a number of occasions in the next year Ann was to show herself capable of a harsh sardonic humour, and from this upstairs vantage point, in a house where she had already suffered greatly, she felt moved to bring off an odd parody of a biblical text. Like many illiterate people she had a quick ear for the cadences and rhetorical strategies of the written word. 'The churning of milk bringeth forth butter,' she announced, 'and the wringing of the nose bringeth forth blood.' One can picture her, a sharp, streetwise Mancunian woman, pausing for effect before adding: 'Do you take care, lest some of you get your noses wrung.'

A man climbed on another's shoulders to get at her. Just as he was reaching up to the window, Hannah Kendall suddenly grabbed at him, crying, 'I'll wring *your* nose.'

The man recoiled straight away and slid down to the ground again.

It had been a good double-act. Hannah was a brave, outgoing person, known as 'friend Hannah, and sometimes valiant', and in due course she was to become joint leader, along with the equally redoubtable Eleazer Rand, of the Harvard–Shirley community.

The crowd now started throwing stones in at the windows. Ann ordered the Shakers to sing, which they did loudly, while some of them tried to reason with their opponents. Sarah Kendall, Hannah's sister, was hit on the head by a stone, and immediately began to bleed heavily. James Whittaker, not one to let a propaganda point go begging, told her to get a candle and show the mob what they had done. Before she could, a man called Benjamin Witt hit the hyperactive Aaron Wood on the head with a club, knocking him down so he lay on the ground apparently dead.

'Mark the man that killed that man!' James called out.

The Shakers picked up the apparent corpse and took a few steps towards the crowd, who immediately began to panic. 'Some ran one way and some another, clambering over fences and stone walls, the falling of which, in the confusion, made a great clattering, which was succeeded by three shouts from the Believers that made the woods echo.' The brethren brought Aaron into the house and laid him on the floor. Jemima later recalled: 'I had no idea but that he was dead, but he soon sprung up & went to dancing.' Having won the day, the Shakers put out the lights so that they could watch some of the rabble creep sheepishly back to get their horses, which they had left behind in their headlong flight.

The next evening the vigilantes were back and David Hammond's house was surrounded again by people hooting and jeering. The Shakers nevertheless continued with their singing, led by the diminutive Eleazer Rand, who stood himself provocatively in front of the window. A shot suddenly rang out, the bullet just missing Eleazer, who didn't 'break his song'. James Whittaker then began leaping, and the believers 'had a powerful time'.

Despite these successive triumphs, tensions inevitably developed among the embattled Shakers. Jemima Blanchard describes another meeting during the stay at Petersham when William Lee received 'a powerful gift of reproof' in which he felt moved to call upon the believers to 'wake up, and labor out of their fallen natures'. It is perhaps a sign of continued rivalry between the British old guard and the American upstarts that he seems to have aimed the reproof particularly in Eleazer's direction, speaking, as Jemima innocently puts it, as 'sharp to Father Eleazer as to any one'.

What happened next gives us another glimpse of an alien world. 'Father William was walking the floor, and the next time he came that way, as soon as he had turned from Father Eleazer, the latter jumped upon Father William's back, and he carried him across the room. We then went into a lively labor,' Jemima says, 'and I saw no more of him at that time.'

Strange though it is, one can figure out a kind of emotional logic behind this behaviour. External pressures and internal jealousies lead to an outburst of unrestrained moral criticism on the part of William. That in turn triggers what almost appears to be an aggressive act (which is also a reminder of previous bravery, of the time when Eleazer leapt on James Shepherd's back to defend him from a whipping, and thereby provides a justification of the status Eleazer has achieved in Ann's eyes – which, given William's obsessive devotion to his sister, is probably what put his nose out of joint in the first place). Eleazer's riposte is immediately converted into a cross between horseplay and ritual, which in turn brings in all the other believers, and the flicker of resentment and antagonism disappears in the general exuberance.

Jemima Blanchard gives us another insight, of a more private and personal kind, into Ann's world during this stay at Petersham. Ann had been working hard with Solomon Frizzle's family, some of whom were falling away from the faith. They had young children, for whom Ann felt a 'peculiar tenderness'. Jemima's bedroom was separated from Ann's by a lathed partition without plastering, and through it she heard Ann sorrowing to God all night 'with such fervent cries that it seemed as if it would break my heart . . . As she wept I heard her say, "O God, I am but a poor woman."' One can conjecture that through the long, miserable darkness Ann was re-enacting in her mind the loss of her biological as well as her spiritual children.

After a stay of twelve days, Ann and the elders continued westward, crossing the Connecticut River at Sunderland and arriving at Joseph Bennet's in New Providence where, the year before, the livestock had been depleted on account, it was thought, of the bestiality of one of the farmhands. They had a public meeting on the Sunday, and as usual it was followed by young people from the town surrounding the house and abusing them. One of the Shaker sisters began calling out, 'She is my Mother!' and William joined in, getting his usual odd frisson from the restructured relationship with his sister. This silenced the crowd outside, giving Ann the opportunity to shame them by reeling off their sins.

After a week Ann and her company went on to Samuel Fitch's house in Richmond, arriving on Thursday 24 July, and continuing to Daniel Goodrich's house in nearby Hancock in the middle of the following week. During her stay at Hancock she spoke on the subject of charity to the poor. Perhaps a memory stirred of the food riots in Manchester that took place the year before she became a Shaker. 'If I owned the whole world,' she said, 'I would turn it all into joyfullness: I would not say to the poor, *Be ye warmed, and be ye clothed,* without giving them wherewith to do it.' These sympathetic sentiments didn't ingratiate her with the locals, however. By the time of worship on Sunday 3 August, a hostile mob had established itself, and was bigger still by the Monday, making false accusations – 'their invention', according to Shaker witnesses, 'was very prolific'.

They were led by 'old Valentine Rathbun', the apostate who had already published a tract attacking the Shakers, and who was still bitter because so many of his family had remained in the fold. He came into the house and began to abuse Ann and the elders. His son Reuben followed him in and told him off for his insults. Valentine backed off through the door, but when he got outside he climbed up some steps, 'taking an advantageous position', and made full use of it by beating his son about the head with a large hickory staff, opening up a three-inch split in his scalp. The dazed Reuben eventually managed to wrest the staff from his father's grasp, take it into the house and throw it on the fire.

Eventually Ann slipped out of the back door into a waiting carriage and returned to Samuel Fitch's. After she had gone Titus Wright, one of the most vociferous of the vigilantes, approached William Lee and abused him. This was not a wise move. Despite his emotional vulnerability William's courage and toughness were never in doubt. He took no notice of the insults, but carried on with his spiritual labours, singing and shouting in his powerful voice. This imperviousness only made Wright raise the stakes. He told William that if he hadn't made himself scarce by the end of fifteen minutes he would 'split his brains out'.

William just gave him a hard look and said, 'You walking devil.' Then he turned away from him and continued to follow his 'gift'.

Wright held his ground, clutching a staff. The trouble with giving a specified time limit to a stand-off is that there is no way of skirting the moment of truth. When the fifteen minutes were up, Wright dropped his weapon and sneaked away.

The elders then left too. But the vigilantes followed, and gathered outside Samuel Fitch's house. The elders tried to reason with them but to no avail, and John Deming was hit on the head. The trouble again demoralised Ann. 'If God does not work for me, it seems as though the wicked would destroy me,' she said. Luckily she received a sign: 'I see a white hand, stretched out before me, which is a . . . promise of my protection.' The white hand, presumably at the opposite end of some iconographic axis from the man who was as black as a negro, failed to prevent a new trial, in the legal sense this time. Rathbun managed to get a warrant served on Ann, the elders, Elizur Goodrich, and Samuel and Dyer Fitch, alleging blasphemy and disorderly conduct.

Years later Daniel Rathbun, Valentine's brother, claimed in a pamphlet that the disorderly conduct charge related to drunkenness on the part of the Shaker leaders, asserting Ann and William in particular were often red-faced with drink. It's a difficult allegation to investigate at this distance in time. When first-generation Shakers were asked for their reminiscences in 1827, they were specifically requested to deal with the issue, and so one after the other repeats a denial, with the counterproductive effect of giving the reader the impression that there must have been some sort of fire to generate so much smoke. On the other hand, there is no reason to doubt the sincerity and honesty of most of the contributors, and some of their specific assertions have the ring of truth about them. Phebe Chase, for example, explains at some length that Ann was not a 'wine-bibber' and that, contrary to what detractors had claimed, 'I never saw the least appearance of intoxication in her, from first to last; nor did I ever see her make any intemperate use of ardent spirits of any kind; indeed I cannot recollect that I ever saw her make use of any at all.' Even more tellingly, Zipporah Cory explains that her father was a drunkard, so that 'even the very smell of rum has ever been nauseous and disgusting to me from my earliest infancy . . . But I never saw any ardent spirits where Mother Ann was, nor did I ever smell any there; and I am confident that I should have smelled it if any had been there'.

It seems unlikely that Ann and the elders would have been able to keep up their prodigious workrate, and convert so many idealistic young New Englanders, if they had been habitually the worse for drink. Moreover, the central features of Shaker worship – talking in tongues, recounting visions, wild dancing, head-shaking and uncontrolled movements of all kinds – were very likely to have reminded observers of drunken behaviour, as was pointed out by Mary Hocknell, the Cheshire girl who had followed Ann through thick and thin from the age of twelve.

Perhaps, in the end, the issue, like that of nakedness, is a bit of a red herring. If drink was sometimes used as an aid to exuberant worship, or as a consolation in times of persecution and struggle, this doesn't compromise the Shaker vision or cast doubt on the leaders' integrity.

The accused were summoned to appear next day at Richmond meeting-house, before Samuel Brown and J. Woodbridge of Stockbridge and James Gates of Richmond, Justices of the Peace. Ann herself spent the night in custody in James Gates's own house where, with typical cheek, she appeared in an upstairs window and 'sung a very lively melodious song' to the believers down below.

The Shaker version of the hearing is that the disorderly conduct charge in effect amounted to an accusation of fomenting the very mobs that were persecuting them. As for blasphemy, the prosecution alleged that Samuel Fitch had declared that the Godhead dwelt bodily in Ann Lee. James Whittaker briefed him on his defence: 'We read in the Scriptures that the fulness of the Godhead dwelt in our Lord Jesus Christ bodily: And again, Except Christ be in you ye are reprobates.' QED, as the magistrates realised. Nevertheless, echoing Ann's own words of two years previously, they concluded that the Shakers 'must be taken care of, or they would turn the world upside down', fined them $20 apiece on the disorderly conduct charge, and ordered them to leave the state.

The Shaker leaders paid their fine on the spot, but reserved the right to stay put. The local accused, Samuel and Dyer Fitch and Elizur Goodrich, were required to give bonds for good behaviour pending an appearance at the county court in Barrington. They refused on the grounds that they had the right to worship God in their own houses, but as far as the court was concerned this would constitute the breaking of the bond on each occasion. They were therefore remanded to Barrington Jail.

Ann and her elders were released. The other side of notoriety is popularity, and the Shakers had received so much local publicity that, on the Sabbath, three of the Goodrich houses, Nathan's, Daniel's and Ezekiel's, had to be requisitioned for worship. In the middle of the following week Ann and her elders appeared at Barrington Jail. 'We have come to see Christ in prison,' Ann announced, making a tart reference to the issue of the Christ-spirit that had been debated in court.

A couple of days later, she resumed her travels. In due course, the charge of blasphemy against the Barrington inmates was dropped on constitutional grounds. Valentine Rathbun brought a new charge of assault and battery against them, for which they were fined a token $1 apiece, plus the court costs, which amounted to '20 pound lawful', presumably because of their refusal to submit to a bond. They were released and given time to pay, which they did.

Meanwhile, Ann and her entourage were staying with Elijah Slosson at West Stockbridge. So many people – both believers and the 'world' – attended on the Sabbath that the meeting had to take place out of doors. A hundred horses were held on Elijah's pasture, and over two hundred people were fed, but in both cases supplies were miraculously replenished, so that one J.H., a tavern-keeper who lived next door, complained. 'How is it?' he asked. 'I keep a tavern and have to pay [be paid] for all I dispose of, and yet I can but just get along. You must have much more company than I do, and entertain them upon free cost, and yet you always have a fulness.' It's the miracle of loaves and fishes again, adapted to an American farming landscape.

Ann and the elders then returned to Hancock, where Ezekiel Goodrich had suddenly died. Ann had a vision, or at least the aural equivalent of one, in which she heard Ezekiel continuing his ministry in the afterlife. 'I heard Ezekiel's voice roar from one prison to another, preaching to the dead.' On Saturday 23 August, Ann's party set off for New Lebanon. In the late morning they arrived at Israel Tallcott's, about halfway between Hancock and New Lebanon, and found Abigail Tallcott cooking a little pot of meat and vegetables over her fire.

Ann told her: 'You must get dinner for us, and all that are with us.'

'Then I must boil more meat and sauce,' Abigail replied.

' "Nay," said Mother, "there is a plenty." '

It was the miracle again, perhaps with an admixture of hospital catering, as Ann remembered strategies of earlier days. What makes the anecdote interesting is the number involved: forty people in all, so it must have been quite a procession wending its way westward. Later that day, the party arrived at New Lebanon, and went from house to house in celebration. Three years previously while in jail in Albany, Ann had promised John Bishop she would visit him in his house, and now she kept her word, going from one room to another singing, 'Now Mother is come! Mother is come now!' One can still catch her exuberance, and her ability to provide a sense of occasion – as well as her talent for orchestrating her own welcome.

On the following Tuesday, at Reuben White's house, James Whittaker sang and danced powerfully. After dinner, Ann was heading out of the room when she suddenly turned and knelt down. She then gave a kind of résumé of her spiritual life, in prayer form, going through her conversion and confession, her imprisonments and her journey to America: 'I crossed the great waters, through many dangers and perils, and by the miraculous power of God I arrived safe to this land.' She thanked the Lord for raising up so many people in America. There was something resonant and elegiac about her testimony on this occasion which led later Shakers to compare it with Christ's prayer in the upper chamber in Jerusalem, before the betrayal of Gethsemane.

Over the next days, she continued her visits to Shakers in New Lebanon and its surroundings, followed by singing believers, and the usual antagonistic crowds demanding 'to see the old woman'. They broke into John Spier's house and crowded round the doorway of a room where the Shakers had assembled. Ann was in the middle, holding a young child of Nathan Farrington's in her arms. She decided, with typically cantankerous bravery, that she had a gift to go into another room, and told the infant's sister, Mehitabel Farrington, to go through the hall and stop for no one. Ann followed: she was as adept, as she had proved in David Meacham's house, at parting hostile crowds as Moses was at parting the Red Sea.

The following day a fateful meeting occurred: Eleazer Grant, Elisha Gilbert and a Dr Averill came to call. If Ann's prayer at Reuben White's heralded her Gethsemane, then Eleazer Grant was to play a portmanteau role in the unfolding passion, half Pontius Pilate, half Judas Iscariot. Ann continued to be in a retrospective mood, talking in detail to the apparently sympathetic listeners about her experiences in England.

A couple of days after this meeting several Indians appeared and William Lee was able to communicate with them in their own language. Soon after, on Friday 29 August, Ann was in ebullient form at Nathan Farrington's nearly completed house. 'Now Mother is come, and you are welcome; you have been faithful to ask, and now you have got a blessing,' she told him, defining the benediction of her presence. Then she turned and gave a good telling-off to Daniel Rathbun's daughter, because though Ann had been all round her father's house, she had never been invited inside: 'While here is a family [the Farringtons], that was so urgent, that it seemed as though I could not get away from them. You know not what a blessing you have lost.'

That weekend was spent at Jebez Spencer's in Stephentown. On the Sunday they were warned by a certain Captain Ichabod Turner that a mob was gathering. The elders assured him they would be off the next day. In the meantime, they began to worship when 'some carnal young men, with their female companions, drew near, and in a scoffing manner, said to some of the brethren, "What, are you dancing to worship God?" '

The elders said they were, and invited the young people to join them.

First the boys, keen to show off, began to dance, no doubt exaggerating, insofar as was possible, the Shaker contortions. Then their girlfriends joined in as well.

What happened next is like something out of Hans Andersen or the Brothers Grimm, where seven-league boots and dancing shoes tend to have a life of their own. Having started dancing, the young people found they couldn't stop. 'They were soon surrounded by the brethren and sisters; and so great was the strength and power of God in the assembly, that they were unable to make any resistance; but were compelled to dance . . . with the head-dresses and hair of the young women flying in every direction, until they were brought down to feel very low and simple; and went off peacable and well mortified.'

Dance was the Shakers' medium: they knew how to use it as a weapon.

On the evening of Monday 1 September, Ann and her party left Jebez's to return to New Lebanon. It was very dark. Ann and Hannah Kendall were in a carriage drawn by two horses. When Eliab Harlow came galloping up out of the night, Ann asked him to let someone else take care of his own horse so that he could lead one of hers along the rough track, while another brother took the bridle of the other animal and Childs Hamlin held on to the carriage at the rear. Thus they wended their way through the darkness, which in late-eighteenth-century America must have been almost absolute, with scant habitation in the rolling hills and forests and no lighting available except candles.

'Brethren be comfortable,' Ann kept calling to her invisible followers, 'brethren be joyful.'

'We will, Mother,' they called back.

To keep their spirits up they sang and shouted so loudly they made the forests ring. It must have chilled the marrow of the lonely farmers in their dark houses.

After a journey of eight miles, Ann and her party arrived at Isaac Harlow's, in New Lebanon. Inevitably, they had a strenuous meeting to celebrate, and things got a little out of hand, with the brethren inveigling themselves in among the sisters and snatching and tugging them about. The Daniel Rathbuns, father and son, were in the forefront of these indiscretions – a sign of their apostasy to come, and, in the more immediate future, a portent, according to Ann, of another outbreak of mob violence. Amazingly, in the early hours of the morning Ann decided to continue her journey, and along with Hannah Kendall, Lucy Wood and the elders, went another mile to George Darrow's house.

They had travelled right into a trap.

As dawn broke, Darrow's house came under attack. A party led by a former militia captain, Thomas Tanner, approached from the north-west, while another under the command of Nehemiah Finch arrived from the south. A warrant was served on George Darrow and David Meacham, charging them with abusing Meacham's daughter.

According to the Shakers themselves this was a cynical strategy to get them out of the house, but we must always remember that theirs was an unbending faith which consistently set itself against normal family relationships. Nevertheless, as far as they were concerned, all the events of 2 September were pre-planned by the malignant genius of Eleazer Grant, before whom, in his capacity as magistrate, Darrow and Meacham were now brought for trial.

Before being taken off to the New Lebanon courthouse, George Darrow put his property in the charge of his brother David and friend Richard Spier, and these two now tried to keep the 'outrageous and horrid mob' at bay, but to no avail. The kitchen door was apparently a floor up from ground-level, and Spier himself was thrown from it three times; other believers were pulled from the house's three doorways by their hair, clothing, arms or legs, and deposited in a nearby mud-puddle. After a struggle lasting fifteen minutes, the attackers broke into the house like 'furious tygers'.

Forty years later some of the intruders swore affidavits to the effect that Ann was so drunk she had no idea what was happening. In reply Rachel Spencer wrote her own account of that night, saying that Ann showed no sign at all of drink. After a long meeting she helped Rachel and a number of the sisters prepare breakfast in George Darrow's kitchen. When the mob attacked, she was whisked off by some of the brethren; Rachel and the other women were beaten and thrown through the kitchen door one after the other.

Ann was concealed in a partitioned-off back bedroom, with brethren guarding it. The assailants made short work of them, however, tearing down the partition and dragging Ann out by her feet, as on several occasions before. They pulled her all the way through the parlour and the kitchen to the raised door. Eliab Harlow had had the presence of mind to get her carriage into position, and Ann was simply hurled head-first into it. Hannah Kendall and Lucy Wood pushed through the throng to get in with her. Prudence Hammond, a twenty-three-year-old sister, came out of the house with Ann's budget, or handbag, and Ann asked her to come with them on the enforced journey to Eleazer Grant's courthouse. There was no room in the carriage, so Prudence and Eliab went on foot beside it.

After they had gone just a few yards, some vindictive lout cut the reins. Eliab went up, took the horse by its head and tried to lead it by hand, but he was dragged away and beaten, meanly, on the throat. One of his attackers, Selah Abbot, later died suddenly; Shakers were always careful to record the balance of their accounts. Some of the rabble then took over the task of towing the horse along by its head. They tried to beat Prudence away from the side of the carriage, but Ann kept her going, repeating, 'Prudence, keep along with us, don't let your faith fail.'

One young man declared in admiration: 'It's the power of God that carries that woman along, in such a manner.' He then tried to capitalise on his praise by inviting Prudence up on his horse, but Ann had her eye on him: 'Prudence, don't be enticed by them.' Obediently Prudence turned down the offer, and carried on running beside the carriage, 'a strangely thrilling experience to the young girl', according to a later Shaker historian.

After a while they came to a steep slope from which a narrow bridge arched out over the river below. Some of the attackers, led by Thomas Law, tried to overturn the carriage, but Medad Curtis grappled with them and Law himself fell down the slope. 'I should have finished the old woman,' he complained subsequently, 'if it had not been for that devil of a Medad.' Half a mile further on he tried to take his revenge, grabbing James Whittaker and attempting to pull him off his horse so that he would brain himself on a rock. One of the Shaker brothers managed to skew him around as he fell, and he hit his chest instead.

Thomas Law: became a vagabond; died in his sleep without warning.

When they arrived at Grant's courthouse, Ann was dragged out of the carriage so roughly she lost her cap and apron. James then asked her if he could make a formal complaint about Law's assault on him, asserting he'd fractured three ribs. Perhaps aware of his tendency to assume the worst of his physical injuries, Ann told James to let it pass, and sure enough he recovered almost immediately.

An odd incident happened in the mêlée outside the courthouse. One man was being particularly offensive, and Hannah Kendall suddenly shouted at him, 'Go off, for you are a thief and a robber.' It may have been that she'd heard rumours or comments to this effect while they travelled along. Threateningly, the man told her to prove her words.

Ann now showed her talent for dramatic improvisation

(and for defusing an awkward situation) by calling out, 'Where is that Hammond girl?'

Prudence stepped forward.

Ann said, 'Hannah has called this man a thief and a robber, and he says she shall prove it.'

Realising it had become her job to get them out of a tight spot, Prudence covered for Hannah, though she didn't know the man concerned. As it happened, her father had just been burgled. 'It is the truth of God, Mother,' she said, 'for he broke into my father's house, and stole twenty-nine dollars.'

Infuriated, the man struck Prudence with a staff, but the extremeness of his response was a give-away. His cronies, who knew about the theft, all burst into laughter: she had fingered the guilty party by pure chance.

When the trial of George Darrow and David Meacham had petered out, Ann was brought before Eleazer Grant. She must have been mortified at the thought that while she had been confiding her spiritual travails to him, all he had been taking on board was that she was a troublemaker, jail-bait on two continents. Instead of answering his charges, she rebuked Grant for abusing his position as a magistrate. As punishment for this *lèse-majesté*, the constable, John Noyes, hit her a severe blow across her bosom with his staff. Her response is another of those moments when her words carry to us through the static of the past. 'It is your day now; but it will be mine by and by, Eleazer Grant,' she told him. 'I'll put you into a cockle-shell yet.'

Grant decided it would be best to get Ann out of the court while he deliberated on the case, so he sent her off to a new house he was building for himself, in the custody of John Noyes and two other men deputed by the court, Ephraim Bowman and Enos Meacham. They manhandled her on the way, so she cried out, 'Must I give up my life into your hands?'

When she got to the house she was shoved into a room, where she sat down and cried like a child.

The crowd surrounded the house, but William and several of the Shaker sisters managed to push their way through. Other believers joined the press of people outside. William's arrival lifted Ann's spirits, and brother and sister went to a window and sang to their followers outside, who responded by dancing. This enraged an elderly man called Asahel King so much that he struck one of the Shakers a heavy blow on the head with his cane.

A Shaker brother was asked to go off to a nearby well to get some water for Ann. He dipped a bowl, and took it back to the house. As he went inside, people in the crowd called out, 'There goes the grog.' Elizabeth Williams, who witnessed this episode, later gave it as an example of how false accusations of Shaker drinking were spread around.

While Ann was held in the house, some of the sisters asked Eleazer Grant's wife to give her food, and like the tavern-keeper's wife following the Black Guard incident, she showed some female sympathy, and obliged.

Eventually Ann was taken back before Grant, and bound over to the county court to keep the peace. David Meacham and George Darrow stood as bondsmen for her appearance. Ann then went out to her carriage. Grant followed her to the door of the court. 'As a magistrate of the state of New York,' he told the crowd outside, 'I desire that there be no mobs or riots.' Then, mischievously, he added, 'Lay hands suddenly on *no man*', emphasising the last two words and repeating the command several times till its implication sank in. The mob then felt free to take over Ann's carriage and they drove her out of town, careering along a rough and muddy road and beating back the Shakers who tried to catch up with them.

The punishment meted out to Eleazer Grant himself was ultimately even more severe. In due course he went 'under a blast': he lost the use of his fingers, then his hands, and confessed to some of the Shakers that he was getting into Ann Lee's cockle-shell at last. As his illness, which may have been Parkinson's disease, developed, his head began to shake so violently that he made involuntary noises with his mouth. Finally, he was unable to have sex with his wife. The Shakers ticked off each item, and gave their acid verdict: 'Thus he became a Shaker in judgement.'

At dusk, Ann and her oppressors drew up outside a tavern. The owner, a man called Ranny, came out and, disgusted at what he saw, berated the crowd for their behaviour. The ringleaders decided it was time to go in any case, but when they tried to take the local Shakers back to New Lebanon with them, they refused to come. A little way beyond Ranny's tavern a log cabin lived in by a poor man called Charles McCarthy. He put up all the believers he could squeeze in, and the rest

slept in an old barn, where they spent a cold and muddy
night.

The next morning the believers cleared some rubbish
from in front of the barn and held a tearful meeting. James
said: 'If these should hold their peace, I believe the very
stones would cry out to God.' After breakfast Ann showed
the followers the bruises she'd received, at least the ones
that could be decently displayed. The sisters vouched for
the others. In a lifetime of adversity, this was perhaps the
lowest point. 'So it has been with me almost continually,
ever since I left Niskeyuna; day and night – day and night,
I have been like a dying creature.'

That afternoon, Ann and the elders returned to Nathan
Farrington's new house. On arrival, Ann felt more secure.
'I feel as though I could take some rest,' she told her
host. As the evening came on, however, people were seen
gathering around the house. They were mostly young men
from the town of Chatham who were known as the 'Indian
club' on account of their violence. They demanded to see
'that old woman'.

Nathan Farrington asked them why.

'She is an old witch,' they told him, 'and she shall not
stay here.'

Nathan told them she was a woman of God, and forbad
them to see her.

Ann wept. 'This comes sudden upon me,' she said.
'What shall I do? I do not feel as though I could endure
any more.'

The vigilantes began to throw stones at the house.
Because the building work wasn't quite finished, they

were able to force some loose boards out, but the brethren on guard still kept them at bay.

'John,' Ann asked Nathan's eldest son, 'can't you go and send these creatures off?'

'Yes, Mother,' he replied.

'Go and shame them. Tell them it is a shame for men to be round, after a woman, in the night; but if they will go off, and come tomorrow peaceably, in the day-time, I will see them.'

John went downstairs and was immediately waylaid by two 'lusty ruffians'. His response was quintessentially Shaker.

'Love,' he said.

'Love,' the men sneered back, and took such tight hold of him they nearly squeezed the breath out of his body.

When their grip slackened off a little, John gasped out, 'More love.'

They squeezed all the harder.

When they finally got tired of it, John said, 'Now, if you have got through, I want to reason with you.' Then he gave them Ann's message.

His stoicism, or the appeal to reason, seemed to do the trick. Perhaps they'd just got bored. Anyway, the rabble had had enough for that night, and dispersed.

The next day only six or eight of them turned up. Ann and several of the sisters went out to meet them. John indulged in some light wordplay: 'This is the woman that you pressed so hard to see last night.'

'What do you want of me?' Ann asked. 'I am a poor weak woman – I do not hurt anybody.'

This made them ashamed, and they began to 'sheer off'. Since it was a firm principle of the Shakers never to relinquish the moral high ground, John invited them to breakfast, but they continued on their way.

At ten o'clock, Ann left Nathan Farrington's on the last leg of her journey. She told the local Shakers not to come with her and her elders because of the danger of triggering more hostility. After a few miles, her horse lost a shoe. They stopped at a blacksmith's belonging to a certain Johnson on White's hill. William asked if he would set the shoe, and in reply Johnson threw a pair of tongs at him, so hard they sank nearly six inches into the earth between his feet. He then announced he'd kill them all if they didn't leave at once.

They made their way as best they could to Ebenezer Knapp's, about a mile further on. His wife Mary and daughter Hannah were converts, and Ebenezer himself was sympathetic to Shakerism. Hannah had hurried home from Nathan Farrington's house to prepare a welcome for them. About twenty minutes later Johnson appeared with a gang of about twenty, all armed with cudgels and whips.

Food had been prepared for the Shakers, but they didn't dare sit down, so ate a few mouthfuls on their feet. Hannah, though young and shy, was so furious that they weren't able to enjoy their meal that she cried out, 'If there was a company of drunkards, whoremongers and whores gathered here to serve the devil, you would not come to drive *them* away.' William joined her on the porch and announced, 'We come here peaceably to refresh ourselves, and we will stay as long as we have a mind to, and do you resist us if you dare.'

Despite the brave words, Ann and the elders left shortly afterwards. One of the mob tried to grab the horse's reins, but Hannah Kendall, who was sitting beside Ann as usual, said, 'Let the horse alone. I am able to drive him myself.' The would-be attackers gave them no more trouble after that.

When they reached the ferry opposite Albany, some Indians were waiting there. They, at least, were welcoming. 'The good woman is come! The good woman is come,' they cried out.

The Shakers crossed the river and travelled through the woods north-west of the town. They stopped in a clearing for a rest, and then continued on their way to Niskeyuna, arriving there at eleven o'clock in the evening of 4 September 1783, the day after the signing of the Peace of Paris had brought the American War of Independence to its triumphant conclusion.

Ann had spent two years and three months on her mission, one year of which was passed at Harvard and Shirley. As the Shaker record has it: 'Mother and the Elders travelled many hundred miles, and suffered indescribable hardships, afflictions, and persecutions, to establish the gospel in this land, and lay the foundation of Christ's Kingdom on earth. Most of the Believers in America had a privilege to see her, either by being visited at their own habitations, or by visiting her where she tarried'. She had been to thirty-six towns and villages, and had established a spiritual community of around a thousand souls.

Now her travels, astounding in their range and enterprise for a woman of her class and time, had come to an end. She had one year left to live.

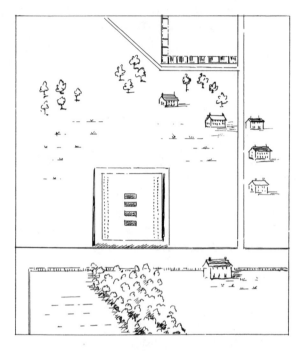

The graveyard in the Watervliet Shaker
community, where Ann's body was buried in
the mid-nineteenth century.

12

Beautiful Messenger

Ann had finished her travels, but her followers still made pilgrimages to her. A group from Harvard did the trip later that year in severe winter weather. Every now and then their sledge would get stuck in the snow, and they would have to get out and walk for a while. Each time this happened their clothes got so frozen they stood in a huddle like so many emperor penguins in order to thaw them out with body heat. At one point they had to stop at a believer's house so as to warm their feet up.

When they arrived at Niskeyuna, Ann, in motherly mode, packed them all off to bed for two hours before they were given a meal and went into meeting. At breakfast the next morning she and the elders waited on the pilgrims in person. Of course, the gesture affirms the very hierarchy it apparently contradicts. Two days later normal life resumed. Jemima Blanchard and another of the Harvard contingent, Lucy Prescott, were assigned kitchen duties. Conditions were still primitive in the overcrowded log building, and the two women had to stand on planks laid upon blocks because water came in over the floor.

One day while Jemima and Lucy were at work, they were both suddenly propelled by the power of God to turn round and fall on their knees in the water. John Hocknell, who had taken responsibility over affairs at Niskeyuna during part of the time Ann was on her mission, was standing in the doorway. He smiled, and said, 'What is the matter. I did but cast my mantle [the shadow of his cape] upon you. You don't mind the water.'

It's a tableau of two awestruck young American women paying homage to an English elder.

Another party of six Shakers arrived from Enfield, Connecticut. By December, the believers were 'taking their lodgings on the floor'. Elizabeth Wood, who had once wanted to shoot Ann with a silver bullet, recorded that after an all-night meeting everybody lay down at sunrise on the straw-covered floor to grab a little sleep. They were so squashed together that if 'one turned over all had to turn also', just as in the children's rhyme. Because the weather was so cold and people were coming in and out all the time, Ann told Thomas Pratt, 'Here, you may be a doorkeeper. You may stand and keep the door shut the day over.'

Ann was as busy as ever, and kept a tight rein on everybody. Elizabeth Wood knitted muffets (gloves) for William Lee and made slippers for Mary Partington. While she was at work one day, Ann came in and noticed that Hannah Knapp was wearing a handkerchief that hadn't been hemmed. 'Take off your handkerchief and make it,' she told her. 'You had never ought to wear a garment before it is made.'

Then she walked over to another sister and asked, 'What are you at work on? And who is it for?'

'Molly Freedom,' the sister replied.

'Where is she? Bring her forward.'

When Molly appeared, Ann said, 'We sent for you to come and work for us, but you bring work and set others at work, do you? Here, take your work and sit down, and do it yourself before you do anything for us.'

A similarly illuminating anecdote, and one which miraculously preserves the cadences of Ann's no-nonsense Manchester voice, comes from Amos Buttrick, one of the Harvard Shakers who had travelled over to work at Niske-yuna. His job was chopping wood, and he describes coming back to the dwelling-house one Saturday afternoon after his week's work. Because Sunday was not far off, he had automatically composed a serious face for himself, and Ann's sharp eyes picked it up.

'A'a't on you! [perhaps "Ah! out on you!"]' she exclaimed with her tight northern vowels. 'Here you have been bright and lively all the week, and now because it is Saturday afternoon you have got an antiChristian face on. When there is any reproof for the old heavens you are all oiled over so that it don't stick to you, because you never made a profession of religion, but I'll have you know that your old religion sticks tighter to you than the shirt on your back.'

Often Shaker testimonies credit Ann, and James Whit-taker for that matter, with closely reasoned theological argument that conveys no sense of the spoken voice. Here, though, we catch a racy idiom and a sharp human percep-tion. Amos likes to disclaim any responsibility for the errors of conventional Christianity because Shakerism was the first religion that he ever properly professed; but he is still enough of a puritan to succumb to Sunday gloom. Ann's authentic voice similarly sneaks through to us on another, undated occasion, when a convert called Stephen Cleverly made the point to her that some philosophers believe that all evil is really good. 'Mother named over many sins that were committed, & said, "Are not them evils?" She was no gram[m]arian, but she spoke with such power, I could not gainsay a word.'

Of course, despite Ann's rebuke to Amos, Shakerism had its own gloomy side. Nathan Tiffany reported that on one occasion the closely compacted sleepers woke up to hear Ann experiencing a dark night of the soul. She was labouring with the dead. 'Come, O ye dead!' she kept crying, 'Come, O ye dead!' She addressed the dark shades in unknown tongues as well. Then she told the elders, 'I feel the jaws of death grasping upon the people – they do not know what we have to go through. I believe you had better call them, and have them go into labours.'

In fact, all-night meetings became the norm, usually stopping at cock-crow, so that the believers could rest till the sun was up, when they had broth for breakfast (with the same to look forward to for supper). During one of these all-night sessions Elizabeth Wood received the gift to spin, and Ann said to William, 'See the bright Angels turning her now.' On another occasion Ann came in among the sisters, raised her hands, and shouted. The sisters gathered round, and hugged and kissed her. Elizabeth Wood knelt down and kissed her feet. Then Ann raised her hands and said, 'Now let me go.'

Receiving the homage of the sisterhood must have been

an extraordinary experience for the girl from Toad Lane. It is true that she tended to balk at assuming supreme authority. Abijah Worster records that he once said to her, 'Mother is my Saviour', and she replied, 'Abijah, you must be careful how you speak. It is Mother in a Saviour and a Saviour in a Mother.' Nevertheless, she dreamed frequently that Christ was her lover, and that they walked in sweet valleys together. The nineteenth-century Shaker Frederick Evans quoted Psalm 45: 'My heart is indicting a good matter: I speak of the things which I have made touching the king . . . King's daughters were among thy honourable women: upon thy right hand did stand the queen in gold of Ophir . . . She shall be brought unto the king in raiment of needlework: the virgins her companions that follow her shall be brought unto thee.'

'No one disputes,' he comments, 'that the King refers to Jesus; but *who* is the *Queen* that stood at his right hand?' At that moment in Niskeyuna, with the sisters embracing Ann and Elizabeth Wood kissing her feet, that question receives its answer.

As winter turned to spring, both Ann and William became ill. One day, Elizabeth Wood was doing some washing in an outbuilding when Ann came in. 'See how sick I am, and how I have puked,' she told her. Of course, for her, illness itself had to have a spiritual meaning. 'I am under great sufferings for some that are coming here,' she went on, 'and they will be here soon.' Elizabeth took this to mean that the new arrivals would prove to be backsliders in due course.

William was confined to bed at this point, but that same afternoon he got up to attend the meeting. Afterwards, though, he had to return to his sickbed. Ann, ill herself, was tense and resentful about the way he was being treated. 'Here is William,' she said, 'under great sufferings, but there are some here now that don't care any more about it than they do for the cocks crowing and the hens cackling.'

The atmosphere became melancholy. When the time came for the Enfield party to leave, William came out and said farewell. 'Desiring us to return home and be faithful,' Elizabeth Wood reports, 'he expressed great thankfulness for the way of God with tears running down his cheeks.'

William grew progressively weaker, and began to bring up 'large mouthfuls of clear fresh blood'. This could have been symptomatic of an ulcer or haemorrhage, but since the illness didn't come to an immediate crisis it is more likely to have had its origin in the lungs, which suggests consumption – hardly surprising, perhaps, given the hardships he had endured. He died a Shaker's death. Though not gifted in public speaking he had always been proud of his fine singing voice. 'He would sometimes go out of doors and his voice would seem to fill the air,' Jemima Blanchard said. Now he could no longer sing, but he asked Aaron Wood to sing for him. With that curious return of energy which is sometimes noted in advanced tuberculosis (if that's what it was) and which receives its most famous artistic celebration in Verdi's *La Traviata*, William got up from his bed and for a few minutes danced to Aaron's singing with great zeal. Then he lay down again and

shortly afterwards died, at about six o'clock in the afternoon of 21 July 1784, in the forty-fifth year of his age.

At the funeral the brothers walked two by two on the
right hand of the coffin, the sisters two by two on the left.
Over the grave, James Whittaker said, 'He has been the
most violent man against sin that ever my eyes beheld,
and if such a one is not saved, I do not know who can
be.' The slight uncertainty of this rhetorical structure suggests the anxiety and trauma William's death had brought
his fellow-Shakers.

How Ann herself behaved at the funeral isn't recorded.
Several Shaker apostates claimed that she and William
fought violently at times in their last phase of life together.
If this is true, it testified just as readily to their closeness
as to their hostility. Shaker observers record that she was
devastated by his death, and ascribe her own, coming just
six weeks later, to grief. Given that Shakerism set itself
to destroy family relationships and replace them with spiritual ones, there is no reason for witnesses to exaggerate
or sentimentalise the bond between brother and sister.
From our distance in time, with our post-Freudian
acknowledgement of unconscious motivation, speculation
becomes tempting. Just as Ann's loss of her children could
have been a factor in her hostility to sexual intercourse,
one can go one step further and wonder if the massive
restructuring of human relationships brought about by
Shakerism could have something to do with enabling William to call his sister his mother, and to love her with an
intensity that could only be justifiable if the subject sat
at the Lord's right hand. Ann herself did not need to rejig

the terminology of her relationship with William. 'Brother William is calling me,' she apparently said many times in the interval between his death and hers. 'Brother William is gone, and it will soon be said of me, that I am gone too.'

The testimony of first-generation American Shakers, collected years later, is inevitably going to be at its least reliable in its account of Ann's utterances during this last period. When she was in the thick of action, travelling from place to place, coping with mobs and confronting the representatives of law and order, there are names and dates and places to provide a convincing ballast of details – reports from believers that normally more or less coincide, and sometimes affidavits from the persecutors themselves to establish that certain events did happen, even if alternative perspectives on them are being offered. But as far as these last weeks are concerned all we have are the believers' accounts of their Mother's last words; and those believers, at the time they put pen to paper, had spent decades in a religious structure that in certain respects was radically different from the one Ann bequeathed, and yet which owed its legitimacy to her example.

Indeed, one can go a step further. Ann Lee did not bequeath a structure at all. She led a charismatic religion which expressed a sense that the final stage of human destiny was currently being enacted, and held that the absolute imperative was to harvest the souls of the living and the dead. It was a religion that believed history was coming to an end, and which therefore offered a point of view outside the temporal process. The Shakers of the nineteenth century, by contrast, lived within a conceptual structure which, however eccentric, showed a fundamental similarity with the mainstream Christian churches: it saw its task as continuing through time, as necessitating the accommodation of spiritual absolutes to historical contingency. Shakerism had become an institution, and an institution has to have a foundation. Ann Lee was needed to provide that foundation, though in fact her conception of Shakerism died with her. The true founder of Shakerism as it is nowadays usually studied and understood was her successor-but-one, Joseph Meacham. It is hardly surprising, therefore, that the Shaker annals insist that in her last days Ann prophesied his succession.

Jonathan Slosson reports that in the summer of 1784, Ann took Joseph Meacham by the hand, and while the two of them walked the floor, announced: 'I see the glories of God in vision and revelation of things to come. Joseph is my first Bishop; he is my apostle in the ministry; my first bishop; what he does, I do! I see the glories of God shine in his face! Joseph! My son Joseph! I feel my time short! I speak that you might understand.'

In fact, Meacham is a shadowy figure at this time. After his initial vital role in delivering the New Light Stir converts, we merely glimpse him going off on missions to remote corners of New England, important work surely, but duties that kept him at a remove from the central drama of early Shakerism. It was quite obvious that James Whittaker would take over the leadership after Ann's death. He had been her most important disciple ever since the early days in Manchester; he played the major part in conducting Shaker meetings; he was her principal spokesman with the authorities; he seems to have exercised much of the moral leadership, and provided the spiritual discipline, of the sect. Whatever happened, he was always there. He was considerably younger than Joseph Meacham, and there was on the face of it no reason to suppose that his interregnum would be short (in fact it only lasted three years before his own death in 1787 at the age of thirty-six). Ann could not have known there would so soon be a vacancy for Joseph Meacham. Unless, of course, she did utter divinely inspired prophecies.

If so, she also foresaw a number of other major developments. Twenty years after her death the Shakers were to take advantage of a religious revival in Kentucky to establish an important base in the region. According to the annals, during her last weeks Ann prophesied this opening of the gospel in the south-west. Similarly, and perhaps more convincingly, she is also credited with proclaiming the future leadership of Lucy Wright, who had already demonstrated her resourceful nature. At the same time she continued to have direct, immediate and provocative visions. Once when she was with Cornelius Thayer and William Scales she said, 'I saw William Scales in vision, writing that which was not according to the simplicity of the gospel; and the evil spirits hovered round him, and administered evil to him. They looked like crows.' In a beatific mood, she said to another brother, 'I see two golden candlesticks, and they stand by each of your legs, and they reach up to your knees.' To a sister she said, 'I see your mouth set open with a wheel of glory.' She might have been describing herself, since the vision reconciles her concept of spiritual travel with her status as Ann the Word. It is through such images – evil spirits like crows, candlesticks up to a man's knees, a mouth set open with a wheel – that we gain access to the strange spiritual world of the early Shakers. Perhaps the most charming of Ann's mystical perceptions occurred when she was talking to Zeruah Clark, the woman who had been forced to make her confession in front of her husband. On this occasion Ann explained the significance of those dust motes that one sees spinning and catching the light in a sunny room: 'When you see little bright lights, like stars, be thankful to God: for they are the specks of angels' wings.'

As her health failed, Ann could still be formidable and wonderfully impressive. 'So great was the manifestation of the power of God, in Mother, at that time,' Eunice Goodrich testified, 'that many were unable to abide by her presence. Her words were like flames of fire, and her voice like peals of thunder.' On a more down-to-earth level she was her usual assertive self when delivering a verdict on a woman who visited Niskeyuna at this period with her children. 'They are old in wickedness,' she told James, 'so they are almost as old as Methuselah.'

But she was clearly ill. It is no more possible to offer a confident diagnosis of her complaint than of her brother's, though once again there are clues. Sarah Kendall reported that on one occasion while she was staying at their house, Ann 'stripped up the sleeve of her dress and showed me her arm which presented the appearance of having been bruised till it had turned black in spots all over it as far

as I had a view of it. Those seeming bruises could be
ascribed to no natural cause as she had not at that time
been abused by her persecutors.' Sarah, of course, puts
the mysterious bruises down to spiritual suffering, but it
is possible that they are evidence of a blood disorder such
as leukaemia. Slight support for this hypothesis is provided
by an arch-enemy of Shakerism, Mary Dyer (not to be
confused with the seventeenth-century Quaker martyr),
who wrote in 1822 that nine years before, 'in the winter
of 1813, a woman who was a Shaker said that she saw
Elder Wm. and Mother Ann when they died. She states
that Elder Wm. bled at his stomach, Mother Ann bled at
the nose, ears, eyes and mouth, and that their death was
unexpected.' As far as Dyer is concerned, this is proof
that brother and sister killed each other while fighting,
but if there is any truth in the story at all, it does suggest
that Ann might have been suffering from a blood disease.

In August 1784, a party of Shakers, twenty-five in all, left
New Gloucester in Maine to visit Ann at Niskeyuna. They
travelled down the coast to New York, then up the
Hudson to Niskeyuna. Though she was very frail, Ann
insisted on meeting them. Her bedroom was in the attic
of the small log house where believers occupied every
inch of floor space, and the party from Maine were shown
in to her a few at a time. One of the visitors, Rachel
Merrill, noticed there was a burn hole in Ann's apron. At
her request, Ann took it off and she darned it for her.

Another large party arrived soon after the Maine contingent, and this time Ann decided to go in person to see

them all at once, perhaps because it would take less energy in the long run. She appeared on the porch outside her room, supported by a sister on each side. After that she wasn't expected to leave her room again, but one day in early September, Hannah Goodrich was sweeping the porch floor when the door opened and out she came.

'Sweep clean,' Ann told her.

'I will, Mother,' she replied.

'Ah, sweep clean, I say.'

'I will.'

'But I say, sweep clean.'

At this point Hannah realised that Ann was talking about sweeping the floor of the heart, and she said no more. Lucy Wright, who was nursing her, came and took Ann by the hand, and told her to go back to bed.

'I will,' Ann replied, 'I will be obedient to you, Lucy, for I am married to you, and I will go with you.'

The terminology used here represents an even stranger appropriation of worldly relationships than usual, but it could well have been part of Ann's campaign to establish Lucy as a future successor. Another source comments that during this period, 'When the sisters would gather round Mother to love her, she would frequently say to them, "Go & love Lucy."'

As her death approached, Ann is reported to have said, 'I see brother William coming, in a golden chariot to take me home.' Then she turned to Mary Hocknell, who was at her bedside, and who had been with her since as a girl of twelve she had been worshipping in the loft of the house in Toad Lane when the constable's men broke in.

'Molly, poor child! I am about to go home, and after I am gone, you will have many sorrows.' That home, to which William had returned already, and where the sorrowing Mary could not yet go, was of course heaven. But for these people, who had travelled so far, and who had never been able to go back to their starting point, maybe it had a tincture of Manchester about it too.

On 8 September 1784, between midnight and one in the morning, Ann Lee died. The chariot she had foreseen did indeed come for her, at least according to John Hocknell, who said that 'when the breath left her body he saw in a vision a golden chariot, drawn by four white horses which received and wafted her soul out of his sight'.

The Maine Shakers had left a little before this time. On the way back their ship was caught in a storm, and nearly foundered. One of them, Dana Thombs, then saw a vision of Ann pacifying the waters, as she had done on the *Mariah* ten years previously, and they were saved. Later she realised that Ann had been dead six hours when she appeared to her.

The funeral announcement in the *Albany Gazette* had an appropriate oddness: 'Departed this life at Nisquenia, Sept. 7th [actually the 8th], Mrs Lee, known by the appellation of the *Elect Lady* or *Mother of Zion*, and the head of that people called Shakers. Her funeral is to be attended this day.'

Abijah Worster and Abiather Eddy made her coffin; Eleazer Rand and Abiather Babbit dug her grave. At the funeral James Whittaker said, 'Here lie my two friends;

God help me! As ever man that is hungry desires to eat, I desire to lie here with them! They are part of myself! ... But I forbear – there is not a man in America that is able to keep the gospel without help.' Samuel Fitch said, 'She has been more persecuted than any other person to my knowledge; and the reason was, she had more of God in her than any other person in my knowledge.'

Ann's story does not end with the grave, however, and she should not be defined by the extent of the persecution she suffered. Unlike Shadrack Ireland, her predecessor at the Square House, she never succumbed to 'the darkness of the flesh' but maintained her spirituality till death and beyond, as testified by Jemima Blanchard, whose witness more than any other gives one a sense of the beauty and strangeness of the Shaker experience of that first American generation. 'When I heard of Mother's decease,' she said, 'I felt so distressed and sorrow-stricken that I thought it was impossible for me to live. I retired in secret and lay prostrate upon the floor, expecting to break out my soul in sorrow – for the more I tried to refrain the deeper my sorrow became. This continued without cessation, until I saw the appearance of Mother Ann, about the size of a child three years old. This beautiful messenger held something in each hand that appeared like a wing which she waved inward, and advancing toward me said, "Hush! Hush!" This took away my sorrow, so that I was able to attend to my duty.'

As powerful as Christ's passion and death is the story of his nativity, the spiritual King appearing as a helpless baby. It is symmetrically appropriate that the story of his female counterpart should end with such an image. It may be that at the heart of the Shaker experience lies one woman's inability to cope with the loss of her own children, and through bereavement to embark on a course that led her to become Mother to thousands. In any case, like Christian evangelists through the ages, she used the imagery of birth to describe the conversion experience and the life after death. With her own death, it was time for Ann the Word to embody that image herself, for the Mother to become the child.

Epilogue

It is significant that James Whittaker saw his task as to provide English leadership for Americans who would otherwise be incapable of looking after themselves. In this respect, as in others, he is following in Ann's footsteps, since she saw her own task as saving America from its pollutions. One day Jemima Blanchard was hurrying down the hallway at Niskeyuna when she heard an altercation between Whittaker and James Shepherd. Whittaker was speaking in a loud voice: 'I will reprove an Old England Devil as quick as a New England Devil. God don't own an Old England Devil any more than a New England Devil and I will reprove it and I am willing that all should know it.'

This accidental eavesdropping is illuminating in a number of ways. James Whittaker is confidently authoritative, but there is a bad-tempered, hectoring edge to his voice that was absent from Ann's, and suggests he lacks the indisputable spiritual status she possessed. There is, too, an assumption that the English Shakers have a privileged position within the sect, but one that cannot be tenable indefinitely. It also suggests that there was internecine warfare among the original band of immigrants, and that is confirmed by the apostasies that soon took place.

Ann's niece, Nancy Lee, had become ill and asked James for help. He told her that her faith would save her, though he admitted that he didn't know at how great a distance from God she was at that time. His suspicion was correct: Nancy left the sect along with another member of the English party, Richard Hocknell, and the two set the seal on their apostasy by getting married. Shepherd himself, the old England devil, left in 1788, a year after Whittaker's death.

Ann Lee described Amos Buttrick's solemn Sunday face as anti-Christian, but that is precisely the demeanour that seems to characterise James Whittaker at this time. In the past he had had his unbuttoned moments, as when chatting to Beulah Cooper in their little weaving room, and laughing about the antics of Aaron Wood, or joking about getting yet another serving of his favourite dinner, buttered potatoes. But now we can discern something hard-headed and dour about many of his utterances. Sometimes he sounds exactly like Jonathan Edwards, telling believers at a meeting in the last month of Ann's life that one day in hell is as a thousand years: 'It is called the bottomless pit, and souls in it feel themselves continually sinking further and further from God; and what still increases their torment, they can see no way out.' On one occasion at Harvard he warned the assembled against feeling any affection or responsibility for unconverted children. A short time after Ann's death, he wrote to his parents in England, after they had tried to send him the money to come and visit them, a letter of unparalleled venom because they had slid away from the faith, telling them they were 'a stink in my nostrils'. Such unfilial sentiments are of course fully legitimised by Shakerism. As a nineteenth-century Shaker song put it:

> Of all my relations that ever I see
> My own fleshly kindred were furtherest from me
> How ugly they look; how distant they feel;
> To hate them – despise them – increases my zeal.
> How ugly they look, & etc.

This uncompromising tendency in Shakerism, a certain emphasis on Thou Shalt Not, seems to have become particularly characteristic of James. Angell Matthewson tells an anecdote about Ann's last year at Niskeyuna which perhaps should be taken with a pinch of salt (he admits he got it second-hand) but which seems to capture this tone. According to Angell, it was during the final period of her life that Ann decided to introduce naked dancing, citing relevant examples from the prophets (one Shaker, an elderly doctor, asked for permission to continue wearing just his shoes on the grounds he suffered from tenderness of the feet). James Whittaker, soon 'out of conceit' with this gift, was 'overheerd to tell the mother viz if you ever make the people strip naked again you shall see my face no more'.

James took his pastoral duties seriously, travelling round New England visiting the believers, and taking some steps to encourage community of property and the beginnings of communal life. He still believed in the imminence of the millennium, however, and even encouraged a hare-brained scheme to build a ship for a final voyage to convert the world. He had been Ann's right-hand man all his adult life, and if he lacked her inspirational qualities and her exuberance, he was deeply loyal to her memory. On his last visit to Harvard during the cold, raw March of 1787, he got out of his sleigh and walked between the brethren and sisters. Then he knelt down and, echoing Ann's words at the first Shaker Christmas celebration, said: 'Brethren put off your shoes from off your feet for the ground whereon we stand is holy.'

During this same visit he also foresaw the end of the English leadership of Shakerism, in effect bringing down the curtain on the drama that had been enacted by Ann and himself: 'The time is at hand when we (meaning those who come from England) will be all gone and then you will have to stand and keep the way of God for yourselves each one for one. Then if you could find us by crossing the ocean or going from one end of the earth to the other you would do it but this you will not be able to do.'

James died on 21 July 1787, the third anniversary of William's death. There was a slightly uneasy interval for a few months while leadership was shared between the Meacham brothers and Calvin Harlow, but in due course the other two men acknowledged Joseph's overall authority. The sixty-four-year-old John Hocknell, who had been so instrumental in bringing about Shakerism's great American project, seems never to have been a candidate, despite the fact that he had taken charge of Niskeyuna for some of the duration of the mission to New England. Perhaps that moment when his nerve failed during the siege of the Square House in August 1782, and he sat under the peach trees of the neighbouring garden wondering what on earth to do until his arm eventually guided him back to Mother, had convinced him (or others) that he did not have what it took to assume the mantle of command, even though the shadow of his mantle could so impress young Shaker sisters like Jemima Blanchard and Lucy Prescott. Perhaps he was too unambitious, or too old, though he wasn't as old as some commentators have believed, since a misprint in a Shaker history suggested he was seventy-six in 1779, when in fact he died at that age in 1799. More probably, despite James Whittaker's scepticism about their ability to manage, the Americans had decided it was time to take over control of a sect that was predominantly American in membership, and fully American in geographical location.

Joseph Meacham had done his best to adapt to the ecstatic, visionary dimension of Shakerism – in the early days after his conversion he had discovered that he had no natural aptitude for the dance, so he taught himself to do it. In 1779, when leading the New Light Stir, he had been as convinced as the English Shakers, who were then living a few miles away unknown to him, that the millennium was imminent. But, by definition, one can't maintain a millennialist perspective indefinitely. It becomes illogical, and disappointing, and exhausting. Shakerism had been expanding explosively (and confrontationally). It was time to withdraw and regroup, to decide what to do next.

Over the next few years Meacham hammered out the beginnings of a social organisation, economic structure and order of worship for the Shakers. The 'gathering' of the society, as this process was called, was begun at New Lebanon which, understandably since it had been the centre of the New Light Stir, Meacham in effect made his headquarters. Social and religious life was there codified and regulated. Three degrees of commitment to the faith were identified and institutionalised: the Novitiate Family, the Junior Family and the Senior Family (as usual, this most anti-family of all faiths showed its addiction to familial terminology). The Novices were only admitted if married to a believing partner or if both partners agreed to a legal separation, with a just sharing-out of their property. The Juniors were fully celibate. Both these orders were able to choose the extent to which they kept their property or donated it to the Church; in any case they would be looked after in sickness and age. The Senior Family consisted of fully committed members who had given their possessions to the church and dedicated themselves to the Shaker way. Leadership was established jointly between men and women at every stage of the hierarchy; and Joseph Meacham appointed Lucy Wright as his partner at the head of the organisation.

Communities became hives of activity, and products began to be sold through local shops, creating a structure of economic interdependence that was to be indispensable in enabling the Shakers to be accepted by the worldly communities adjacent to them. Their reputation for quality, inventiveness, and technological and agricultural skill began to be established.

Rigid timetables and codes of conduct were laid down. Worship took place at set times, in a set order. Meetings became solemn; spontaneous, inspired behaviour gave way to prescribed ritual. The man who had had to teach himself to dance, Shaker style, had no hesitation in choreographing the movements of the believers, so that the 'Square Order Shuffle', where the carefully segregated dancers went through a sequence of movements in slow formation, became the norm. This was more than a matter of tidying up; it was a conceptual shift. The physical manifestations of Shaker meetings were no longer a tussle between the human and the divine, but a form of spiritual discipline. And discipline was the word. Formality replaced spontaneity; prescription imposed itself upon exuberance. The blueprint for America's most successful utopian experiment was being drawn up. It had nothing to do with Ann Lee, who had never shown the slightest interest in long-term solutions.

In 1790, Joseph Meacham published his *Concise Statement* of Shaker principles, in which he enumerated four occasions when the Holy Spirit had descended to earth: it had visited Abraham, Moses, Jesus and the Shaker sect *in toto*, beginning in 1747. Ann Lee's name isn't mentioned. Of course, there had always been a certain ambivalence about her status. Jesus, when he had manifested the Christ-spirit, had had the unique task of establishing a spiritual world for humankind to occupy; when Ann Lee had received it, she was simply the first to find her way to that heaven while on earth, *prima inter pares*, the leader of the charge. She was the guide, the Word, the Mother. There must be a kind of egalitarianism among the saved. She had maintained a hierarchy of elders, of course, but the logic behind it was simply one of chronology, neatly establishing itself in terms of the precedence of the English contingent. Now she was gone there was a class structure to mirror that of society, and an ecclesiastical hierarchy that had its points of similarity with Catholicism and episcopalianism in general. The charismatic leadership of an individual had been supplanted by a structure built to persist through time. Ann had denounced concupiescence as the original sin, and had no interest in reproduction because there was no future to fill with people. In nineteenth-century Shakerism celibacy became a matter of austerity and mortification, of a spiritual discipline that had its points of similarity with that other long-lived utopian structure, the monastic tradition. The nineteenth-century American essayist Ralph Waldo Emerson once said that an institution is the lengthened shadow of one man; in terms of the historical phenomenon of Shakerism, of Shakerism as it is popularly understood, that shadow was cast by Joseph Meacham.

But of course a religion has to have a soul as well as a body. Meacham died in 1796, having consolidated and institutionalised the faith, leaving Lucy Wright in sole charge until her own death twenty-five years later. She shared Meacham's organisational skills, but she also allowed some missionary zeal to creep back into Shaker culture. Formal devotions remained the prevailing mode, but some scope for spontaneous dancing returned. The former Shaker Thomas Brown records exuberant worship to the accompaniment of jig tunes from 1798, for example.

Shakerism prospered. A mission was sent into the Ohio valley in 1805 to take advantage of the revivalism that had broken out in the mid-west (and in conformity to the prophecies Ann Lee had allegedly made during her last months). This established an enormously important western base for the religion, and it was from here that leaders such as David Darrow, Benjamin Seth Youngs and John Dunlavy began to write works of Shaker theology and history, giving the religion a coherent intellectual basis and establishing as its most important characteristic its emphasis on a female dimension to the godhead that had been embodied in Ann Lee, bringing her back centre-stage after having been consigned to obscurity by Joseph Meacham. This work was boosted by the compilation in 1816 of a vital collection of anecdotes and sayings of Ann Lee and the other early leaders in a book entitled *Testimonies of the Life, Character, Revelations and Doctrines of Mother Ann Lee, and the Elders with Her.*

The book was printed in the Shaker community of Hancock, Massachusetts, and circulated and read out in public for a couple of years before being withdrawn. The Ann Lee it depicted no longer conveniently fitted the version of her that was current in the organised religion of the time. Leaders were uncomfortable at reading about her threat to wring people's noses. Given the rigid hierarchy that had by now been established for the running of the different communities, and for the central administration of the faith on a national basis, those in authority felt that their positions were challenged by accounts of Ann's habit of imparting her doctrines to all and sundry, including the weak-minded, when really she should have confided in intellectuals like Joseph Meacham. Of course, the main problem, as usual, was that Ann had given no thought to the future, since she hadn't believed in one. But these were people of the future, and they found it hard to live with her assertion that she would be unable to give further help to anyone after her work was completed. In the light of these problems the decision was made to withdraw the book from circulation, and to allow only the most senior Shakers access to it. It became therefore a most mysterious document, known as the 'Secret Book of the Elders', until its republication in 1888.

When Lucy Wright died in 1821 there were four thousand Shakers, about four times the number Ann Lee had left behind, housed in sixteen orderly communities that stretched from Maine to Connecticut and from Massachusetts to Ohio, Kentucky and Indiana. But like any historical institution, however effectively organised it might be, Shakerism needed an occasional input of energy, and in 1837 it received one, when a ten-year period known as Mother Ann's Work began.

It started with visions, appropriately enough, given the number Ann herself had experienced. Some pubescent girls in the Shaker community at Watervliet, as Niskeyuna was by then known, began to have trances. One of them in particular, fourteen-year-old Ann Goff, went on a spiritual journey in which she was taken to a room where Ann Lee was enthroned, and invited to sit on her right hand. Shortly afterwards Lucy Wright entered, and sat on the left. It was a wish-fulfilment fantasy, a young girl imagining herself part of a female triumvirate in power; but it expressed the most original, powerful and long-lasting element of Shakerism, the affirmation of the importance of the feminine in spiritual life, and the explicit claim of femaleness as an aspect of the divinity.

Other Shakers had similar encounters, receiving guidance and comfort from William Lee and James Whittaker as well as from Ann. Shaker behaviour, for decades characterised by orderliness and propriety, became bizarre and ecstatic again. Believers shivered for hours on end and then passed out. They bent down and ate 'simplicity' from off the floor. They even danced with partners instead of shuffling in long lines. A kind of abstract debauchery took place, with brethren and sisters laughing for hours on end, getting drunk with invisible wine, adorning themselves with spiritual jewellery. Those old allies, the Native Americans, spoke to them from the afterlife in strange truncated English that brings to mind Tonto in *The Lone Ranger*: 'Dare me will sing lobe lobe lobe.' On one occasion, at the Watervliet community, six brothers and eight or nine sisters became possessed by the tribal spirits and began a powwow, with 'whooping, yelling and strange antics'. Shakers conversed with these earliest Americans in their 'Native Language', or spoke in tongues of their

own, or even sang inspired hymns in a mixture of tongues
and English:

> Selera vae van vo canara van se lava
> Dilera van se lane cinara van se vo,
> 'Tis Mother's Holy love, love, she sent it by her dove,
>   dove,
> 'Twas vane van se vane, 'twill ever more endure.

Ann visited frequently in spirit: this exuberance and
excess was 'her work', a sudden infusion of vitality to give
the sect momentum again fifty years after her death. She
was often impersonalised as Holy Mother Wisdom.
According to Shaker theology the doctrine of the Trinity,
as elaborated in the fourth century, was flawed, since the
three persons all possessed the masculine gender.
Shakerism replaced it with duality, the 'manifestation of
Father and Mother in the Deity'. The male force is power,
and creates; the female one is wisdom, and shapes.

On other occasions she appeared in her own right, with
her old companions, William and James. There are more
records of these spiritual communications in the Shaker
Archives than any other kind of document. In the Enfield
Shaker community in 1842, one believer was visited by
the founders of Shakerism on successive sabbaths, and on
20 February of that year Fathers William and James, and
Mothers Lucy and Sarah (Kendall) all came together,
bringing crowns for each of the Enfield elders. Then they
left, but that afternoon Father William was back once
more, insisting that the seer bathe himself in the waters
of humiliation.

Symbolic water of this kind became a landscape feature too. With typical Shaker energy, and in response to their deep need to convert inspiration into ritual through labour, 'spiritual fountains' were erected on hills near Shaker villages, and hundreds of hours were spent excavating and building these sacred sites, where no actual water would ever be seen. On appointed days Shakers would march to the spots playing imaginary musical instruments, and when they arrived would consume large, but completely insubstantial feasts.

In 1842 Philemon Stewart received 'A Holy Sacred and Divine Roll and Book' by dictation from an angel called Al'sign te're Jak, in which Ann is identified as the Second Coming of Christ, who as first female witness of the divinity completes the 'foundation of the kingdom'. Angels were busy at this period. On 11 November 1841, an unnamed angel belonging to the fifth band of the angels of love at Holy Selan brought the words of Holy Mother to the Shakers at New Lebanon. The whole experience of these spiritual manifestations involved a new confrontation with the original energies of the religion, and a release of pent-up enthusiasm. Shaker artists gleefully drew pictures, under spiritual guidance, of Ann's epic voyage across the Atlantic in the *Mariah*.

In due course, the excitement died down. By about 1847, one hundred years after the Wardleys had founded the sect in Bolton, Mother Ann's Work was petering out. Several of the instruments through whom the spirit messages were conveyed left the society, finding the religious discipline too austere.

Shakerism continued, though it now began a slow decline. In a sketchy and vestigial form it still just about exists today. It has developed an enormous reputation for achievements Ann Lee knew nothing of, and in which she would have taken no interest: the stability of its institutional structures, its buildings and, especially, its beautiful furniture; its skill at cultivation, its arts and crafts and technology (a Shaker sister invented the circular saw). Many see it as a repository of old American values, of an innocent way of life in touch with the environment, where self-help is combined with caring, and spiritual integrity and purity are all-important.

There is some validity in that perspective, but it sentimentalises and marginalises the original strangeness and energy of the movement, its assault upon family life and sexual love, its encouragement of bizarre and irrational behaviour. Ann Lee remains such a powerful figure because she was utterly uncompromising and completely certain of herself. One can apprehend her in terms of her historical significance and her cultural importance, particularly for her enormous and undervalued contribution to feminism. But in the end one must experience Ann Lee as she herself experienced her faith, directly, personally, viscerally.

Notes

Sources are cited by a key name or word, cross-referenced to the bold type in the Bibliography; np means no page numbers.

Epigraph

vii *'To such as addressed her'*: Darrow, xxviii

1: *Toad Lane*

3 *Toad Lane*: Victoria, 177
3 *Spelling was only just becoming standardised*: Scragg, 80, 90–91
4 *two Manchester engravers*: Casson, np
5 *Acres Field*: Victoria, 180; Aston, 40
6 *'meer village'*: Defoe, ii, 262
6 *two thousand houses*: Victoria, 180
6 *a population of around eight thousand*: Aston, 46
7 *'fleshly cohabitation'*: Testimonies, 3
7 *'heavenly visions, instead of trifling toys'*: Green, *View*, 31
7 *dreaded the sound*: Blanchard, np
9 *Ann had to go to work*: Green, *View*, 60

9 *'earn their own bread'*: Rule, 42

10 *a cutter of velvet*: *Testimonies*, 3

10 *a poor woman called Beulah Rude*: *Testimonies*, 313

11 *'I saw them clothed with blackness'*: *Testimonies*, 42

13 *a quixotic character called Sergeant Dickson*: Selby, 73

13 *One of the local loyalists, Peter Mainwaring*: Byrom, 15–16

14 *The Manchester Regiment was picked out*: Lenman, 273

14 *student called Edward Hall*: Brockbank, E. M., 11

14 *The hatting trade in Manchester*: Aikin, 162

15 *establishment of the Manchester Infirmary*: Brockbank, W., *Address*, 9; Brockbank, W., *History*, 8

15 *'daub-hole field'*: Manchester Infirmary Board Minutes for 21 August 1753, quoted Brockbank, W., *Portrait*, 14

16 *according to Beppy Byrom*: quoted Brockbank, E. M., 18

16 *The only descriptions we have*: Green, *View*, 25; *Testimonies*, 343

16 *diet sheet*: *Rules*, 25–6

17 *'cheapening some Potatoes'*: *Mercury*, 14 June 1757

17 *'Great Cheese Riot'*: Thompson, 64

19 *a sense of injustice*: Thompson, 64

19 *Shude Hill Fight*: *Whitworth's*, 22 November 1757

20 *nine hundred, according to one source*: Procter, 43

20 *In the Thames Valley in 1766*: Thompson, 64

21 *a letter to the* Mercury: *Mercury*, 14 December 1757

23 *a reward of £5*: *Mercury*, 19 July 1762

23 *Food riots during the second half of the eighteenth century*: Thompson, 9–14

2: *Clothed with the Sun*

25 *an early-nineteenth-century Shaker textbook*: Darrow, xxv
26 *'ye steeplehouse shooke'*: Fox, *Journals*, i, 54
26 *Margaret Fell*: Barbour and Frost, 28
26 *One convert, John Gilpin*: Barbour, 118
27 *In 1650 Fox appeared*: Fox, *Journals*, i, 4
27 *As the Shakers said of their own label*: Darrow, xxv
28 *'receiving the spirit of the French prophets'*: Darrow, xxiii
28 *a fifteen-year-old called Isabeau Vincent*: Schwartz, 17–18
29 *Persecution inevitably began*: Schwartz, 26–7
29 *'Holy Maid of Kent'*: Owen, 67–8
30 *presided over by Thomas Dutton*: Owen, vii-viii; Schwartz, 154
30 *preacher called Howell Harris*: quoted Garrett, 85
31 *Mary Dyer deliberately went to Boston*: Bacon, 29
31 *the Quaker Elizabeth Adams*: Bacon, 19
31 *Mary Keimer . . . Dorothy Harling*: Garrett, 57, 56
32 *the* Virginia Gazette: *Virginia*, 9 Nov 1769, 1
32 *The Bible . . . can be resonant*: these quotes and others in Darrow, xxv
35 *if they were 'two babes'*: Testimonies, 49
35 *'low temporal circumstances'*: Darrow, xxii
37 *began to establish a base in north Cheshire*: Darrow, xxii, xxiv
38 *'I laid myself down upon the ice'*: Testimonies, 59
38 *A certain nobleman*: Testimonies, 55–6
40 *'Many times, when I was about my work'*: Testimonies, 46–7
41 *a mid-nineteenth-century Shaker*: Evans, 128
41 *'In my travail and tribulation'*: Testimonies, 48
42 *'When I felt my eyes closing'*: Testimonies, 44
42 *Shaker sources claim*: Green, *View*, 7; *Testimonies*, 6

42 *Ann's 'first imprisonment'*: Andrews, *Shakers*, 299, reported by
   Seth Youngs Wells

43 *The records . . . show that patients*: *Manchester Infirmary Records*,
   admission records up to 1769; Cheadle admission records
   from 1773

44 *the institution was a therapeutic one*: Brockbank, W., *Portrait*,
   27

44 *'My soul broke forth'*: *Testimonies*, 47

44 *'And when I was brought through'*: *Testimonies*, 48

45 *This process was best described*: Evans, 128

46 *She was in a position*: *Testimonies*, 3; Darrow, xxviii

46 *One of the key texts of Shakerism*: Green, *View*, 187–93

47 *Ann Lee was born the very next year*: Green, *View*, 193

48 *An early-twentieth-century Shaker sister, Catherine Allen*: Allen,
   3

48 *As Thankful Barce . . . was to put it*: Wells, 94

48 *'Christ did verily make his second appearance'*: *Testimonies*, vi

49 *five of the French Prophets*: Garrett, 56

49 *an American convert to Shakerism named Cornelius Thayer*: *Testimonies*, 236–7

50 *'I love the day when I first received the gospel'*: *Testimonies*, 44

50 *astonishing power*: *Testimonies*, 49

3: *The House of Correction*

53 *twenty-four 'assistants'*: *Manchester Constables'*, 227, entry for
   14 July 1772

54 *Other members of the family*: Andrews, *Shakers*, 9

54 *Another of her brothers*: *Testimonies*, 53–4

54 *William, four years younger than Ann*: Green, *View*, 39–41;
   Testimonies, 333–42; Haskett, 66

55 *'I love my Mother,'*: Green, *View*, 41

56 *First thing on that Sunday morning*: *Testimonies*, 60–2

57 *The constables' accounts*: *Manchester Constables'*, 228, entry for 14 July 1772

57 *imprisoned in the local lock-up*: Green, *View*, 12

57 *When talking about this period*: *Testimonies*, 50–1

57 *According to the constables' accounts, however*: *Manchester Constables'*, 228, entries for 14 and 15 July 1772

57 *The Houses had been set up by Elizabeth I*: Harrison, 89–90, 96

57 *'evil, disease-ridden places'*: Thompson, 61

58 *When the House was modernised*: Harrison, 96

59 *by the name of James Whittaker*: Green, *View*, 42; *Testimonies*, 354

60 *James was just twenty-one*: *Testimonies*, 52–3

61 *A historian writing just thirty years after*: Aston, 246

61 *The governor in the early 1770s was Thomas Whitlow*: *Lancashire Quarter Sessions*, np, record for October 1772

62 *when Ann was jailed in Albany*: *Testimonies*, 32–6

62 *many inmates at this period managed to escape*: Harrison, 92

62 *When she was being held in Albany*: Wells, 44

62 *On 23 July 1772 Thomas Whitlow*: *Lancashire Quarter Sessions*, np

63 *Once again a tavern was taken over*: *Manchester Constables'*, 230, entry for 30 July 1772

63 *half of the eight witnesses*: *Manchester Constables'*, 229, entry for 23 July 1772

64 *he would give her* 'true desires': *Testimonies*, 44

64 *2s 6d for 'Cryers Fees'*: *Manchester Constables'*, 229, entry for 23 July 1772

65 *On the 3rd, the constables claimed*: *Manchester Constables'*, 235

65 *A couple of weeks later, on 19 October:* Manchester Constables',
    241

65 *struck William over the head with a firehook:* White, 64; Bishop,
    np, entry for 12 May 1835

65 *She got out of her house with a mob:* Testimonies, 57

66 *Her brother James was not quite so lucky:* Manchester Constables',
    241

66 *On other occasions Ann, too, failed:* Testimonies, 59

66 *Sunday 23 May 1773:* Lancashire Quarter Sessions, np

67 *There were precedents in the history of the French Prophets:* Gar-
    rett, 30–1

67 *'Woe unto ye bloddy citty':* Fox, *Journals,* i,15

67 *The disruption of a service at the Old Church:* Testimonies,
    57–8

68 *Once when recounting the tale:* Testimonies, 65

68 *Timothy Dwight, President of Yale:* Dwight, iii, 149–69

69 *An eccentric commentator called Thomas Brown:* Brown, 297

69 *'To Ann Lees a shaker appre[he]nded':* Manchester Constables',
    256, entry for 30 May 1773

70 *This took place on 24 July 1773:* Lancashire Quarter Sessions,
    np

70 *All we have is a note in the accounts for 28 July:* Manchester
    Constables', 265

4: *The* Mariah

75 *One Saturday, as they sat down by the roadside:* Testimonies, 66

76 *Once, as she neared the end of her life, Ann:* Green, *View,* 35

76 *He also addressed enormous crowds in Manchester:* Dallimore,
    ii, 286, 348, 465

77 *Some years later, in the early 1780s:* Testimonies, 64

78 *In Harvard town, Massachusetts, in 1781*: Testimonies, 225

79 *John Townley, who had stood in the dock*: Darrow, xxix

80 *John and Jane Wardley, now getting along in years*: White, 35

80 *Shakerism in north-west England peaked*: Garrett, 158

80 *'those of the society who remained in* England': Darrow, xxix

81 *the ship had apparently been condemned*: Testimonies, 67

82 *In the close confines of the* Mariah: Testimonies, 67–8

83 *This account comes from a Shaker called Morrell Baker*: Darrow, xxx

83 *Another source gives a more melodramatic version*: Testimonies, 68

84 *The motley group of Shakers made their way*: Green, *View*, 15

85 *She herself was given the job of washing*: Testimonies, 8

87 *they believed their leader to be the woman 'clothed with the sun'*: Plumer, 306

87 *it was John Hocknell who found the spot*: Filley, 11–12

87 *Hocknell found his arm rising upward*: Bathrick, 'Wise Sayings', 183

87 *one Valentine Rathbun*: Rathbun, 11

88 *he found himself in Wisdom's Valley*: Filley, 52

89 *Shakers were able to arrange the lease*: Filley, 11, 20

89 *he had sold his farm ... for eight hundred guineas*: Bathrick, 'Wise Sayings', 183

89 *James Shepherd joined William Lee and James Whittaker*: Testimonies, 6

89 *The experience of Hannah Goodrich and her husband Nathan*: Testimonies, 31–2

90 *Ann had a vision of 'a large black cloud'*: Testimonies, 304

90 *a Shaker apologist, Benjamin Seth Youngs*: quoted Brown, 20

91 *Some years after the conversion of the Goodriches*: Testimonies, 295

91 *'Tho he never had been considered'*: Green, *View*, 15

91 *'The man to whom I was married'*: Testimonies, 45

91 *in the autumn of 1775, he became seriously ill*: Blinn, 9

92 *to join with 'the wicked at public houses'*: Green, *View*, 16

92 *he 'loved his beef'*: White, 15

93 *'When I first gained victory'*: Testimonies, 208

94 *'her only shelter from the inclemency'*: Testimonies, 11

94 *The vessels that plied the river*: Carmer, 142–3, 147

94 *Their sloop moored*: Testimonies, 235

95 *Someone then fired the shot*: Emerson, *Poems*, 125

95 *the man-of-war* Asia: Schaukirk, 2–3

96 *On Christmas Day 1775*: Testimonies, 9

5: *Niskeyuna*

99 *though John Hocknell and John Partington*: Filley, 11–12; Wells, 67

99 *Iroquois Nation*: Graymont, 13–14

99 *more correctly* Nis-ka-yu-na: Filley, 11

100 *They built a bigger dwelling-house*: White, 33

100 *by 1778 they had erected another*: Filley, 12

101 *Eleanor Vedder*: Filley, 12

101 *William is described*: Testimonies, 179, 201

101 *The Iroquois Nation gave women more status*: Graymont, 13,11

102 *a military physician called James Thacher*: Thacher, 141–2

103 *Thomas Brown*: Brown, 82, 47

104 *by the name of William Haskett*: Haskett, 52–3

105 *Hannah Hocknell found her hands were shaking*: Andrews, *Christmas*, np

105 *One day Ann led her little group*: Testimonies, 14

105 *William said later that this moment*: White, 34

106 *One day she stood on the bank*: Testimonies, 12

106 *In the spring of that year*: Testimonies, 14
107 *'Sinners in the Hands of an Angry God'*: Edwards, 365, 372, 377
109 *One of the leading families in Enfield*: Garrett, 165–6
110 *Richard Treat*: Wells, 40
110 *Amos Stower*: Wells, 84
110 *Samuel Johnson, a graduate*: Wells, 106
111 *Many others shared this anxiety*: Wells, 39
111 *'a virgin life would be required'*: Wells, 157
112 *Another of them, Joseph Main*: Wells, 97
112 *Job Bishop gives*: Wells, 158
112 *All those assembled at New Lebanon*: Green, *View*, 17
112 *Meacham himself was gripped*: Wells, 158
113 *All the revivalists could do*: Green, *View*, 17
113 *Richard Treat was one*: Wells, 40–1
116 *The New Light pilgrims*: Testimonies, 19
116 *Ann . . . had gone through*: Evans, 116–17
116 *Hannah Shipley*: Testimonies, 38
117 *another vegetable analogy*: Worcester, 'Testimony', np
117 *Another of the pilgrims, Abijah Worster*: Wells, 138–40
117 *Nineteen-year-old John Farrington*: Wells, 13
118 *She then led him out*: Testimonies, 20
119 *the doctrine was explicitly stated*: Green, *View*, 98
119 *The original sin*: Green, *View*, 124
119 *The 'prince of darkness'*: Green, *View*, 130
119 *Adam and Eve didn't mate*: Green, *View*, 133
119 *'Jesus Christ, the second Adam'*: Green, *View*, 151
120 *'So when a man comes up to'*: Green, *View*, 320
121 *Richard Treat again set off*: Wells, 41
122 *'Some are of such a hard make'*: Testimonies, 326–7
122 *One of them, Daniel Moseley*: Wells, 74
122 *Abigail Cook*: Wells, 36

122 *They would say to visitors*: Wells, 42

122 *Eliab Harlow at eighteen*: Wells, 19–24

123 *The Rev. Samuel Johnson acknowledges*: Wells, 109

123 *the case of Lucy Wight*: Wells, 67–8

124 *Thankful Barce's testimony*: Wells, 92

125 *John Deming, having confessed*: Testimonies, 37

125 *Hezekiah Hammond did his best*: Testimonies, 27–8

6: *The Dark Day*

129 *the Rev. Mr Cutler*: Boston, 29 May 1780

130 *John Howland . . . the Rev. Isaac Backus*: McLoughlin, 88–90

130 *a farmer called Issachar Bates*: Bates, np

131 *Olney Winsor . . . Samuel Williams*: McLoughlin, 88–90

132 *Whether Ann Lee and Joseph Meacham*: Green, 'Meacham', 11

132 *William Plumer*: Plumer, 306

133 *Calvin Green, who was born*: Green, 'Memoirs', 4

133 *Joseph Meacham and his colleague Calvin Harlow made their way*: Green, 'Meacham', 9

133 *Meacham pointed out that St Paul*: Testimonies, 21

134 *As Anne Matthewson*: Wells, 51

134 *As Shaker theology was later to have it*: Green, *View*, 217

135 *In 1781 she talked to Eunice Goodrich*: Testimonies, 205

136 *'A body without a head'*: Blanchard, np

136 *On arrival, Rathbun tells us*: Rathbun, V., 4–6

137 *This severe attitude is confirmed*: Plumer, 308

137 *Rathbun explains that if the novice*: Rathbun, V., 6, 9–10, 7

139 *'They sing the song'*: Goodrich, np

140 *'You ought to pass by each other like angels'*: Testimonies, 339

140 *Sometimes an individual's impulses*: Blanchard, np

140 *Often they would run wild*: Rathbun, V., 12; Backus, *History*, 298

141 *The experience of Elizabeth Johnson*: Wells, 88

142 *Nathan Tiffany*: Wells, 170

142 *A family called Ingrahams*: Carmer, 137–9

143 ' "*Tell them,*" *said Mother*': Testimonies, 318

143 '*Commissioners for Detecting*': Minutes, 452

144 *Darrow fought on the Rebel side*: White, 45

144 *at a hearing on 17 July*: Minutes, 461

144 *$23,633.54 was owed in pensions*: Nourse, 267

145 *The week after, on 24 July*: Minutes, 469

145 *Jacob Kidney*: Minutes, 441

145 '*The wicked are plotting*': Testimonies, 45

145 '*that they had also been guilty*': Minutes, 470

145 *Thankful Barce described*: Wells, 94

146 *Richard Treat says*: Wells, 44

147 '*grates of the prison*': Darrow, xxxiii

147 *a Shaker called Mary Knapp*: Testimonies, 33–4

148 *Zadock Wright*: Testimonies, 35–6

148 *meeting on 26 August*: Minutes, 504

149 *A Shaker called John Bishop*: Testimonies, 235

149 *the Baltus Van Kleek house*: Filley, 23

149 *the turn of Samuel Johnson*: Minutes, 507, 517–18; *Testimonies*, 74; Wells, 90

151 *the home of James Boyd*: Testimonies, 78

152 *The Shakers held in Albany*: Minutes, 569–75

152 *William Lee promptly went*: Filley, 23

152 '*mockers and scoffers*': Green, *View*, 20

152 *a young man called Jonathan Slosson*: Testimonies, 284

153 *A couple called Rufus and Zeruah Clark*: Testimonies, 219–20

154 *as it was for Hannah Cogswell*: Wells, 28–9

154 '*You are called in relation*': Green, *View*, 34

7: *The Journey to Harvard*

157 *'If you could see the glory'*: Testimonies, 288–9

157 *one of the believers described James Whittaker*: Barret, np

157 *Rachel Spencer*: Wells, 26

159 *a certain Dr Hollibert*: Testimonies, 83–4

159 *A young girl called Elizabeth Wood*: Wood, np

161 *Ann impressed other local people*: Testimonies, 231; Wood, np

162 *the Rev. Solomon Prentice*: Garrett, 135–6

163 *a resident . . . by the name of Nat Smith*: Stiles, 418

163 *a splinter group of Whitefield's English followers*: Dallimore, ii, 423

163 *Any offspring produced*: Cooper, B., np

163 *Sarah had long ago*: Garrett, 138

164 *Things had become hot for Shadrack Ireland*: Manifesto, December 1899, 233; Bathrick, 'Testimonies', 119

165 *A Shaker annalist*: Manifesto, December 1899, 287

166 *referred to him as 'The Man'*: Bathrick, 'Wise Sayings', 233

166 *'Sister Nabay,' he said*: Isaac Holden, quoted Garrett, 179; similar version in Backus, *History*, 462

166 *The other account shows him*: Bathrick, 'Wise Sayings', 227

167 *They barred the Square House*: Manifesto, December 1899, 287; Bathrick, 'Wise Sayings', 228

167 *Charles Owen*: Owen, 96–7

167 *Dr Thomas Emes*: Owen, 97–103; Schwartz, 113–25

168 *They buried him in a cornfield*: Bathrick, 'Wise Sayings', 228

168 *'As I was tossing – tumbling'*: Extract, np

169 *The two daughters of Abel Jewett*: Cooper, B., np

169 *A twenty-two-year-old woman called Jemima Blanchard*: Blanchard, np

170 *As Jemima later described it*: Bathrick, 'Wise Sayings', 33

171 *the census of 1776*: Baldwin, 3; Horgan, 20

171 *a reasonably sized New England township*: Horgan, 21

171 *Isaac Backus*: Backus, *History*, 462

171 *Thirty years previously he and his wife*: Horgan, 28

171 *She told a group of people*: Testimonies, 224

172 *One night she had a vision*: Testimonies, 85

172 *This is the house*: Bathrick, 'Testimonies', 120

173 *The door was answered*: Bathrick, 'Wise Sayings', 212–15;
Sears, 37

175 *You are now old people*: Wells, 62

175 *One day, Ann announced*: Testimonies, 225

175 *Ann often had vivid and Dantesque visions*: Testimonies, 43

176 *'There being quite a heft'*: Sears, 4

177 *the sum of five hundred dollars*: Nourse, 258

8: *The Experience of Jemima Blanchard*

179 *Jemima Blanchard continued to work*: Blanchard, np

180 *He was a preacher himself*: Bathrick, 'Wise Sayings', 33

180 *William Lee told him*: Blanchard, np

181 *James Whittaker, describing an early mystical experience*: Green,
View, 43

181 *by the name of George Keith*: Keith, 51

182 *Jemima, along with the Cutters*: Blanchard, np

183 *the poet Emily Dickinson*: Dickinson, 551

183 *Nathan Tiffany*: Wells, 170

183 *At this point Jemima decided*: Blanchard, np

185 *Zipporah Cory*: Wells, 57

185 *Jemima's father had arrived*: Blanchard, np

185 *he was hovering on the edge*: Bathrick, 'Wise Sayings', 43

186 *He urged her to conform*: Blanchard, np

189 *James Whittaker suddenly extended*: Testimonies, 355

189 *While Jemima knelt*: Blanchard, np

190 *gathering up the 'driblets'*: Testimonies, 349

190 *'The American people are so full fed'*: Blanchard, np

191 *'heavy dancing'*: Taylor, 15–16

192 *Susannah Barret's experience*: Barret, np

192 *In Jemima's case*: Blanchard, np

194 *'slandering, mocking, scoffing'*: Testimonies, 97

194 *'a cage of unclean birds'*: Testimonies, 247

194 *In nearby Acton*: Nourse, 259

194 *Ann got headaches*: Cooper, B., np

194 *making gowns for . . . Ann Lee*: Hammond, np

194 *Beulah Cooper would often join him*: Cooper, B., np

194 *according to one ex-Shaker*: Matthewson, letter 4, np

195 *Once, the elders were about to go on a visit*: Blanchard, np

195 *he dismissed a meeting at Elijah Wilds's house*: Wilds, np

196 *The first time Susannah Barret*: Barret, np

196 *'wild and strange' behaviour*: Cooper, B., np

197 *he had 'no more lust'*: Testimonies, 369

197 *Whittaker . . . could hold the attention*: Matthewson, letter 4, np

198 *they had appeared like an invading army*: Testimonies, 87

198 *A town meeting was held in Harvard*: Sears, 62

198 *Committee of Correspondence and Safety*: Nourse, 260

198 *James listened to them at the door*: Testimonies, 89–90

199 *William 'sparkled with rage'*: Haskett, 66–7

199 *Jemima Blanchard had a vision of hell*: Blanchard, np

201 *the kitchen cupboards had got very dirty*: Cooper, B., np

201 *'There is no dirt in heaven'*: Testimonies, 265

201 *Ann called . . . Jonathan Slosson*: Testimonies, 91

9: *Black Guards*

205 *Ann and her entourage*: Testimonies, 92–7

209 *Peckham's wife treated Ann*: Wells, 177

209 *David Hammond and William Lee also tried*: Testimonies, 97

209 *Meanwhile James Whittaker had been too badly injured*: Robinson, np

210 *When her cap and fillet*: Testimonies, 97

210 *rumours about witchcraft*: Testimonies, 98

210 *General James Sullivan*: Testimonies, 314–5

211 *Captain Phineas Farnsworth*: Testimonies, 100–1

212 *A certain Elias Sawyer*: Backus, *Diary*, ii, 1091

212 *their usefulness was 'nearly hedged up'*: Testimonies, 102

213 *Their exit was in the nick*: Testimonies, 102–3

213 *Lucy was born*: Green, 'Wright', 7; *Testimonies*, 222

214 *The hierarchical structure of Shakerism*: Taylor, 4–5

215 *Ann and the elders arrived at Enfield*: Testimonies, 104–5

215 *A woman called Tryphena Perkins*: Testimonies, 226–7

216 *some two hundred people*: Wood, np

217 *Valentine Rathbun*: Rathburn, V., 3, 7

217 *Ann walked out of the house*: Wood, np

218 *James Whittaker addressed*: Testimonies, 104

218 *Eliphalet Comstock reported*: Wells, 177

218 *pulled out the lynchpin*: Wood, np

218 *The brethren and sisters sang*: Testimonies, 104–5

219 *one Ebenezer Burbanks*: Testimonies, 386

219 *Ann and the elders journeyed*: Testimonies, 107

220 *a Committee of Safety*: Garrett, 183

220 *Lucy Bishop*: Testimonies, 314, 313

221 *Jemima Blanchard reports*: Blanchard, np

221 *She had the same advice*: Testimonies, 313

221 *Ann went five miles*: *Testimonies*, 108; Matthewson, letter 5, np

222 *the poem 'Out, Out – '*: Frost, 160

223 *things had cooled off at Harvard*: *Testimonies*, 108

223 *One of the Wilds family*: *Testimonies*, 319

223 *another Susannah from Shirley*: Barret, np

223 *Calvin Green, for example, was born*: Green, 'Memoirs', 6–9

225 *the man, 'in a fondling manner'*: *Testimonies*, 328

225 *a 'man of the world'*: *Testimonies*, 324

226 *the young lawyer William Plumer*: Plumer, 305–6

228 *resentment was building*: *Testimonies*, 108–10

228 *'The world used to notice'*: Blanchard, np

228 *William Plumer quickly penetrated*: Plumer, 304

229 *A young woman called Polly Swain*: Worcester, 'Sayings', np

229 *In late July 1782*: *Testimonies*, 108–10

231 *Parker probably had mixed feelings*: Backus, *History*, 463–4

232 *the crowd, fuelled*: *Testimonies*, 111

233 *Lucy Wright joined the ranks*: *Testimonies*, 256

233 *In August Ann had another vision*: *Testimonies*, 112–13

10: *Exasperating the Devil*

237 *On 18 August 1782*: *Testimonies*, 114

237 *'Mother used to say'*: Blanchard, np

237 *Their zealousness*: *Testimonies*, 114–15

240 *One of them, Elizabeth Jewett*: Jewett, np

240 *John Hocknell himself managed*: *Testimonies*, 116–27

241 *He had been a fifer*: Nourse, 267

242 *He was put under guard*: *Testimonies*, 116–27

248 *After a short stay at Woburn*: *Testimonies*, 129

248 *'I saw your father'*: *Testimonies*, 241

249 *The next port of call*: Testimonies, 129

249 *Here Ann pronounced on the morals*: Testimonies, 226

250 *proceeding to Preston*: Testimonies, 130–1

251 *She pushed her way into the thick*: Wood, np

252 *Luckily the town constable*: Testimonies, 131–2

253 *David Meacham later recorded*: Testimonies, 132–3

253 *Ann had an intriguing little conversation*: Testimonies, 330

254 *Deborah Williams reported*: Williams, D., np

254 *During this stay at New Providence*: Testimonies, 133–5

256 *building the first meeting-house*: Matthewson, letters 3 and 4, np

257 *he sobbed his way through a whole meal*: Green, *View*, 41

257 *multitudes being satisfactorily fed on almost nothing*: Testimonies, 137–8

257 *vivid displays of Northern lights*: Testimonies, 228

257 *one meeting was audible . . . seven miles away*: Testimonies, 135–6

257 *A man called Peter Dodge*: Wells, 122

258 *Lydia Matthewson confided to her*: Testimonies, 242

259 *Ann had a similar vision*: Testimonies, 238

259 *David Slosson*: Testimonies, 240

260 *James Whittaker claimed schools*: Matthewson, letter 4, np

261 *One of Aaron Wood's exorcism subjects*: Matthewson, letter 5, np

262 *Ann Lee 'casteth out devils'*: Darrow, xxxi

262 *'Every trew believer'*: Matthewson, letter 3, np

262 *Jemima Blanchard*: Blanchard, np

263 *'some of you are hawking and spitting'*: Testimonies, 287

263 *the predicament of Joseph Bennet*: Testimonies, 251

263 *Ann had addressed the problem of bestiality*: Testimonies, 303, 278–80

264 *The catalyst . . . seems to have been Daniel Bacon*: Testimonies, 138

264 *the Ashfield residents appointed a committee*: Testimonies, 139–43

268 *Ann sent out three teams*: Matthewson, letter 7, np

269 *This evangelism played an important part*: Garrett, 184–9

11: *The Journey Back*

271 *A woman called Sarah Turner*: Testimonies, 146

271 *The Kendalls were a rich family*: Warner, 7

272 *women tended to wear their dresses short*: Blanchard, np

272 *Sarah Turner managed to persuade*: Testimonies, 146–7

273 *'I have seen the poor negroes'*: Testimonies, 43

273 *'as a contemptible stripling'*: Testimonies, 286

273 *On 1 June 1783*: Testimonies, 148

274 *Elijah Wilds cut up bread*: Wells, 143

274 *James Whittaker tried to address*: Testimonies, 148–9

276 *This refuge was thereafter . . . known*: White, 51

276 *Those searching for her*: Nourse, 262–3

276 *the crowd agreed to accept James Whittaker*: Testimonies, 150–2

278 *According to Elijah Wilds*: Wells, 149

278 *He then turned to Ivory Wilds*: Testimonies, 153–4

278 *The leaders of the Harvard persecution*: Testimonies, 385

279 *Hannah offered Ann a silk handkerchief*: Bathrick, 'Wise Sayings', 57–8

279 *Their first port of call*: Testimonies, 155–8

281 *Hannah was a brave, outgoing person*: Warner, 7

281 *The crowd now started throwing stones*: Bathrick, 'Wise Sayings', 9–10

281 *a man called Benjamin Witt*: Testimonies, 157

282 *Jemima later recalled*: Bathrick, 'Wise Sayings', 58–9

282 *The next evening the vigilantes*: Testimonies, 158

282 *Jemima Blanchard describes*: Blanchard, np

284 *After a stay of twelve days*: Testimonies, 159–60

284 *'If I owned the whole world'*: Testimonies, 270

285 *'their invention'*: Testimonies, 161–3

286 *Years later Daniel Rathbun*: Rathbun, D., 14–17

287 *Phebe Chase*: Wells, 34

287 *Even more tellingly, Zipporah Cory*: Wells, 59

287 *pointed out by Mary Hocknell*: Brown, 47

288 *The accused were summoned*: Testimonies, 165

288 *Ann herself spent the night*: Rude, np

288 *James Whittaker briefed him*: Testimonies, 166–7

289 *Valentine Rathbun brought a new charge*: Testimonies, 204

289 *Ann and her entourage were staying with Elijah Slosson*: Testimonies, 167–70

290 *'I heard Ezekiel's voice'*: Testimonies, 239

290 *On Saturday 23 August*: Testimonies, 172–7

291 *later Shakers to compare it with Christ's prayer*: White, 55

291 *she continued her visits*: Testimonies, 178–86

295 *After a struggle*: Wells, 26–7

295 *Ann was concealed*: Testimonies, 187

296 *One of his attackers, Selah Abbot*: Testimonies, 383

296 *Some of the rabble*: Testimonies, 187–8

296 *'a strangely thrilling experience'*: White, 56

297 *they came to a steep slope*: Testimonies, 188

297 *Thomas Law: became a vagabond*: Testimonies, 382

297 *When they arrived at Grant's courthouse*: Testimonies, 188–92

299 *an elderly man called Asahel King*: Rude, np

299 *A Shaker brother was asked*: Williams, E., np

299 *Ann was taken back before Grant*: Testimonies, 192

300 *'Lay hands suddenly on no man'*: Testimonies, 193; White, 58

300 *The punishment meted out to Eleazer Grant*: Testimonies, 384

300 *At dusk, Ann*: Testimonies, 194–202
304 *She had been to thirty-six towns*: White, 48
304 *around a thousand souls*: Garrett, 237

12: *Beautiful Messenger*

307 *A group from Harvard*: Blanchard, np
307 *their clothes got so frozen*: Bathrick, 'Wise Sayings', 63
307 *Ann, in motherly mode*: Blanchard, np
308 *Another party of six Shakers*: Wood, np
309 *Amos Buttrick*: Bathrick, 'Testimonies', ii, 4
310 *a convert called Stephen Cleverly*: Bathrick, 'Testimonies', 51–2
310 *Nathan Tiffany reported*: Testimonies, 243
310 *During one of these all-night sessions*: Wood, np
311 *Abijah Worster records*: Worcester, 'Sayings', np
311 *she dreamed frequently that Christ*: Testimonies, 204–8
311 *Frederick Evans quoted*: Evans, 129–30
311 *Elizabeth Wood was doing some washing*: Wood, np
312 *William grew progressively weaker*: Testimonies, 337
312 *Jemima Blanchard said*: Blanchard, np
312 *he asked Aaron Wood to sing*: Testimonies, 341
313 *At the funeral*: Testimonies, 342
314 *'Brother William is calling me'*: Testimonies, 351
315 *Jonathan Slosson reports*: Testimonies, 220–2
316 *future leadership of Lucy Wright*: Green, 'Wright', 9
316 *'I saw William Scales'*: Testimonies, 231–2
317 *Perhaps the most charming of Ann's mystical perceptions*: Testimonies, 331
317 *'So great was the manifestation'*: Testimonies, 205
317 *'They are old in wickedness'*: Wood, np

317 *Ann 'stripped up the sleeve'*: Bathrick, 'Wise Sayings', 4

318 *'in the winter of 1813'*: Dyer, 42

318 *Rachel Merrill, noticed*: Aurelia, np

318 *Another large party arrived*: Sawyer, np

319 *Hannah Goodrich was sweeping*: Testimonies, 332–3

319 *'When the sisters would gather round Mother'*: Green, 'Wright', 9

319 *'I see brother William'*: Testimonies, 333

320 *'when the breath left her body'*: Green, *View*, 37

320 *their ship was caught in a storm*: Sawyer, np; White, 94

320 *The funeral announcement*: Munsell, ii, 288

320 *Abijah Worster and Abiather Eddy*: Testimonies, 352

321 *Samuel Fitch said*: Wells, 50

321 *as testified by Jemima Blanchard*: Blanchard, np

Epilogue

323 *'I will reprove an Old England Devil'*: Blanchard, np

324 *Nancy Lee, had become ill*: Cooper, B., np

324 *telling believers at a meeting*: Testimonies, 244

324 *he warned the assembled*: Testimonies, 291

325 *'a stink in my nostrils'*: Meacham, 13

325 *Of all my relations that ever I see*: Axon, 24

325 *Angell Matthewson tells an anecdote*: Matthewson, letter 7

326 *a hare-brained scheme*: Garrett, 217–19

326 *On his last visit to Harvard*: Hammond, np

327 *as some commentators have believed*: Garrett, for example, 158

327 *a misprint*: White, 71

327 *he had no natural aptitude for the dance*: Green, 'Meacham', 13

328 *Meacham hammered out the beginnings of a social organisation*:

Green, *View*, 51; Sears, 181; Garrett, 223–37; Stein, 44–9

329 *Meacham published his* Concise Statement: Meacham, 6–10

330 *Emerson once said*: Emerson, *Essays*, 35

331 *Thomas Brown records exuberant worship*: Brown, 82–4

331 *A mission was sent*: Stein, 57–76

332 *there were four thousand Shakers*: Stein, 87; Garrett, 237

333 *fourteen-year-old Ann Goff*: Stein, 170–83

333 *six brothers . . . became possessed*: Andrews, *Shakers*, 170

333 *Shakers conversed with these earliest Americans in their 'Native Language'*: Andrews, *Shakers*, 166

334 *Selera vae van vo*: Sears, 216

334 *According to Shaker theology*: Green, *View*, 92

334 *In the Enfield Shaker community*: 'Sixty-Nine', np

335 *'spiritual fountains'*: Andrews, *Shakers*, 161–9

335 *In 1842 Philemon Stewart*: Stein, 180–3

335 *an unnamed angel*: Youth's, 3

335 *Shaker artists gleefully drew*: Promey, *passim*

Bibliographical Note

Ann Lee was illiterate, so she left behind no diaries or letters. Most of the information we have about her was collected after her death when the next generation of Shakers felt the need to ensure that anecdotes and reminiscences were recorded before those believers who had known her and witnessed her accomplishments in America took their memories with them to the grave. The most important collection of this material, anthologised in a book called *Testimonies of the Life, Character, Revelations and Doctrines of Mother Ann Lee, and the Elders with Her*, was compiled by Rufus Bishop and Seth Youngs Wells in 1816 for circulation within the Shaker community. As mentioned in the Epilogue to this book, it was withdrawn shortly after its release, the authorities believing that the Ann Lee presented within its pages was incompatible with the icon that had been established in the years since her death. It was thereafter only circulated at senior levels in what had by then turned into a most hierarchical religion, and became known, rather romantically, as the 'Secret Book of the Elders'. It wasn't republished until 1888.

The story of this collection is told in some detail in Stephen J. Stein's *The Shaker Experience in America*, yet somewhat oddly he endorses Clarke Garrett's view that the *Testimonies* is fundamentally unreliable because the witnesses would inevitably have slanted their reminiscences to shed the best possible light on themselves and on their religion as they currently observed it (Stein, 25–8, 78–85). There is always going to be a danger of this in any collection of material produced after the event, particularly when the contributors feel the need to justify the way of life they have chosen, but the fact that the book proved such a hot potato when it was first published suggests that the material had not been extensively sanitised and adapted. Moreover, the richness of detail, the agreement of many witnesses about central events and issues, even the minor inconsistencies and frequent chronological vagueness, point to the authenticity of these testimonies rather than otherwise. I share the opinion of one of the important Shaker scholars of our time, Stephen A. Marini, that the *Testimonies* provides an invaluable and underrated source of material. Marini concedes that

During the three decades that separated Mother Ann from these accounts of her, Shakerism had developed a theology that inevitably shaped both individual memory and collective understanding of her life. Yet those who had known her longest were the very ones who constructed Shaker theology. And although some interpreters will assume that this later intellectual structure must have determined the form of the *Testimonies*, it is just possible, both in theory and historical reality, that the reverse is true ... For the Shakers the danger of the *Testimonies* was not its theological distortion but rather its historical veracity and the peril of public misinterpretation. All this leads me to conclude that the *Testimonies* are as close to Mother Ann as we are going to get. (Marini, 51)

Other important compilations are a collection by Seth Youngs Wells with a confusingly similar title, *Testimonies Concerning the Character and Ministry of Mother Ann Lee and the First Witnesses of the Gospel of Christ's Second Appearing*, and some later records collected by the Shaker annalists Eunice Bathrick and Roxalana

Grosvenor. Accounts by the impartial outsider William Plumer, and far from impartial apostates like Valentine Rathbun and William Haskett, provide valuable supplements to these reminiscences.

In 1916 the Shaker enthusiast Clara Endicott Sears anthologised some of this material in a volume called *Gleanings from Old Shaker Journals*. Though the book made no attribution of sources and was written in a gushing and sentimental style, it served a valuable purpose in making part at least of this fascinating story available to the general reader.

Up till now no serious biography of Ann Lee has been written. An amateurish though enthusiastic account by Arthur Joy was published by a small press in Minnesota in 1960. A young people's biography by Nardi Reeder Campion entitled *Mother Ann Lee: Morning Star of the Shakers*, is sentimental, superficial and so poorly researched as to be almost useless (she places Ann Lee in nineteenth-century industrial Manchester, and devotes a chapter of her book to a meeting between Ann and Lafayette that never took place). Campion's book was originally published as *Ann the Word*, but since that resonant phrase, which was attributed to Ann by followers and enemies alike, has been discarded by the author, I have felt free to make use of it as my own title.

The best accounts of Ann Lee's life have come as parts of books on larger issues. The great Shaker scholar, Edward Deming Andrews, covers her story in the first three chapters (amounting to fifty pages in all) of his *The People Called Shakers*. The definitive history of Shakerism of our time, Stein's *The Shaker Experience in America*, devotes fewer than forty of its 442 pages to Ann Lee (while giving almost a hundred to coverage of Shakerism's decline after the Second World War). This prioritising is determined not just by the distrust of sources already mentioned but also because Ann Lee's story fits uneasily into the history of the religion that she more or less inaugurated. She didn't intend to create a long-standing institution, and she showed no interest whatsoever in utopian communities or the design of furniture. American Shakerism as it has come to be perceived was a kind of accidental by-product of her life's mission.

Clarke Garrett establishes a different context for Ann in his book *Spirit Possession and Popular Religion*, now republished as *Origins of the Shakers: From the Old World to the New World*. He traces the tradition of sacred theatre and in particular the history of the French Prophets or Camisards, arriving at Ann's story in chapter 6, and devoting four chapters (seventy-three pages) to her. It seems to me perverse that Garrett's distrust of the *Testimonies* leads him to favour the accounts given by enemies of Shakerism like Rathbun and Haskett, since the evidence of indignant apostates is surely likely to be less reliable than that of people who are trying to express what it is they actually believe in. Despite this, Garrett's version is the most valuable one we have of Ann Lee to date: it is scholarly, sympathetic and vividly written, and has been by far the most important secondary source used in the making of this book.

Bibliography

Keyword references to sources, as given in the Notes, are in bold type.

Abbreviations:

LoC	Library of Congress Shaker Collection
NYPL	New York Public Library Shaker Collection
SLC	Sabbathday Lake Shaker Collection
WRHS	Western Reserve Historical Society Shaker Collection

All MS citations are to microfilms where possible.

Aikin, J. A., *Description of the Country from Thirty to Forty Miles Distant Around Manchester* (London: J. Stockdale, 1795)

Allen, Eldress M. Catherine, *The American Shakers* (Sabbathday Lake, Maine: The United Society, 1974)

Andrews, Edward Deming, *The People Called **Shakers*** (New York: Dover, 1963)

Andrews, Edward, and Andrews, Faith, *The Shaker Order of **Christmas*** (New York: Oxford University Press, 1954)

Andrews, Edward, and Andrews, Faith, *Visions of the Heavenly Sphere: A Study in Shaker Spiritual Art* (Charlottesville: University of Virginia, 1969)

Aston, Joseph, *The Manchester Guide* (Manchester: J. Aston, 1804)

Aurelia, Sister, 'Journal', 14-DJ-120, SLC

Axon, William E. A., 'Biographical Notice of Ann Lee' (pamphlet), from *Transactions of the Historical Society of Lancashire and Cheshire* (Liverpool: T. Brakell, 1876), quoting *Report of the Examination of the Shakers of Canterbury and Enfield before the New Hampshire Legislature, 1848*

Backus, Isaac, *A History of New England* (1871; repr. New York: Arno Press, 1969)

Backus, Isaac, *The Diary of Isaac Backus*, ed. William G. McLoughlin, 3 vols (Providence: Brown University Press, 1979)

Bacon, Margaret Hope, *Mothers of Feminism: The Story of Quaker Women in America* (San Francisco: Harper & Row, 1986)

Bailey, Derrick S., *Sexual Relation in Christian Thought* (New York: Harper, 1959)

Baldwin, Thomas W., *Vital Records of Harvard, Mass. to the Year 1850* (Boston: Wright & Potter, 1917)

Barbé-Marbois, François de, *Our Revolutionary Forefathers: The Letters*, trans. E. P. Chase (New York: Duffield, 1929)

Barbour, Hugh, *The Quakers in Puritan England* (New Haven and London: Yale University Press, 1964)

Barbour, Hugh, **and Frost**, J. William, *The Quakers* (New York and London: Greenwood Press, 1988)

Barret, Susannah, 'Testimony', VI: B-9, WRHS

Bates, Issachar, 'Sketch of the Life and Experience of Issachar Bates', VI, B-9, WRHS

Bathrick, Eunice, 'Book ii, **Testimonies** . . .', VI: B-12, WRHS

Bathrick, Eunice, 'Testimonies and **Wise Sayings** . . . of Mother Ann and the Elders . . . gathered from Different Witnesses', VI: B-10, WRHS

Bishop, Rufus, 'Daily Journal', Reel 1, NYPL

Blanchard, Jemima, 'Testimony', recorded by Roxalana Grosvenor, VI: B-9, WRHS

Blinn, Elder Henry Clay, *The Life and Gospel Experience of Mother Ann Lee* (East Canterbury, NH: Shakers, 1883)

Boston Gazette (eighteenth-century newspaper)

Braithwaite, William C., *The Beginnings of Quakerism* (Cambridge: Cambridge University Press, 1955)

Brockbank, E.M., *Honorary Medical Staff of the Manchester Infirmary 1752–1830* (Manchester: Manchester University Press, 1904)

Brockbank, William, *Portrait of a Hospital* (London: Heinemann, 1952)

Brockbank, William, *An Historic Address on the Manchester Royal Infirmary* (Manchester: Manchester Royal Infirmary, 1952)

Brockbank, William, *History of Nursing at the M.R.I.* (Manchester: Manchester University Press, 1970)

Brown, Thomas, *An Account of the People Called Shakers* (Troy, New York: Parker & Bliss, 1812)

Byrom, Elizabeth [Beppy], *The Journal of Elizabeth Byrom in 1745*, ed. Richard Parkinson (Manchester: Chetham Society, 1857)

Campion, Nardi Reeder, *Mother Ann Lee: Morning Star of the Shakers* (Hanover, N.H.: University Press of New England, 1990)

Carmer, Carl, *The Hudson* (London: Hodge & Co., 1951)

Casson, R., and Berry, I., *A Plan of the Towns of Manchester and Salford in the County Palatine of Lancaster* (Manchester: John Berry, 1746)

Cogswell, Anna, 'Testimony', VI: A-4, WRHS

Cooper, Beulah, 'Testimony', VI: B-9, WRHS

Cooper, Deliverance, 'Testimony', VI: B-4, WRHS

'Corrections and Additional Testimonies . . .', VI: B-11, WRHS

Dallimore, Arnold A., *George Whitefield*, 2 vols (Edinburgh: Banner of Truth, 1980)

Darrow, David, Meacham, John, and Youngs, Benjamin S., *The Testimony of Christ's Second Appearing, Containing a General Statement of All Things Pertaining to the Faith and Practice of the Church of God in this Latter Day* (Albany, NY: E. & E. Halford, 1810; originally published in an imperfect edition in 1808)

Defoe, Daniel, *A Tour Through England and Wales* (1724–6), ed. G. D. H. Cole, 2 vols (London: J. M. Dent, 1948)

Deming, Martha, 'Testimony', VI: A-2, WRHS

Dexter, Elizabeth Anthony, *Colonial Women of Affairs* (Boston: Houghton Mifflin, 1931)

Dickinson, Emily, *The Complete Poems*, ed. by Thomas H. Johnson (London: Faber & Faber, 1970)

Dwight, Timothy, *Travels in New England and New York*, 3 vols (New Haven, Conn.: 1822)

Dyer, Mary M., *A Portraiture of Shakerism* (printed for the author, 1822)

Edwards, Jonathan, *Puritan Sage: The Collected Writings*, ed. Vergilius Ferm (New York: Library Publishers, 1953)

Elkins, Hervey, *Fifteen Years in the Senior Order of Shakers* (Hanover, NH: Dartmouth Press, 1858)

Emerson, Ralph Waldo, *Essays: First Series*, ed. Joseph Slater et al. (Cambridge, Mass.: Belknap Press of Harvard University Press, 1979)

Emerson, Ralph Waldo, *Poems*, ed. Harold Bloom and Paul Kane (New York: Library of America, 1994)

Evans, Frederick W., *Shakers: Compendium of the Origin, History, Principles, Rules and Regulations, Government and Doctrines of the United Society of Believers in Christ's Second Appearing*

(New Lebanon, NY: Auchampaugh Brothers, 1859, 3rd edn)

Evans, Frederick W., *Autobiography of a Shaker* (Albany, NY: 1869)

Extract *from an Unpublished Manuscript on Shaker History* (1850), 22: 300, LoC

Faxon, Alicia Craig, *Women and Jesus* (Philadelphia: United Church Press, 1973)

Filley, Dorothy M., *Recapturing Wisdom's Valley: The Watervliet Shaker Heritage* (Albany, NY: Albany Institute of History and Art, 1975)

Fox, George, *The Woman learning in Silence; or, the **Mysterie** of the womans Subjection to her Husband, as also, the Daughter prophesying, wherein the Lord hath, and is fulfilling that he spake by the Prophet Joel, I will pour out my Spirit unto all Flesh* (London: 1656)

Fox, George, *The **Journals** of George Fox*, ed. Norman Penney, 2 vols (New York: Octagon Books, 1973)

Frost, Robert, *The Complete Poems* (London: Jonathan Cape, 1967)

Garrett, Clarke, *Spirit Possession and Popular Religion: From the Camisards to the Shakers* (Baltimore: Johns Hopkins University Press, 1987; reissued as *Origins of the Shakers: From the Old World to the New World*, 1998)

Gilpin, John, *The Quakers Shaken* (London: 1653)

Goodrich, Thankful, 'Experience', 3: 14, NYPL

Goodrich, Thankful, 'Testimony', VI: B-9, WRHS

Graymont, Barbara, *The Iroquois in the American Revolution* (New York: Syracuse University Press, 1972)

Green, Calvin, 'Biographical Account of the Life, Character and Ministry of Father Joseph **Meacham**', 8: 110, NYPL

Green, Calvin, 'Biographical Memoir of Mother Lucy **Wright**', VI: B-27, WRHS

Green, Calvin, 'Biographic **Memoirs** of the Life and the Experience of Calvin Green', 5: 78, LoC

Green, Calvin, and Wells, Seth Y., *A Summary View of the Millennial Church or United Society of Believers, Commonly Called Shakers, Comprising the Rise, Progress and Practical Order of the Society together with the General Principles of their Faith and Testimony* (Albany, NY: 1823)

Hammond, Thomas, 'Sketches of Shadrack Ireland', VI: A-8, WRHS

Hammond, Thomas, 'Testimony', VI: B-9, WRHS

Harkness, Georgia, *Women in Church and Society* (Nashville, Tenn.: Abington Press, 1972)

Harris, Howell, *Howell Harris's Visits to London*, ed. Tom Benyon (Aberystwyth: Cambrian New Press 1960)

Harrison, William, 'The Old House of Correction at Hunt's Bank, Manchester', *Transactions of the Lancashire and Cheshire Antiquarian Society* (Manchester: Ireland & Co., 1886)

Haskett, William J., *Shakerism Unmasked, or the History of the Shakers* (Pittsfield, Mass.: published by the author, 1812)

Horgan, Edward R., *The Shaker Holy Land: A Community Portrait* (Harvard, Mass.: The Harvard Common Press, 1982)

Humez, Jean M. (ed.), *Mother's First-Born Daughters: Early Shaker Writings on Women and Religion* (Bloomington: Indiana University Press, 1993)

Jewett, Elizabeth, 'Testimony', VI: B-9, WRHS

Joy, Arthur F., *The Queen of the Shakers* (Minneapolis: T. S. Denison, 1960)

Keith, George, *The Magick Of Quakerism* (London: 1707)

Lancashire Quarter Sessions Records (1772–4), Lancashire Archive Office, Preston, Lancs

Lenman, Bruce, *The Jacobite Risings in Britain 1689–1746* (London: Eyre Methuen, 1980)

Manchester Constables' Accounts (1743–76), ed. J. P. Earwacker, vol. 3 (Manchester: J. E. Cornish, 1892)

Manchester Infirmary Records, Jefferson Library, Manchester Royal Infirmary; Cheadle Royal Hospital

Manchester Mercury (eighteenth-century newspaper)

Manifesto, The, Shaker journal, founded in 1871 as *The Shaker*; then *The Shaker and Shakeress*, *The Shaker Manifesto*; finally *The Manifesto*

Marini, Stephen A., *Radical Sects of Revolutionary New England* (Cambridge, Mass.: Harvard University Press, 1982)

Marini, Stephen A., 'A New View of Mother Ann Lee and the Rise of American Shakerism', *Shaker Quarterly* 18 (1990): 47–62, 95–114

Matthewson, Angell, 'Reminiscences in the Form of a Series of Thirty-Nine Letters to his Brother Jeffrey', 9: 119, NYPL

Mayo, Margot, 'The Incredible Journey of Mother Ann', *Shaker Quarterly* 2 (1962): 42–52

McLoughlin, William G., 'Olney Winsor's "Memorandum" of the "Phenomenal Dark Day" of May 19, 1780', *Rhode Island History* 26 (1967): 88–91

Meacham, Joseph, *A Concise Statement of the Principles of the Only True Church, According to the Gospel of the Present Appearance of Christ . . . Together with a Letter from James Whittaker, Minister of the Gospel in this Day of Christ's Second Appearing – to his natural Relations in England, dated October 9th, 1785* (Bennington, Vt.: Haswell & Russell, 1790; repr. United Society, 1963)

Minutes *of the Commissioners for Detecting and Defeating Con-spiracies in the State of New York, 1780–1*, ed. V. H. Paltsits (Albany, NY: State of New York, 1910)

M'Nemar, Richard, *The Kentucky Revival; or, A Short History of the Late Outpouring of the Spirit of God in the Western States of America* (Cincinnati, Ohio: John W. Browne, 1807; repr. New York: Edward Jenkins, 1846)

Morse, Flo, *The Shakers and the World's People* (New York: Dodd, Mead & Co., 1980)

Munsell, Joel, *Annals of Albany*, 2 vols (Albany, NY: J. Munsell, 1869)

Nourse, Henry S., *History of the Town of Harvard, Massachusetts, 1732–1893* (Harvard, Mass.: Warren Hapgood, 1894)

Owen, Charles, *The Scene of Delusions Open'd in an Historical account of Prophetick Impostures, . . . wherein the Pretensions of the New Prophets, are Considered and Confuted* (London: John Lawrence, 1712)

Patterson, Daniel, *The Shaker Spiritual* (Princeton, NJ: Princeton University Press, 1979)

Pelham, R. W., *A Shaker's Answer to the Oft-Repeated Question, What Would Become of the World if All Should Become Shakers?* (Boston: Rand, Avery, 1874)

Plumer, William, 'The Original Shaker Communities in New England', ed. F. B. Sanborn, *The New England Magazine*, May 1900, 303–9

Procter, Richard Wright, *Memorials of Bygone Manchester* (Manchester: Palmer & Howe, 1880)

Promey, Sally M., *Spiritual Spectacles: Vision and Image in Mid-nineteenth-century Shakerism* (Bloomington: Indiana University Press, 1993)

Rathbun, Daniel, *A Letter to James Whittacor* (Springfield, Mass.: published by the author, 1785)

Rathbun, Valentine, *An Account of the Matter, Form, and Manner of a New and Strange Religion, Taught and Propagated by a Number of Europeans, living in a Place called Nisqueunia* ... (Providence: Bennett Wheeler, 1781)

Register of Baptisms and Deaths, Christ Church, Manchester, Manchester Cathedral Archives

Report of the Examination of the Shakers of Canterbury and Enfield before the New Hampshire Legislature ... (Concord, NH: Ervin B. Tripp, 1849)

Robinson, Charles Edson, *Concise History of the United Society of Believers Called Shakers* (East Canterbury, NH: 1893)

Robinson, John, 'Testimony', VI: B-9, WRHS

Robinson, John, 'Testimony, February 1830', VI: A-8, WRHS

Rude, Alphus, 'Testimony', VI: A-4, WRHS

Rule, John, *The Experience of Labour in Eighteenth-Century Industry* (London: Croom Helm, 1981)

Rules and Orders of the Public Infirmary at Manchester (Manchester: Joseph Harrop, 1769)

Sasson, Diane, *The Shaker Spiritual Narrative* (Knoxville: Tennessee University Press, 1983)

Sawyer, Otis, 'History of Alfred, Maine', 1-AS-030, SLC

Schaukirk, Ewald Gustav, *Occupation of New York City by the British* (New York: New York Times and Arno Press, 1969)

Schwartz, Hillel, *The French Prophets: The History of a Millenarian Group in Eighteenth-Century England* (Berkeley: University of California Press, 1980)

Scragg, D. G., *A History of English Spelling* (Manchester: Manchester University Press, 1974)

Sears, Clara Endicott (ed.), *Gleanings from Old Shaker Journals* (Boston: Houghton Mifflin, 1916)

Selby, John, *Over the Sea to Skye* (London: Hamish Hamilton, 1973)

'Short Account of the Rise of Believers', V: B-60, WRHS

'Sixty-Nine Spirit Communications ... to Individuals in Enfield, Conn.', 1: 13, LoC

Stein, Stephen J., *The Shaker Experience in America* (New Haven: Yale University Press, 1992)

Stiles, Ezra, *Extracts from the Itineraries*, ed. F. B. Dexter (New Haven, Conn.: Yale University Press, 1916)

Taylor, Amos, *Narrative of the Strange Principles, Conduct and Character of the People Known by the Name of Shakers* (Worcester, Mass.: 1782)

Testimonies *of the Life, Character, Revelations and Doctrines of Mother Ann Lee, and the Elders with Her, through Whom the world of Eternal Life, Was Opened in this Day of Christ's Second Appearing, Collected from Living Witnesses in Union with the Church . . .*, compiled by Rufus Bishop and Seth Youngs Wells (Hancock, Mass.: J. Tallcott & J. Deming, 1816; 2nd ed, Albany, NY: Weed, Parsons & Co., 1888). (My references are to the 1816 edition)

Thacher, James, *Military Journal of the American Revolution* (Hartford, Conn.: Hurlbut, Williams & Co., 1862)

Thompson, E. P. *The Making of the English Working Class* (London: Gollancz, 1965)

Victoria *County History of Lancashire*, ed. William Farrar and John Brownbill (London: Dawson's, 1911)

Virginia *Gazette* (eighteenth-century newspaper)

Warner, John, 'A Short account of ... Father Eleazer and Mother Hannah', VI: B-7, WRHS

Wells, Seth Y., *Testimonies Concerning the Character and Ministry of Mother Ann Lee and the First Witnesses of the Gospel of Christ's Second Appearing; Given by Some of the Aged Brethren and Sisters of the United Society, including a few sketches of their own religious experience: approved by the Church* (Albany, NY:

Packard & Van Benthuysen, 1827; originals in individual handwriting in VI: A-4, WRHS)

West, Benjamin, *Scriptural Cautions against embracing a Religious Scheme, Taught by a Number of Europeans* ... (Hartford, Conn.: Basil Webster, 1783)

White, Anna, and Taylor, Leila S., *Shakerism: Its Meaning and Message* (Columbus, Ohio: Fred J. Heer, 1904; repr. New York: AMS Press, 1971)

Whitson, Robley Edward (ed.), *The Shakers: Two Centuries of Spiritual Reflection* (New York: Paulist Press, 1983)

Whittaker, James, 'Letter [to Josiah Talcott], 25 Feb 1782', 5: 80, LoC

Whitworth's Manchester Advertiser and Weekly Magazine (eighteenth-century newspaper)

Wilds, Eunice, 'Testimony', VI: B-9, WRHS

Williams, Deborah, 'Testimony', VI: B-9, WRHS

Williams, Elizabeth, 'Testimony', VI: A-4, WRHS

Wood, Elizabeth, 'Testimony', VI: B-1, WRHS

Worcester, [spelt Worster elsewhere] Abijah, '**Sayings** of Mother Ann and the first Elders', VI: B-9, WRHS

Worcester, Abijah, '**Testimony**', VI: B-9, WRHS

Youth's Guide in Zion and Holy Mother's Promises (Canterbury, NH: 1842; repr. United Society, 1963)

Illustration Credits

p. 4 View of Manchester towards the south-west: from Casson & Berry's plan of Manchester and Salford, 1746; p. 43 Manchester Infirmary from the Medical Collection of the John Rylands University of Manchester, and reproduced by courtesy of the Director and Librarian; p. 58 House of Correction at Hunt's Bank from Richard Wright Procter's *Memorials of Bygone Manchester* (Manchester: Palmer & Howe, 1880); p. 74 Map of New York drawn after the plan by Bernard Ratzer (1767); p. 98 Map of Niskeyuna wilderness drawn after the survey of Manor Rensselaerwyck (1767) by J. R. Bleeker; p. 146 Court House and Prison at Albany and p. 150 Van Kleek house, both reproduced by permission of the Albany Institute of History and Art; p. 239 Square House and p. 275 Elijah Wilds's house in Shirley, both reproduced courtesy of the Fruitlands Museums, Harvard, Massachusetts; p. 306 Ann Lee's grave drawn after the plan of Watervliet, N.Y., in the Albany Institute of History and Art.

Front endpaper shows detail of Casson & Berry's plan of Manchester and Salford, 1746. Details from this are shown on pp. 2, 24, 52. Back endpaper shows map of New England and New York drawn by Vera Brice after eighteenth-century originals. Details from this are shown on pp. 98, 128, 156, 178, 204, 236, 270.

Index